THE PRACTICE OF READING

The Practice of Reading

Interpreting the Novel

Derek Alsop
and
Chris Walsh

St. Martin's Press
New York

THE PRACTICE OF READING

Copyright © 1999 by D. K. Alsop and C. J. Walsh

St. Martin's Press, Scholarly and Reference Division, 175 Fifth Avenue, New York, N.Y. 10010

First published in the United States of America in 1999

This book is printed on paper suitable for recycling and made from fully managed and sustained forest sources.

Printed in Hong Kong

ISBN 0–312–22156–8 clothbound
ISBN 0–312–22157–6 paperback

Library of Congress Cataloging-in-Publication Data
Alsop, Derek, 1960–
The practice of reading : interpreting the novel / Derek Alsop and Chris Walsh.
p. cm.
Includes bibliographical references and index.
ISBN 0–312–22156–8 (cloth). — ISBN 0–312–22157–6 (pbk.)
1. English fiction—History and criticism. 2. Books and reading.
I. Walsh, Chris, 1956– . II. Title.
PR821.A45 1999
823.009—dc21 98–49468
CIP

For Angela and Linden

with love

However much thou art read in theory, if thou hast no practice thou art ignorant.

Muslih-al-Din Sheikh Sa'adi, *Gulistan* (1258), trans. James Ross

This book is not directed to academics, because only a small remnant of them still read for the love of reading.

Harold Bloom, *The Western Canon* (1994)

What I have been saying is that whatever they do, it will only be interpretation in another guise because, like it or not, interpretation is the only game in town.

Stanley Fish, *Is There a Text in This Class?* (1980)

A novel is a living thing, all one and continuous, like any other organism, and in proportion as it lives will it be found, I think, that in each of the parts there is something of each of the other parts.

Henry James, 'The Art of Fiction' (1884)

Contents

Contents

Preface

A preface is a good place to tell readers what to expect – and what not to expect – in a book. Although, in this book, the challenging and flouting of expectations are shown to be an important part of the novel-reading experience, it would be a trifle perverse were we to require our readers to proceed to the following chapters in uncertain anticipation of their contents. So what kind of book is *The Practice of Reading: Interpreting the Novel?* And what kind of book is it not?

First, this book is *not* an introductory survey or synopsis of established theoretical and critical approaches. Neither does it attempt to help readers catch up with the latest developments in accounts of the reader in current literary theory. The present proliferation of introductory books is partly the response to a certain feeling of helplessness we all experience when faced with so many new, and often complex, theoretical books. Geoffrey Bennington has aptly acknowledged the shared 'recognition of the need to "gain time" . . . allow[ing] readers to make conversation . . . about thinkers whose work there has not been time to read'.[1] *The Practice of Reading*, in this sense, will not save readers much (if any) time. In our references to influential critical thinkers of the late twentieth century, we do not attempt to provide a concise survey of their achievements, or a broad outline of their careers and summaries of their contributions to current thinking. Although we do hope that readers will find many informed points of departure for their own further reading of criticism, the main aim of our book is to encourage a return to the close reading of novels. Our use of theory in the pages that follow is eclectic; our aim is always the elucidation of the *experience of reading* the novels selected, and the revelation of the problems – and pleasures! – which reading entails. Therefore, there is no single favoured critical discourse: we are interested in all theories which offer insights into reading novels. Far from offering a short-cut, we aim to celebrate the pleasures of careful, detailed attention, and if this volume belongs to any tradition it might be best placed alongside those texts (whatever their critical persuasion) which demonstrate a commitment to close reading. However, this is not to say that this book has no introductory qualities: those unfamiliar with theories of reading will find a range of approaches explained and applied. We do not assume previous intensive critical reading on the part of our readers, and so do not take for granted complex technical issues. Our aim is to be lucid about the helpfulness of certain ideas and perspectives in defining the importance of the reader's role in the production of meaning. To do this we must at times simplify, but we aim not to oversimplify; we use terminology when it is helpful, not because it is fashionable. This book is not written as a reaction against theory: we do not, for instance, lament the excesses of postmodernism. Neither do we wish to provide a critique aimed at exposing the weaknesses of particular theoretical approaches. But nor do we pay lip-service to current critical orthodoxies. Ultimately, we are much more interested in readings of novels than in the use of novels to validate preferred theories.

The Practice of Reading has a few, simple premises: that reading novels demands the skills of careful textual analysis; that no thoroughgoing analysis of the novel can ignore those theoretical developments, from reception aesthetics to poststructuralism and beyond, which have placed the activity of reading at the centre of critical debate; and that the best way to examine theoretical concepts is through the practice of reading. Most importantly, behind every claim made in the following pages is the governing idea that *reading is a creative, interpretational activity with profound and transforming implications*. We hope this book conveys our sense of the urgency and the intensity of the reading experience. As we will see, though, what we call 'the experience of reading' is infinitely complex. We will not be suggesting that there is some simple 'experience' to be valued above and beyond more sophisticated reflections on reading. It is the nature and quality of the experience which matters, not the mere fact that when we read we inevitably have some kind of experience. Our aim is to return the reader to the practice of close reading in the light of the various issues and questions which any detailed consideration of reading inevitably raises. With its emphasis on practice, the book explores acts of interpretation in terms of the dynamics of the reading process.

It is no accident, though, that the book opens and closes by referring to the thrill of reading, as expressed by commentators as different as Richard Rorty and A. S. Byatt. We agree with Rorty (and his critical practice never oversimplifies the matter) that 'books should make a difference', and our treasured memories of the experience of reading are, like Byatt's, those which 'make the hairs on the neck . . . stand on end'. It is worth stressing here that wherever critics express their commitment to reading there is likely to be some virtue. To take an example from Chapter 2: although we have reservations about Melvyn New's view of *Tristram Shandy*, his idea that 'our interpretations are our lives' suggests that we have more in common with his approach than with the approaches of others for whom criticism has nothing to do with values.

We ought, perhaps, in this preface, to remark on the method which takes one major novel per chapter (or, in the case of Chapter 7, a major trilogy of novels) to illustrate particular aspects of the reading process. Most important, here, is the assumption throughout that reading is an *intertextual* activity. To read *Tristram Shandy* is to be told (explicitly, by Tristram) to 'read, read, read', and no close attention to Sterne's novel could leave the reader without the strongest sense that the novel owes much of its textual existence to the writings of others, and that its indebtedness has a convoluted intertextual history. According to Derek Attridge, in a statement with which we entirely agree, we can never read Joyce for the first time: his texts intersect with all aspects of our reading culture. Similarly, Byatt's novel *Possession*, with which we end our discussion, has the final word on the intertextual nature of the reading experience, with its impressive collection of interpolated texts, merging a fictional recreation of the past with the threads of actual literary history. The range of novels we have chosen to discuss exemplifies the diverse nature of textual relations and interrelations.

We have also chosen these novels because they are themselves books which highlight the *significance* of reading: they offer plenty of particular instances of reading proper (for example, Elizabeth Bennet's crucial reading of Darcy's letter, or Pip's profoundly self-conscious reading of a note telling him to 'Please read this, here'); and they are more generally suggestive about the formative connections between reading and other experiences.

The novels selected allow us to introduce a range of complex issues arising from our overarching emphasis on the practice of reading. The choice of novels allows us to differentiate between the various kinds of issues which reading experiences raise, and the individual works

allow us to find continuity and coherence in their acknowledgement
of the central role of reading. At the same time the chronological
ordering of the chapters serves to give some sense of the historical
development of novelistic assumptions about reading.

It is not our aim to enter into debate about the legitimacy of different ideas of the literary canon, and we do not wish to proclaim some
great new tradition. Generally, we have chosen novelists whose work
is likely to be reasonably familiar to students of literature. Admittedly,
such students are more likely to be familiar with Beckett's plays than
with his *Trilogy* – if so, they will recognize some of Beckett's preoccupations discussed in these pages. In taking a relatively recent novel
there is more uncertainty about readership, but the choice of
Possession, as a Booker Prize-winner, at least ensures the fairly wide-
spread reading associated with literary bestsellers. It is an assumption
vital to the success of this book that the approaches and insights
which can be applied to reading these novels can certainly be applied
to reading other novels. But we find that *these* novels give us a particular flexibility in examining the role of the reader, and provoke in
profound and compelling ways crucial questions about the nature of
the practice of reading.

And here, for the first time, surfaces one of the paradoxes of this
book, which some will welcome and others perhaps will condemn.
Though it is our aim always to emphasize the creative, constitutive
role of the reader, and though we believe that literature is an experience and that reading novels creates them as they thereafter come to
be known, nevertheless we often discuss the novels as if they invited
the responses we give. And, worse undoubtedly in some eyes, we
continue to celebrate the texts themselves, as if they were responsible
for our experiences. However, our understanding of the problems
attendant upon such a view of texts is throughout a central issue in
this book, as we acknowledge the complexities of the hermeneutic
circle which takes us from subject to object and back again.

Finally, it might be asked why we wish to concentrate on the novel
in our account of the practice of reading. In a sense the answers are
simple. We are interested in the particular kinds of reading that novel-
reading entails. It might fairly be urged that some of the claims about
what happens when we read this or that novel are equally relevant to
poems, plays, biographies, essays, or indeed any other texts; but, as
we argue below, we have specific kinds of reading agenda when we
come to read novels. We enter, as it were, 'novel-reading mode', and

this leads to a different experience from, for instance, reading lyric poetry or dramatic tragedy. We would not wish to be exclusive in this claim – indeed, in some of the discussions which follow we make use of poetic and dramatic comparisons where we feel they are interesting – but we do aim at a coherence which would otherwise be impossible were we to try to over-generalize about what is involved in the practice(s) of reading. Broadly, and not surprisingly, the features which distinguish novel-reading from other kinds of reading have to do with narration, plot, time, point of view and the complex interactions between such features. Wherever, in the chapters that follow, we discuss such topics as the temporal aspect of the reading experience, the processes of anticipation and retrospection; the reader's shifting expectations of narrative development, the reader's relationship with the narrator, and the reader's self-conscious role as reader, we are raising issues which have a special application to the novel, and which it would not be possible to raise in quite the same way were we to attempt to deal also with the conventions which circumscribe the reading of poetry, drama, and other kinds of prose. Put another way, the reader of the novel encounters such issues in a context which has its own special implications and makes its own special demands, and this book aims to deal with that context.

As practising teachers, we believe that the issues considered in this book will be of relevance to all students of the novel. The choice of novels reflects as broadly as possible the field of study normally open to such students through numerous university and college courses. For this reason, we hope this book will not only stimulate reading and thought, but will be useful.

Derek Alsop
Chris Walsh
23 April 1998

Acknowledgements

We both register here our indebtedness to numerous colleagues, tutors and students with whom we have had so many fruitful discussions down the years.

More particularly, Derek Alsop would like to thank Tim Burke for his most helpful suggestions on an earlier draft of part of the book.

Chris Walsh would like to thank: Glyn Turton for his kindly interest in the project since its inception; and Michael Wheeler, whose guidance, support and encouragement over a quarter of a century have been invaluable.

Any faults in the book are ours.

List of editions used

All quotations from, and page references to, the main novels discussed in this study are to the following editions, unless otherwise specified.

Jane Austen, *Pride and Prejudice*, ed. Vivien Jones (London: Penguin, 1996).

Samuel Beckett, *Trilogy: Molloy; Malone Dies; The Unnamable* (London: John Calder, 1994).

A. S. Byatt, *Possession: A Romance* (London: Vintage, 1991).

Charles Dickens, *Great Expectations*, ed. Charlotte Mitchell (London: Penguin, 1996).

George Eliot, *Daniel Deronda*, ed. Terence Cave (London: Penguin, 1995).

James Joyce, *A Portrait of the Artist as a Young Man*, ed. Seamus Deane (London: Penguin, 1992).

Laurence Sterne, *The Life and Opinions of Tristram Shandy, Gentleman*, ed. Melvyn New and Joan New (London: Penguin, 1997).

1 Reading and Interpretation

What happens when someone reads a novel? What do novel-readers actually do? Is it really possible to generalize about 'the role of the reader' and 'the experience of reading'? How is meaning produced? How far does meaning depend on the reader, and how far on the text of the novel itself? To what extent – if any – should the novelist's stated intentions be taken into account in discussing the process of reading? How important are language and context to reading practices? How significant are various modern developments in literary theory and criticism for our understanding of what is involved in the process of reading novels?

These and other related questions will be explored in the chapters which follow. In this introductory chapter, however, the focus will be on the nature of reading and interpretation, and the relationship between them, in the context of recent critical and theoretical discussions. It is often the practice, in those books which aim to examine and apply the insights of theory to the description of reading, to attempt a kind of catalogue of critical approaches. But if the motive for trying to provide an inclusive, balanced and exhaustive summary of positions is understandable, the result can too easily be an utterly routine and predictable orthodoxy – the re-establishment of the current canon of acceptable theories, rather than an engagement with the realities of the process of reading and understanding literary texts. Our experience might well echo Richard Rorty's feeling when he came to 'slog through' a 'methodical' anthology of readings on Joseph Conrad's *Heart of Darkness* (1902):

> . . . one psychoanalytic reading, one reader-response reading, one feminist reading, one deconstructionist reading, and one new historicist reading. None of the readers had, as far as I could see, been enraptured or destabilized by *Heart of Darkness*. I got no sense that

the book had made a big difference to them, that they cared much about Kurtz or Marlow or the woman 'with helmeted head and tawny cheeks' whom Marlow sees on the bank of the river. These people, and that book, had no more changed these readers' purposes than the specimen under the microscope changes the purpose of the histologist.[1]

Rorty's claim needs qualifying, perhaps: the nature of the specimen will certainly affect the *conclusions* the histologist draws. (An 'histologist' is someone who examines the minute structures of biological tissues.) But the key word above is *purpose*. We shall argue later that every reading of a novel has its own history, and its own context; and that these histories and contexts are locatable in a wider, shared historical context. There is, however, a risk here of emphasizing the general context at the expense of the personal situation of the reader. For all readers read with purpose (with design, with intention). This is so basic a notion that it is easy (even for critics!) to overlook it: it is fundamental – the very ground on which we stand. We read *on purpose*, as the idiom has it. And the purposes of no two readers are quite the same, precisely because of the personal element. Only persons can read. Individual readers read on the basis of different personal motives and, unsurprisingly, different particular readings result. This is what makes the critical discussion of alternative readings interesting: otherwise we would find ourselves not only reading the same texts in the same contexts, we would be producing readings which could only be differentiated on the basis of their ideological positions and associated critical methodologies. And the result would be the kind of bland monotony Rorty describes.

We identify, then, with Rorty's assumption that the critical properly includes the personal, that reading books should, somehow, *make a difference*. We intend to convey, in the chapters which follow, a sense both of the rapture and the rupture that reading entails. Though a range of methods is employed in critically discussing the novels in *The Practice of Reading*, we aim not to be methodical in the tedious sense described by Rorty. Our approach is consistently eclectic. Whatever approaches to reading are useful to describe the practice of reading particular novels, we use. You will not find a monolithic new historicist, psychoanalytical, or feminist 'reading' in this volume, though you will find insights related to each of these broad and over-lapping theoretical discourses. But, though we are eclectic, we are not neutral. We agree, for instance, with Matei Calinescu's observation on politicized readings:

> Our relationship to texts that have acquired a personal significance for us – texts that have once occasioned moments of self-revelation or otherwise memorable reading experiences – cannot be erased in one act of one-dimensional political rereading.[2]

Retrospectively, if we wanted to, we could choose which theoretical or critical label to apply to our reading of a text, but no label would summarize adequately our total personal response to that text. In the passage just quoted, Calinescu has just been considering certain feminist accounts of the reading experience, having cited Patrocinio Schweickart's argument that 'the feminist inquiry into the activity of reading begins with the realisation that the literary canon is androcentric' (in other words, male-centred).[3] Schweickart herself offers an excellent example of the immediacy and excitement of a memorable reading experience. Though, ostensibly, she uses the experience to support a *theoretical* agenda (the full title of her essay is 'Reading Ourselves: Toward a Feminist Theory of Reading'), her account actually bears witness to the intensity of personal conviction which attends good reading. The sense of engagement remains vivid despite, rather than because of, the theoretical claims. Schweickart's paradigm for the 'feminist story' is Adrienne Rich's account of visiting the nineteenth-century American poet Emily Dickinson's home. At times, here, Rich's experience is universalized to serve Schweickart's theoretical agenda, but the claims are less convincing as part of a feminist manifesto than they are as testimony to the importance of a personal response. To illustrate our point, here are three extracts from Schweickart's essay:

> The metaphor of visiting points to another feature of feminist readings of women's writing, namely, the tendency to construe the text not as an object, but as the manifestation of the subjectivity of the absent author – the 'voice' of another woman.[4]

> Rich's metaphors together with her use of the personal voice indicate some key issues underlying feminist readings of female texts. On the one hand, reading is necessarily subjective. On the other hand, it must not be wholly so. One must respect the autonomy of the text. The reader is a visitor and, as such, must observe the necessary courtesies.[5]

In the feminist story, the key to the problem is the awareness of the double context of reading and writing. Rich's essay is wonderfully illustrative. To avoid imposing an alien perspective on Dickinson's poetry, Rich informs her reading with the knowledge of the circumstances in which Dickinson lived and worked.[6]

In literary-critical terms each of these claims could be said to be highly traditional: the first involves a sense of the author's 'presence' and communication with the reader; the second advocates a deferential respect for the text; the third endorses the connection between imaginative biography and criticism. In the history of literary criticism these are amongst the commonest of all critical stances, and, in that they have often served a critical canon as androcentric as the literary one, it is questionable how useful they can be in developing a specifically *feminist* theory of reading. Schweickart goes on to suggest that feminists should not choose what she calls the 'deconstructive plot' because it is important, politically, not 'to be overly enamored with the theme of impossibility': 'Instead, we should strive to redeem the claim that it is possible for a woman, reading as a woman, to read literature written by women.'[7] According to this argument, we could simply side-step the implications of those theories which seriously challenge models of identity and presence, were we to favour a feminist agenda which asserts the importance of 'real' women readers and writers. Thus, Roland Barthes's announcement of 'the death of the author' would not be helpful to those wishing to recover the achievements of female authors. Responding to the following passage from Rich's essay, Schweickart celebrates its attempt to 'connect' with the author (choosing rather to ignore the ease of the claim that there were 'two mid-nineteenth century American geniuses'):

> I am traveling at the speed of time, along the Massachusetts Turnpike
> . . . 'Home is not where the heart is', she wrote in a letter, 'but the
> house and adjacent buildings' . . . I am traveling at the speed of time,
> in the direction of the house and buildings . . . For years, I have been
> not so much envisioning Emily Dickinson as trying to visit, to enter
> her mind through her poems and letters, and through my own inti-
> mations of what it could have meant to be one of the two mid-nine-
> teenth century American geniuses, and a woman, living in Amherst,
> Massachusetts.[8]

It is unrealistic to present this familiar idea of imaginative empathy as if it offered some new perspective available only to feminist strategies of interpretation. Further, an acknowledgement that the ideas of 'genius' and the pantheon of greats are highly problematical would perhaps allow for an intriguing critical debate about the persistence of such ideas in an age which (wrongly) believes it has laid them to rest. But, despite these critical blind spots, Schweickart is not wrong to celebrate the imaginative power of Rich's response. It is the recognition of the intensity of the female reading experience which makes Schweickart's discussion interesting, not her attempt to make it serve a new orthodoxy. Indeed, so vital is this sense of response that it *cannot* be new. We have the clearest feeling, to return to Rorty's point, that Dickinson has changed the purpose of her reader, and that her poems have made 'a big difference'. So well has Rich conveyed this that her writing in turn has also made a difference and thus has changed the purposes of *her* reader, Patrocinio Schweickart. *Critical* reading has become *personal* reading.

It is hardly surprising that we should find Schweickart's commentary reprinted in a recent collection of essays on *Readers and Reading*, or that, being there, it should raise again the issue which has most dominated accounts of the reading experience. When Schweickart notes that 'On the one hand, reading is necessarily subjective. On the other hand, it must not be wholly so. One must respect the autonomy of the text',[9] she is participating in the most recurrent debate affecting theories of reading. Though the General Editors' Preface to the volume where her essay appears notes that lecturers and teachers need 'guidance in a rapidly changing critical environment' and 'help in understanding the latest revisions in literary theory'[10] there is really no resolving help or guidance to be had concerning the relationship between text and reader in the production of textual meaning. The rapidly changing critical environment has not changed very rapidly in this respect. Schweickart's position, though put forward as part of a feminist agenda, is actually close to Wolfgang Iser's, and the opening essay in *Readers and Reading* is Iser's 'Interaction between Text and Reader', where we find the following:

> . . . the phenomenological theory of art has emphatically drawn attention to the fact that the study of a literary work should concern not only the actual text but also, and in equal measure, the actions involved in responding to that text. The text itself simply offers

'schematized aspects' through which the aesthetic object of the work can be produced. From this we may conclude that the literary work has two poles, which we might call the artistic and the aesthetic: the artistic pole is the author's text, and the aesthetic is the realization accomplished by the reader. In view of this polarity, it is clear that the work itself cannot be identical with the text or with its actualization but must be situated somewhere between the two.[11]

For those who fear that criticism moves too fast, and that they are forever trying to catch up with the latest revelations, it is heartening to find this essay by Iser at the opening of a collection first published in 1995. Iser's essay, indeed, exists in many forms, and goes back in English at least to 1972. We can find more or less the same comment, verbatim, on the 'phenomenological theory of art' in 'The Reading Process: A Phenomenological Approach', *New Literary History* 3 (1972), or in *The Implied Reader: Patterns of Communication in Prose Fiction from Bunyan to Beckett* (1974), or in *The Act of Reading: A Theory of Aesthetic Response* (1978), or in Chapter 2 of *Prospecting: From Reader Response to Literary Anthropology* (1989). And, if we do not have Andrew Bennett's recent edited collection conveniently to hand, we can find the same essay already republished in Susan R. Suleiman and Inge Crosman, *The Reader in the Text: Essays on Audience and Interpretation* (1980), or in David Lodge's *Modern Criticism and Theory: A Reader* (1988). No need here to worry that we may have missed out on something! When we say 'more or less the same comment', however, it is interesting to compare variant readings. Here is the 'same' passage from 'The Reading Process: A Phenomenological Approach' (1972):

> The phenomenological theory of art lays full stress on the idea that, in considering a literary work, one must take into account not only the actual text, but also, and in equal measure, the actions involved in responding to that text . . . The text as such offers different 'schematized views' through which the subject matter of the work can come to light . . . If this is so, then the literary work has two poles, which we might call the artistic and the aesthetic: the artistic refers to the text created by the author, and the aesthetic to the realization accomplished by the reader. From this polarity it follows that the literary work cannot be completely identical with the text, or with the realization of the text, but in fact must lie halfway between the two.[12]

We can notice here that though the subtle changes attempt to give increased authority to Iser's idea they move no further forward in defining the crucial relationship between the text and the reader. So what was an *idea stressed* by the phenomenological theory of art has become, apparently, an *emphatic fact*, not because of any change in the argument, but simply because of a change in the words. The 'schematized views' have become 'schematized aspects'. In one version they allow the 'subject matter' to 'come to light'; then again they are something 'through which the subject matter of the work can be produced'. In the earlier version, the literary work 'in fact must lie halfway' between its two poles; later it 'must be situated somewhere between the two'. These subtle changes in expression reveal the problems with Iser's theory. Putting the point more generously, the changes indicate the polar paradox. Where a textualist view might imply that subject matter 'comes to light', a readerly view might prefer to suggest the reader's 'production'. In a version of literary meaning which depends on the idea of an interaction between the text and the reader, the exact location of meaning will always be uncertain. Iser retains the idea of a criticism which considers text and response 'in equal measure' but drops the idea that the work exists 'halfway' between text and actualization (or, in the later version, its 'realization'), because the vaguer form 'somewhere between the two' seems less committal and therefore less susceptible to objection. It leaves itself open, though, to the devastating question, where, *exactly?*

It is not only Iser who has not moved forward in this respect. Indeed it is almost impossible *to* move forward, in this line of thought. Pragmatists such as Stanley Fish and Richard Rorty have cornered the market in irrefutable arguments to counter anyone who wants, even partly, to locate meaning either in the text or in the author's intention. Since such arguments must be important to a book about the practice of reading, it is worth rehearsing them here, as they will surface time and again in the chapters that follow. The pattern of the debate can be observed in the similarity of Fish's response to Iser and Rorty's response to Umberto Eco. Iser and Eco broadly satisfy Fish's description of the pluralists:

> Pluralists wish neither to embrace a theory in which literary texts have one and only one correct reading (because that would be as they see it to violate the essence of literature), nor to embrace a theory in which a literary text can receive as many correct or legitimate read-

ings as there are readers (because then words like 'correct' and 'legitimate' would lose their force). It is their contention, therefore, that while a literary text is distinguished by its openness to a number of readings, it is not open to any and all readings.[13]

This position, as embodied by Iser, Fish argues, depends on a notion of something 'given'. The text constrains and controls the possible 'concretizations' (or 'realizations' or 'actualizations') performed by the reader. We are 'concretizing' something already inherently there. The reader is an active participant in meaning because literary texts have varying degrees of 'indeterminacy', but the reader is not a free agent and has to meet the text half-way or at least somewhere in the middle. And the very concept of 'indeterminacy' depends on a notion of otherwise determined texts relating to a determined world.

To illustrate these points, let us turn to an example from the beginning of Chapter 11 of *Pride and Prejudice*:

> WHEN the ladies removed after dinner, Elizabeth ran up to her sister, and seeing her well guarded from cold, attended her into the drawing-room; where she was welcomed by her two friends with many professions of pleasure . . . (p. 48)

Inasmuch as this refers to a fictional world there can be no determinate verification of its statements. To say 'Derek Alsop and Chris Walsh wrote a book' *seems* to be a completely different order of statement from 'Elizabeth ran up to her sister'. The first statement has real referents (a real book, real people, a real action); the second does not (there is no Elizabeth, she does not have a sister, non-existent people cannot run). This is what Iser means when he comments: 'How can we describe the status of a literary text? The first point is that it differs from any text presenting an object that exists independently of the text.' In this sense a literary text is different from a piece of writing which 'describes an object that exists with equal determinacy outside it'.[14] Alsop and Walsh are 'determined' beings, beings of flesh and blood, whose flesh and blood fingers tap computer keyboards. Elizabeth Bennet is not 'determined' – she 'exists' in the space between her textual graphemes (the printed letters that form her name) and her 'realization' in the reader's imagination (Hamlet's 'the mind's eye'). But, in terms of the imaginative response to Jane Austen's words, Iser would also say that there are *degrees* of indeterminacy. We could say, for instance, that as long as the reader knows that in polite society to leave the dinner table and go into (or 'withdraw' into) the drawing-room is called 'removing', and that to go politely with someone is called 'attending', then the imagination does not struggle to 'determine' what 'happens' in this bit of text – Elizabeth courteously and attentively goes with her sister into the drawing-room. But when she is welcomed 'with many professions of pleasure', the reader has more to do than if the text had said she was welcomed by someone saying 'What a delight it is to see you!' What exactly was supposed to have been said is not given. Some linguists would describe this as the 'narrator's representation of speech acts': there were 'professions' but we do not know exactly what they were. Our imagination has to supply the kind of statements that would qualify as speech acts expressing such pleasure.[15]

There are two main aspects to Fish's response to these kinds of points. First, the reader supplies everything. Every aspect of our reading of these lines from *Pride and Prejudice* is a matter of our readerly construction of 'the text'. Nothing is 'given' by the text. 'Elizabeth ran up to her sister' is no more or less 'determined' than 'she was welcomed . . . with many professions of pleasure'. Indeed the reader might completely ignore the normal meaning of the word 'run' – after all, ladies do not normally 'run' about polite houses. Even if we imagine that Elizabeth's solicitude for her sister was such that she moved with indecorous haste, we do not know, from some 'given' in the text, exactly how she ran. She *could* have sprinted, she *could* have jogged – if such ideas are comical they are so only because of what *we* bring to the text: our sense of propriety, our sense of Jane Austen's world, our sense of how to behave in a house and in polite company, and the sense of absurdity, linguistically, that such words would bring to such a context. Even if the text had read 'Elizabeth moved at a velocity of two metres per second up to her sister' that would still not have determined the matter comprehensively. The example, fortuitously, anticipates Fish's very words, in another context:

> Talk of angles and ratios and velocities may have more cachet in the game of 'accurate' description than talk of running and jogging, but it is still talk made possible in its intelligibility by a dimension of assessment; and therefore the accuracy such talk achieves will be relative to the facts as they are within that dimension.[16]

Fish, here, has been discussing examples of 'constatives' (referential statements) from speech act theory, and specifically J. L. Austin's (not Austen's!) citing of the expression 'He is running' as a 'model constative': 'because its truth can be determined simply by checking it against "the fact that he is running"'.[17] We can see, now, where the second phase of Fish's argument leads. Not only is literary language not constative (Elizabeth does not 'run' in any interpretation of the word – she does not even exist), no language is constative:

> One need only imagine someone saying to the speaker, 'You call that running, it's barely jogging,' to see that the fit between the description and the 'fact' will only be obvious to those for whom the articulations of the language of description correspond to their beliefs about the articulations in nature.[18]

We could of course complicate the issue further, by arguing, for instance, that Fish's example is compromised by the fact that no one would take the running/jogging person to be swimming, but that would miss the real point of Fish's argument. Fish is claiming – and doing so in a philosophical tradition that stretches back at least as far as to the eighteenth-century idealist philosopher Bishop Berkeley – that everything is a matter of mediation, that nothing is 'given', either in the world or in the text as something fully determined before the act of interpretation that comprehends it. Furthermore, the 'it' that is comprehended is entirely what it is through the act of comprehension.

Theories of reading tend forever to run (as it were) into the implications of this claim. Lennard Davis, in his book *Resisting Novels: Ideology and Fiction*, depends on the notion that fictions lie about the real world and that we must resist their ideologically loaded falsifications. (He identifies himself, humorously, with the Puritan book burners who 'did not like fiction' because 'it was a pack of invented lies'.)[19] In the context of this overarching view there is an interesting discussion of contemporary responses to Dickens's description of the sordid poverty of Jacob's Island in *Oliver Twist* (1837–8). Davis notes that, after reading the Dickens passage, the Bishop of London suggested reforms, but that Sir Peter Laurie, an opponent of such reforms, mocked the Bishop's 'mistake' by claiming that Jacob's Island 'ONLY existed in a work of fiction'. Davis gives Dickens's own brilliant response to this point, with its uncompromising development of Laurie's logic:

When Fielding described Newgate, the prison immediately ceased to exist . . . when Smollett took Roderick Random to Bath, that city instantly sank into the earth . . . when Scott exercised his genius on Whitefriars, it incontinently glided into the Thames . . . an ancient place called Windsor was entirely destroyed in the reign of Queen Elizabeth by two Merry Wives of that town . . . and . . . Mr. Pope, after having at a great expense completed his grotto at Twickenham, incautiously reduced it to ashes by writing a poem upon it.[20]

Davis's gloss on this argument is that 'Dickens rightly attacks Laurie for a kind of myopia, but the myopia operates on a larger scale than Dickens might wish to admit.'[21] For Davis, in line with his thesis, Dickens's description of Jacob's Island is not an innocent, determined description of an external reality, but an ideological description with its own agenda. Thus far, Fish would agree. Davis, though, wants to use this claim to support the argument that fiction lures us into dangerous and false ideologies. But how can there be a basis for a critique of the novel's self-interested perversion of reality, unless an alternative, disinterested and true account of reality can be imagined? In fact, the impossibility of imagining a 'true', perspectiveless account does not challenge the thrust of Dickens's satire. Pragmatists like Fish are not arguing the facile point that because response mediates reality there is no reality. Rather, they are asserting that whatever we say about fiction's representation of its 'reality' holds true for any representation of reality. Lennard Davis views character in the same way in which he views place. Novels present us with a deliberate falsification of human reality for ideological purposes, and they are able to impose upon us because 'fictional characters have a different level of existence and creation than people we meet'.[22] For real people we have 'corroboration, evidence and proof'. It is hardly surprising, here, that Davis should cite Iser:

Here Wolfgang Iser . . . can help because he spends a good deal of time trying to distinguish between literary speech and ordinary speech – that is, between language in a literary work and language in our lives.[23]

But, according to Fish, this is precisely where Iser *cannot* help. Fish rejects the set of assumptions which he believes belongs to Iser's theory:

... the assumption that looking at real objects is different from *imag-ining* objects in a poem or novel; the assumption that in the one activity the viewer simply and passively takes in an already formed reality, while in the other he must participate in the construction of a reality; the assumption that knowledge of real people is more direct and immediate than knowledge of characters or lyric speakers; and, finally, the assumption that these two kinds of experience come to us in two kinds of language, one that requires only that we check its structure against the already constituted structure it reproduces or describes, and the other that requires us to produce the objects, events, and persons to which it (in a curious, even mysterious, liter-ary way) refers.[24]

Fish hinges his argument on what he considers to be a false distinc-tion in Iser between 'determinate' reality and 'indeterminate' fiction. If reality itself is never the already given, but always the effect of some act of mediation (usually, here, a linguistic act), then the distinction, Fish believes, does not hold. There is nothing that can be determined, so the idea of indeterminacy becomes redundant. But, however strong this argument, we still need the distinction. Scepticism, here, has practical limits. We depend, as readers, on the dualism which separates our response from the text and from the world we believe the text is trying to depict. Practically we cannot even begin to talk about response unless we posit a something to respond to, outside our response. For the pragmatists this might be just a way of talking, but it is the absolute precondition for talking about texts. However persuaded we may be that response is everything, we remain as readers of texts and as readers of the world around us, convinced that there *is* something external to our grasp, something which our language cannot encompass. The mistake is to assume that there are ways of defining and finally determining this something *without* responding to it and in the process creating it anew. Here, as readers, we face the paradoxical sense both of our own power over the text together with the feeling that the text and the world it describes always elude our attempts at closure. We can, then, restore the word 'indeterminacy' in a rather different sense: what Geoffrey Hartman means by it when he uses it to counter those theories which ignore 'the resistance of art to the meanings it provokes' and therefore underestimate the inexhaustibility of response.[25] Here, then, the term 'indeterminacy' expands beyond an acknowledgement that art cannot determine (any more than any other form of representation or response) an external world, to include the idea that readers can never determine texts. For the pragmatists such claims are pointless, but the experience of readers is often that such confidence in the face of the unknown is misplaced. It is one thing to say that the world cannot be conceived outside our response to it; it is another thing to be perfectly comfortable about this. Hartman's view suggests, however, that the unsayable and the unknowable can be seen as preconditions for the reader's creativity.

Other nuances of this debate about the source of meaning – text or reader? – are explored in the collection of lectures, *Interpretation and Overinterpretation*, edited by Stefan Collini. This volume collects Umberto Eco's three *Tanner Lectures* and the response to them by Richard Rorty and others. In his lectures Eco provides a critique of the tendency in recent criticism towards what he calls 'unlimited semiosis' (where the process of signifying continues beyond and against anything signified). This he sees as linked to 'hermetic' and 'gnostic' traditions. Broadly, hermetic thought takes its cue from Hermes – a shape-changer who knows no spatial or temporal constraints and who confounds the principles of identity and causality. Equally elusive, the gnostic tradition has come to celebrate a kind of mystic, intuitive knowledge, not dependent on perception or received opinion for its truths. Combined, Eco argues, the influence of these traditions has led some to see the text as open to 'infinite interconnections', a site for an 'uninterrupted chain of infinite deferrals'; to see language as inadequate to reality; and to see the reader as the *Übermensch* (superman), free to impose intention on the text and to 'discover that texts can say everything, except what their author wanted them to mean'.[26]

Eco offers an allegory to express his idea of a necessary respect for the *intentio operis* (the intention of the work, within the work) as compared with the wilful, disrespectful imposition of the *intentio lectoris* (the intention of the reader, imposed upon the work). A slave, bringing figs to someone, with a letter from his master noting the number of figs, eats some of the figs on the way and is upbraided by the recipient, on discovering that fewer figs have been delivered than the letter specified. Next time, on the same errand, the slave hides the letter under a stone, so 'it' will not see him eating some of the figs. He is still upbraided, however, when the letter does not correspond with the figs left. His response is to think that the letter is miraculous. Eco comments: 'we cannot disregard the point of view of the slave who witnessed for the first time the miracle of texts and of their interpretation. If there is something to be interpreted, the interpretation must speak of something which must be found somewhere, and in some way respected.'[27] Eco goes on to give many amusing examples of what he thinks of as over-(and therefore 'mis-') interpretation. Respect for the text, though it allows the pluralism noted above, means an acknowledgement of the stability of the text:

> Between the mysterious history of a textual production [which includes for Eco, the 'intent of the author'] and the uncontrollable drift of its future readings [which include the 'intent of the readers'] the text qua text still represents a comfortable presence, the point to which we can stick.[28]

But, of course, for the pragmatist this textual intention is the construct of the reader. Indeed Eco has acknowledged that 'it is possible to speak of the text's intention only as the result of a conjecture on the part of the reader'.[29] In other terms, Eco calls this conjecture an 'interpretive bet'. Let us return to the figs. Imagine the letter reads: 'Here I send you the 100 figs I promised' – the recipient counts only 95 figs, and turns to the slave to accuse him of eating them. What would the slave be likely to say? It is of course possible that he would acknowledge 'a fair cop'. But he might say: 'Well, I swear I haven't eaten any, they must have fallen out' or 'Well, I swear I haven't eaten or dropped any, my master has tried to trick you out of five figs' or 'Well, I swear it's not my fault, my master must have miscounted' or 'Yes, I was attacked by a fig-eating creature'. The words of the letter do not refer to a reality (there are five figs fewer than noted) but neither do they declare their intention (the slave's master might have intended the letter to trick the recipient out of five figs, assuming that the slave will be blamed). Even if there were complete agreement between the letter and the number of figs, the intention of the letter would not necessarily be clear: 'Here I send you the 100 figs I promised' might conceal the meaning 'and I hope you choke on them' as easily as 'and I hope you enjoy them'. As far as the likes of Fish and Rorty are concerned, texts do not have intentions that are not the result of interpretation. Intention is not a 'given': it is a 'made'. So Rorty, answering Eco, asserts that texts cannot proclaim of readings: 'you get me all wrong; this is what I really mean':

My disinclination to admit that any text can say such a thing is rein-
forced by the following passage in Eco's article. He says 'the text is an
object that the interpretation builds up in the course of the circular
effort of validating itself on the basis of what it makes up as its result'.
We pragmatists relish this way of blurring the distinction between
finding an object and making it.[30]

Actually Rorty, elsewhere, has taken the blurring of this distinction to
its fullest conclusion, in a debate which links directly with the discussion of external reality. Considering the question as to whether scien-
tists 'make' or 'find' the phenomena they describe, Rorty concludes:

> Nothing deep turns on the choice between these two phrases –
> between the imagery of making and of finding . . . It is less paradoxi-
> cal, however, to stick to the classic notion of 'better describing what
> was already there' for physics. This is not because of deep epistemo-
> logical or metaphysical considerations, but simply because, when we
> tell our Whiggish stories about how our ancestors gradually crawled
> up the mountain on whose (possibly false) summit we stand, we need
> to keep some things constant throughout the story. The forces of
> nature and the small bits of matter, as conceived by current physical
> theory, are good choices for this role. Physics is the paradigm of
> 'finding' simply because it is hard (at least in the West) to tell a story
> of changing physical universes against the background of an
> unchanging Moral Law or poetic canon, but very easy to tell the
> reverse sort of story.[31]

Jonathan Culler is rightly impressed with this marvellous passage, and
quotes it in his section 'Stories of Reading' in *On Deconstruction*,
adding: 'Reader-oriented critics have themselves found that it makes
a better story to talk of texts inviting or provoking responses than to
describe readers creating texts, but the distinctions that structure
these stories are open to question and accounts that rely on them
prove vulnerable to criticism.'[32]

This is certainly Rorty's own view of Eco's account, to return to that
debate. Rorty challenges Eco's central distinction: 'I ask why he *wants*
to make a great big distinction between the text and the reader,
between *intentio operis* and *intentio lectoris*.'[33] For Rorty there is no
such distinction. The intention of the text is the intention we have
given it in the process of reading it. We can, of course, give it 'daft'
intentions but we will then be called 'daft'. The text does not prohibit

'daft' readings: the constraints of the rhetorical context in which we persuade others by the convention of citing the text in support of our claims makes us generally avoid them. Fish would put this differently – he would say that what we mean by a 'daft' reading is a reading not recognized by the literary-critical system within which all literary-critical readings must be recognized. So, in Fish's legal arguments, a judge cannot make 'bad' judgements and remain a judge. To judge is to judge within a system which allows the various judgements that it allows. A judge may follow a precedent, or the constitution, or a sense of moral law allowed by the legal system, but a judge may not make judgements outside the system. (A judge cannot say 'I sentence you on the basis that I don't like your hair': even if this is the secret reason for the judgement it cannot be given as the reason – the reason given must be a reasonable one within the law.) According to Fish and Rorty, then, it is not the case that the mediation of all meaning leads to a free-for-all. There are always constraints, but they are not the constraints of linguistic signification or textual intention.

But, in another sense, Rorty himself has already answered his question to Eco. The reason Eco '*wants* to make a great big distinction between the text and the reader' concerns the power of that story Rorty has described as the 'scientific' paradigm. It conforms to the idea of a comforting and comfortable physical universe where we find, rather than make, the objects of our investigation, and where our experience is therefore rooted in measurable certainties.

Ultimately, we agree with the positions of Fish and Rorty, but with qualifications. In that the concern of this book is *practice* we further agree that 'theory' is 'the name for all of the ways people have tried to stand outside practice in order to govern practice from without'.[34] But we concur also with Elizabeth Freund in her synopsis of approaches supporting *The Return of the Reader*:

> Theoretically the distinction between the objective and the subjective, between the literary fact (or the author's text) and the interpretive act (or the reader's construction) cannot be maintained. In practice, however, the distinction always returns; it is always being made so that acts of interpretation can continue to be produced.[35]

To return, briefly, to Fish's description of the pluralists' position, it is as true of Fish as it is of Iser that, in practice 'while a literary text is distinguished by its openness to a number of readings, it is not open to any and all readings'. It is true that this would mean something rather different as applied to Fish or Rorty: for them there could be as many texts as there are readers, but, practically, *only certain readings are allowed or legitimized within the context in which readings take place*. Privately we can believe that Elizabeth Bennet sped across the room at full tilt to be with her sister: the text clearly allows us to arrive at such an interpretation. The text will not declare its intentions. It will not tell us 'you get me all wrong; this is what I really mean'. But, practically, other readers would tell us 'it can't possibly be like that', and they would tell us so in the name of the text. They might argue, for instance, that Elizabeth 'runs' to her sister not literally: actually she 'moves quickly' but Austen uses the word to express the degree of her sympathy for her sister. Such a reading would not be true to some determined meaning *in* the text, but it would be offered as such, and rightly so. We cannot, in practice, maintain a distinction which all the time asserts that whatever we say about the text represents our reading intention and not some textual reality. Our interpretation makes the text what it is, and it then *is* what we take it to be. The text comes to be known as the source of meanings that can only, theoretically, be situated in the reader's response and in the negotiation of that response within groups of readers. The text, then, is the *site* where readers justify and validate their readings. As such it is never fixed, creating the inescapable paradox that though the text is *cited* as the origin of interpretation, the interpretation changes the nature of the origin. Neither is this as controversial a point as it is sometimes believed to be. The history of textual criticism shows that even the words on the page are created by acts of interpretation. What the text of *Hamlet*, or *The Prelude*, or *Ulysses*, actually *is* is the subject of often vehement debate, before we even get to the problem of what those texts mean. The outrage of a recent letter to the *Times Literary Supplement* reveals the urgent importance that readers attach to the issue of textual determination. The letter's author wants to reject an edition of *Ulysses* prepared by Danis Rose:

> The perceived requirement that there was a need for an edition 'as a novel to be read' is the first of many self-justificatory claims; as an 'ordinary reader' I have read it at least half a dozen times (in the 1968 edition) and each time am more awed by the astounding richness, flexibility and creativity of the language and images that it contains . . . The arrogance of Rose's stated 'correction' of 'hundreds

> of manifest errors in the syntactical structure' leads one to ask who actually wrote this book, Joyce or Rose? Is Rose not aware that the linguistic creativity and flexibility, and the poetic development of the language, are largely what make the work so extraordinary in the first place? . . . Hyphens were inserted, we are told, 'where required': by whom? Clearly not by the author . . . Fortunately, Joyce has enough defenders (most of them by no means 'frozen in academia', simply lovers of the book that he actually wrote) to ensure that more authentic versions of the text will survive very much longer than this one.[36]

What is interesting here is that the writer seems not only unaware of some serious contradictions, but consummately confident of views which are compromised in the very process of expressing them. The issue is what *Ulysses* 'really is', and the writer is sure it is not what Rose makes it. What it *should* be, the writer is sure, is the book Joyce 'actually wrote', the quintessence of its author, whose name becomes its metonym ('Joyce has enough defenders'). But the defenders of the true 'Joyce' must base their defence *on* something and the letter-writer seems sure of his ground here. *Ulysses*, serialized in one form in 1918, published in another in Paris in 1922, is to be saved from outrage by 'the 1968 edition' or, at least by editions 'more authentic' than Rose's. The writer is perfectly at ease in proclaiming the absolute standard of an authentic *Ulysses*, when all that is available, by his own account, are competing versions of *Ulysses*. The truest Joyce is to be found in an edition published twenty-seven years after Joyce's death. There can, of course, be no true defenders of Joyce if the measure of their love is access to the book 'he actually wrote'. But where, we might ask, does the anger in the letter come from? The anger seems to exist in proportion to the intensity of response: the letter-writer has been 'awed' by *Ulysses*, 'astounded' by it, and has become a 'lover' of the novel. It 'contains' both 'richness' and 'creativity' (also 'flexibility', but considering the importance of fixing the text this is perhaps an unfortunate term). We cannot talk about the object of our love as if it might be the projection of our love, because our own powers and virtues are at stake – that we find the text 'rich' or 'extraordinary' is a testimony to our capacity to find it so, but we would like others to verify our skills by pointing to the same text and agreeing. And, despite the manifest contradictions of this letter, it offers a legitimate discourse – the editor of the *Times Literary Supplement* printed it, allowing it to contribute to the public debate about what *Ulysses* really is, despite the fact that all its assumptions have been challenged by modern theory. In turn, we should not be outraged by the letter when, no matter how conscious we are of the naïvety of its gestures, we, too, have always to talk about *Ulysses* as if it was the undisputed source of our response. We cannot do otherwise than call the text the cause of readings that undoubtedly cause it to be what it is.

So the fears of those who take a reactionary view of developments in theories accounting for meaning are, in one sense, pointless. George Steiner's arguments are interesting here. Necessary to Steiner's belief in the primacy of art is recourse to what Hartman refers to as 'the Arnoldian Concordat' (after the Victorian critic, Matthew Arnold), 'which assigns to criticism a specific, delimited sphere distinct from the creative'.[37] Criticism becomes the expression of a secondary response to the primary text. For Steiner, art 'causes' our response: 'the poem comes before the commentary'. The intent of the creator and the act of creation, what Steiner calls 'the bringing into being of the work of art', is 'prior to all other modes of its subsequent existence'.[38] Not only, though, does art have 'precedence' over response. Response, at least in its critical expression, is parasitical. Criticism provides a living 'for all manner of secondary souls'. This last expression is followed by the parenthesis 'how could I not know and acknowledge this to be so', which is hardly convincing. (Steiner, of all people, does not consider himself to be a 'secondary soul'!)[39]

Actually, according to Steiner's cult of authorship, authors not only deprive us of the right to claim primary creativity but also take the secondary laurels as well. The best respondents to literature are creative writers; the best critics of music are musicians. The point is, though, that arguments asserting the primary nature of art and the pre-eminence of its creators paradoxically resist such a hierarchy. There is nothing a Steiner can say about the greatness of art that is not equally a testimony to the intensity of *response*. The rest is silence. That is why Steiner wants to insist that the expression of response is redundant – words about art are ultimately futile and pointless. Art is the experience of the primary which transcends language. Our engagement with art is akin to religious experience. It is ineffable, and therefore, in Beckett's formulation, not to be 'effed'. It is not so much, for Steiner as for others in his tradition, that we read texts – we rather 'live in them'.

We can admire Steiner's celebration of art as experience without accepting the gag. Of course we feel things when we read. Of course our response is emotional and – therefore – always partly inexpressible. Yet it is pointless developing a tone of elegiac regretfulness about the assignment of primary and secondary roles. Steiner assigns to us 'an anxious desire for interposition, for explicative-evaluative mediation between ourselves and the primary'.[40] But how could we ever allocate primacy *without* mediation? And what is threatened by assigning the reader a creative role? 'The big push comes', writes Rorty of Eco, 'when I ask why he *wants* to make a great big distinction between the text and the reader.'[41] The answer, perhaps, is that what is at stake is the myth of origins. Seeing art as the sign of God's originating power puts the pressure on. If readers were allowed to create authors then the light might die before their uncreating words. But, again, this should give no real cause for concern. Response can say nothing about an origin outside of response. Either, practically, the origin is our version of it, or it exists beyond our response. If there is an origin without mediation then we literally have to be silent about it, so Steiner need not fear our words. We certainly cannot threaten its existence. In practice, the (false) distinction between primary and secondary is trivial. Reading is an experience which is partly communicable and always communal. We can never separate ourselves from the text. Whatever the text is, our reading has made it so.

However, this is not to deny that connected with our experience is a wish to assign value to something other than our own response. This idea persists despite the rigorous theoretical challenges of the last thirty years. In practice, if our experience of art seems profound, moving, uplifting, transcendental, it must be because we, as readers, are – in some sense – profound, moved, uplifted and transcendent. But the story of origin is a powerful one, and the feelings of admiration we have for other supposed 'authors' of our experiences, it could be argued, are manifestations of deep human needs. As theorists we can 'problematize' sources beyond redemption, we can even 'prove' that any such bases (calling them, oddly, 'transcendental signifiers') are unstable, but as readers such 'ontological groundedness' is none the less vital to our sense that reading matters. Rorty would not have wanted readers to be 'enraptured' by *Heart of Darkness* unless he believed *Heart of Darkness* to be both a likely and a worthy *source* of rapture. Adrienne Rich was not travelling to anyone's house: she was travelling to the house of a 'genius'. Eco takes it as a law that he must 'respect' the miraculous text. An account of reading which denies (as misguided) or ignores (as irrelevant) this aspect of our response is deluding itself. But Steiner takes too little care. Ideas of greatness, genius, and miracle are created *by* response. It will not do to ostracize only those forms of response which do not explicitly worship at the altar of authorship. The view our culture holds of common worth – that Shakespeare was a genius; that *Ulysses* is miraculous; that *Middlemarch* is a masterpiece; that Jane Austen has to be admired – derives as much from professional criticism as does the challenge to those values. As readers we have an originating responsibility for such claims.

But who are we? What, or whom, do we mean by 'the reader' in this book about reading? It has become something of a routine to list the types of reader that different accounts of the activity of reading have posited. As the authors of *The Practice of Reading*, we believe that, nearly always, the different kinds of readers offered as models are ultimately euphemisms for the authors-as-readers who write about them. Even when researchers genuinely want to give an account of the experiences of 'real' readers they actually create stories about the process of reading which tell us more about their *own* perspectives and agendas than about those supposed readings which are the subject of their debate. Many examples might be given to prove this point, but we can take, as typical, Ben Knights's empirical account of reading groups in *From Reader to Reader: Theory and Practice in the Study Group*.

'What I offer', writes Ben Knights, 'is a series of "process readings": accounts of the reading of literary texts not from the standpoint of achieved wisdom, but in a way that seeks to represent the reading as event. At this point my argument is closest to that of reader theorists like Wolfgang Iser, and Stanley Fish.'[42] (Actually, Knights's approach, in that it posits a relationship between constraining text and mediating reader is broadly comparable with that of Iser, and in so far as it is interested in 'interpretive communities' is loosely indebted to Fish.) It is Knights's aim to be faithful, in his representation, to the study group's response to the texts. But he does not attempt to present their 'actual' contributions. To do so would involve transcribing all the features of what linguists call normal non-fluency (the stops and starts of spoken discourse, the abandoned structures, the voiced fillers, the overlapping talk). What we have instead is a story, a narrative construct. Indeed, he suggests that the teacher's role 'parallels in many respects the role of the narrator in realist fiction'.[43] And he proceeds to fictionalize the readers. How can we be sure of this?

Because, to adapt Barthes's maxim about fiction, 'everything functions'. The group cannot behave dysfunctionally without the experience being meaningful. Even when there *appears* to be
non-participation it proves to be rich with meaning – far from the
acknowledgement that we little understand the ways of the wayward.
One man, who becomes a character in a mini-drama, is given the
name 'Eric'. The pseudonym, in keeping with Knights's narrative
approach, serves the realist purpose of those abbreviations and
hyphens in the realist novel (so characters have to be named 'Mr B.',
dates and places have to be censored with dashes or asterisks). 'Eric'
is a real man, with a real life, and we must not upset him by betraying
the trust of the seminar-confessional. Of course Eric never existed, by
which we do not mean that Knights does not have a real person or a
real event in mind, but rather that his transposition is a piece of
coherent fiction writing:

> After withdrawing into the pages of a volume of Larkin's essays . . .
> Eric launched in with the avowed purpose of bringing the class back
> to reality . . . He accused the class of being trivial and boring . . . and,
> when other members pressed him to say what in that case he would
> prefer, spoke of admiring great authors. After some acrimonious
> minutes, he left, shouting from the door that he was the only honest
> person in the room.[44]

Just consider the fictionalizing construct here. In actuality, the person
represented as 'Eric' might have been reading Larkin's *Required
Writing* (though the failure to name the volume serves the realist
agenda again). But, as given in this account, the detail contributes to a
piece of narrative characterization. Knights's view is that groups work
with a feminine dialectic; and Larkin, as we know, is an easy target for
feminist orthodoxy. That 'Eric' 'withdraws' into the Larkin pages is
oddly rich. Not allowed the right of penetrative phallocentric engagement with the female group, Eric withdraws to enjoy the masturba-
tory pleasures of Larkin, until roused to assert his ritual of dominance.
And what, exactly, did Eric say? We doubt whether he said 'I accuse
you of being trivial and boring.' He would, of course, have to 'launch
into' such a speech. One always 'launches'. What are 'acrimonious
minutes'? Knights is creating a character, not representing the
member of the group. This always happens when we try to talk about
real readers. They come to serve our reading purposes. They become

the constructs of our system of reading. As such they come to epitomize a spurious coherence so often assumed to be the goal of our interpretative strategies. Eric's behaviour as 'reader', even as a kind of resisting reader who will not conform, is perfectly incorporated within a narrative of coherent psychodynamic interaction. He is incapable of irrelevance. 'Empirically', writes Elizabeth Freund, 'most of us tend to think of ourselves and others in terms of distinctive and recognizable "styles" which integrate and unify different aspects and details of our behaviour into recurrent patterns.'[45] The creation of Eric depends on these styles (conservative, anti-feminist, phallocentric, authoritarian, isolated, threatened, vulnerable, etc.).

The context for Freund's remark just quoted is actually her discussion of Norman Holland's models for 'the reader' in his *5 Readers Reading*. Her conclusion is that Holland's model for transactive psychoanalytical accounts of the reading experience tends to run into problems, merging the idea of the 'self' with that of 'identity' as if the self were a unified presence:

> Basically, the model totters over its inability to decide whether the 'self' is the provisional product of interpretation or an 'unchanging essence'. This is due to the fact that Holland seems unable to shake off the empirical conviction that the 'self', like the text, is an objective or real entity, a conviction reinforced by his analyses of real readers the impression of whose abiding 'personality' serves as the key to an explanation of their reading practices.[46]

The assumption that there are 'real readers', with abiding personalities, ignores what Derrida has called the 'transformational' nature of reading. Here is Andrew Bennett's neat synopsis of the idea:

> 'Reading', Derrida declares, 'is transformational.' Reading may be understood in terms of what we might call the 'trance of reading' – 'trance' as in transition or transit, transference, transposition, translation, transformation, transgression and, finally, entrancement. In the trance of reading, the identity of the reading subject is itself unstable, yet to be determined or constituted in the 'experience' of reading.[47]

It is interesting that many theorists of reading who readily see the text as unstable nevertheless posit real readers as models of stability.

Moving, then, from the text's status as an external object to the reader's status as an external being, we encounter similar problems, and return to the provisional, mediated nature of the reality we would seek to describe.

These central debates about the source and locus of meaning, the nature of the reader's role, and the identity of the reader, which have been the subject of this introductory chapter, will be of recurring importance in this book. But they will be investigated through a detailed analysis of the processes involved in reading particular novels.

Such a commitment to 'close reading' means that we are drawn towards theories of reading which can 'be assimilated into a tradition of textual criticism'. This description belongs to Robert Holub, who uses it to explain why American criticism has taken the work of Wolfgang Iser as representative of reception theory, and has comparatively neglected the work of other reception theorists. His view is that the American textualist tradition finds it more comfortable to engage with a theorist whose view is that the reader must fill textual gaps and indeterminacies, because this involves a detailed attention to the text and the strategies used in reading it. Holub sees the work of Stanley Fish, paradoxically, as confirming this textualist bias:

> It may seem that the only constant feature in the vicissitudes of [Fish's] theoretical quest during the seventies was the premise that it is only the reader, and not the text, that determines meaning. But his actual critical practice depends, as he shows time and again, on following closely the words printed on the page before him.[48]

Fish would have several answers to this criticism. First, he would claim that he has not been doing 'theory' but 'practice'. Secondly, he would argue that 'practice' within the disciplined community of literary studies *means* 'textual practice'. Finally, he would say that this practice, far from asserting the given nature of the 'words printed on the page', actually constitutes the text. In other words, Holub's assumption returns to the idea that the text is a given which the reader interprets. The word 'depends' here is important: it implies that Fish is 'dependent' on the text.

As the authors of this book we have to confess that we are entirely open to the terms of Holub's critique. *The Practice of Reading* is much more interested in Iser, Fish, and other theorists, whose practice is a practice of close reading, than in the work of those who prefer to examine the ideological and historical contexts of reading and textual production. We, like Elizabeth Freund, find R. P. Blackmur's idea of 'technical' criticism useful:

> 'A critic's job of work', the essay from which I quote, argues strongly and eloquently against 'tendencious' [sic] criticism, the kind which strives for omnipotence and represses self-awareness and the awareness of gaps. Blackmur's ironic ideal is 'technical' criticism (playing on the root meaning of *techne* – an art). We need whatever 'techniques' (tools and speculative instruments) we can muster for performing the unceasing acts of mediation we call . . . criticism. But these techniques should be employed to *enact* the experience of reading – provisionally, speculatively, dramatically – not to totalize it. It is not the knowledge to be obtained or the object to be seized that concerns Blackmur, but the ways of knowing, the 'habit (not a theory) of imagination'.[49]

Of course, this kind of practice, though its end is not the monolithic interpretation of texts, nevertheless needs texts to work with. In this book, therefore, we have taken seven texts which we find rich ground for a broad range of reading techniques. J. Hillis Miller's apology for his choice of texts in *The Ethics of Reading* might equally serve here:

> It may be seen from my use of examples that I think my topic is one that cannot be adequately discussed in the abstract. It *must* be analyzed and demonstrated in terms of specific cases . . . It is easy to see that no choice of examples is innocent. It is a somewhat arbitrary selection for which the chooser must take responsibility. On the other hand there is no doing, in this region of the conduct of life, without examples.[50]

The expression 'somewhat arbitrary' is an interesting one for an author like Hillis Miller who, the reader feels, weighs each word chosen. One would have thought the choice of examples is *entirely* arbitrary. But the critic's 'will' is always to some extent constrained by the cultural context from which the examples are to be chosen. We have been happy to select narrative texts which could be said to belong to a highly constrained, even conservative, canon of prose fiction in English. They are, if you will, 'classic' texts. (This idea of the 'classic' perhaps demands a sense of the test of time which *Possession* cannot fulfil as yet, but it is clearly written within the academy, and has already acquired the status of prize-winning novel, which might be said immediately to relegate it to the status of a heritage object.) We are not embarrassed about this. The novels are ones we greatly admire, but, more importantly, they allow us to explore a spectrum of reading experiences across the period of the novel's mature growth. Moreover, there is no way of escaping a canon. That we have chosen texts which belong to one of the canons of Western academic literary studies does not mean that we look with disapproval upon alternative canons. It rather means that students and teachers of literature within that academic context are more likely to have read the books we discuss. It is true that students are more likely to have read *Great Expectations* than Beckett's *Trilogy* but Beckett's work is similarly obsessed with reading the human self and with interpreting constructions of identity. Indeed, even those who have not yet read Beckett's *Trilogy* have, in another sense, already read it. This is an advantage with the 'classic' text, as noted by Calinescu: 'reading the classics, as Italo Calvino once observed, is always an act of rereading; even though "every rereading of a classic is as much a voyage of discovery as the first reading"'.[51]

This anticipates Derek Attridge's claims about Joyce quoted at the beginning of Chapter 6. On the one hand 'we can never read Joyce's works for the first time'; on the other hand 'we can also never come to the end of our reading of them'. The ideas behind both observations here are central to *The Practice of Reading*. We have always already 'read' these novels because they are a part of our culture, and have had an impact on that culture. But they are also inexhaustible. To take just one point: the idea of the intertextuality of the reading experience supports both these claims. To read Sterne we must read Rabelais (and Montaigne, and Burton, and Cervantes . . .), and if we have already read them then we have literally read parts of *Tristram Shandy* without ever picking up the book. And if *Tristram Shandy* is full of 'foreign' texts, then *Possession* is a thorough exercise in polyphony, with its writings by seven Victorian and ten twentieth-century figures. We cannot exhaust such novels partly because our reading depends on other reading(s).

The Practice of Reading, though, also examines the yearning for completion and coherence, the passion for truth that motivates the urge to read on. 'We hunger for ends and for crises,' argues Kermode; '[w]e are driven by endings as by hunger,' reveals *Possession*. It is, for the reader as for Elizabeth Bennet, always 'impossible not to long to know', because reading is driven by the deep desire for narrative closure. But the reading experience can often seem to be one of endless deferral where our expectations are scarcely ever fulfilled and our desire for order and coherence is disabled by impossible attempts to structure chaos. It seems, depending on which source one follows, that the idea of postmodern openness creates anxiety in directly opposite senses. On the one hand, there is the academic fear that it is unacceptable to reach for closure, completion and coherence. Robert Holub expresses the situation well:

> Far more disturbing for me is the tendency in many contemporary humanities departments to instill another type of anxiety. It is most manifest among young critics and students who find that in the current academic climate, particularly among theorists, it is not chic to embrace any principles except those that maintain the inevitability of aporia, contradiction, and nihilism.[52]

On the other hand, as Ben Knights argues, 'In existential terms, ambiguity and relativity can be hard things to bear, and yet the literary class is expected to make no bones about its sojourn in the emotional state implied by the reading of text.'[53] While willingly considering the openness of the novel-reading experience, and bowing neither to postmodernist orthodoxies nor to the manœuvres of counter-modernism, we have tried in this book to hold many different perspectives in mind. The 'pathless path' of the aporia, as we argue below, can be both unnerving *and* liberating, and an acknowledgement of the reader's desire for ends should inform any judgement which ventures to suggest that there are no ends to be had. Readings and interpretations may be end*less*, but all readers and interpreters have at least one common end in mind, without which reading and interpretation would never, could never, happen – the wish itself *to* read, *to* interpret. In our beginnings are our ends.

2 The Role of the
Reader: *Tristram Shandy*

There can be few other novels that so comprehensively evoke and
explore the central importance of the reader's response than
Laurence Sterne's *The Life and Opinions of Tristram Shandy,
Gentleman* (1759–67). A novel which makes use of every conceivable
kind of vacancy (including missing pages, blank pages, misplaced
chapters, empty chapters) and, in place of words, gives rows of asterisks, squiggles, and black and marbled pages, offers an abundance of
easy material for those who wish to stress the crucial productive
involvement of the reader's imagination in the generation of
meaning. Equally helpful are Tristram's and Sterne's explicit statements concerning the creative and active participation of the reader.
Here is Tristram's colloquial analogy, which gives the idea of a 'mediated' response in its etymological sense (from the Latin *mediāre*,
meaning to halve or be in the middle):

> WRiting, when properly managed, (as you may be sure I think mine
> is) is but a different name for conversation: As no one, who knows
> what he is about in good company, would venture to talk all; — so no
> author, who understands the just boundaries of decorum and good
> breeding, would presume to think all: The truest respect which you
> can pay to the reader's understanding, is to halve this matter amica-
> bly, and leave him something to imagine, in his turn, as well as your-
> self. (p. 88)

In that such a comment explicitly acknowledges the importance of an
'interaction' between novel (or fictional autobiography) and reader, it
is hardly surprising that Wolfgang Iser, whose theory of response is
based on such an idea, should want to quote this passage in his
volume on *Tristram Shandy*.[1] Tristram's sentence even anticipates
the terms of Iser's debate. Just as Tristram moves from '*halving* the

matter' to 'leaving the reader *something* to imagine' so Iser moves from situating the 'literary work' '*halfway*' between the text and response to putting it '*somewhere*' between the two. Iser also quotes Sterne's thanks to an American reader who had given him a present of a walking stick:

> Your walking stick is in no sense more *shandaic* than in that of its having *more handles than one* – The parallel breaks only in this, that in using the stick, every one will take the handle which suits his convenience. In *Tristram Shandy*, the handle is taken which suits their passions, their ignorance or sensibility. There is so little true feeling in the *herd* of the *world*, that I wish I could have got an act of parliament, when the books first appear'd, 'that none but wise men should look into them.' It is too much to write books and find heads to understand them.[2]

These two quotations alone seem to touch on the whole enterprise of theories of reader response: reading is not passive but active, participatory, and the meaning of the text is a matter of the subjective involvement of the reader. Consequently there are no single meanings or single readings. There are many different 'handles' for different readers to grasp. The 'author', be it the 'real' Sterne or the 'fictional' Tristram does not, *cannot*, exercise an authoritarian control over the reception of the text. This is confirmed by Sterne's helpless, but comic, wish for an Act of Parliament. Whatever the authorial intentions, whichever handles Sterne would prefer us to grasp, the novel allows multiple readings. But Iser argues that Sterne encourages the grasping of handles other than those which simply suit us. Hence, by imaginative involvement in other perspectives, we avoid the narrow confines of our own limited subjectivity. The two quotations, then, would seem to offer uncontroversial support to a theory of reading which stresses the central role of the reader.

However, at a conference entitled *Laurence Sterne in Modernism and Postmodernism* at the University of York in 1993, Iser's use of both these quotations *was* an issue of controversy. It is worth recalling (here, and later in this chapter) some of the proceedings of this major conference, not only because the occasion prompted much astute and engaging commentary (not all of which has been subsequently published), but also because it showed how often debate about *Tristram Shandy* in the 1990s has concerned itself with the role of the reader. Tom Keymer, in a paper entitled 'Sterne and Reader-Response Theory', took issue with Iser's interpretation of the first quotation, arguing that, far from encouraging an anachronistic sense of post-modern openness, the passage is to be read ironically. Tristram, in the same section, goes on to claim that it is now the reader's 'turn' to do the imagining, but no sooner is this freedom granted than it is denied; the self-absorbed narrator dictates rather than enlists the reader's response:

> Let the reader imagine then, that Dr. *Slop* has told his tale; —— and in what words, and with what aggravations his fancy chooses: —— Let him suppose that *Obadiah* has told his tale also, and with such rueful looks of affected concern, as he thinks best will contrast the two figures as they stand by each other: Let him imagine that my father has stepp'd up stairs to see my mother: — And, to conclude this work of imagination, — let him imagine the Doctor wash'd, —— rubb'd down, — condoled with, — felicitated, — got into a pair of *Obadiah*'s pumps, stepping forwards towards the door, upon the very point of entering upon action. (p. 88)

Keymer's argument here is not dissimilar to A. S. Byatt's, quoted below in Chapter 8: 'It is Sterne who manipulates, who teases the reader and demands total admiration and assent.'

The use of the second quotation was disputed by Melvyn New in his keynote lecture, 'Sterne, Nietzsche, and Tartuffery' (subsequently revised as 'Tartuffery' in his *Tristram Shandy: A Book for Free Spirits*). Here, New argued that the point is not, to use Iser's terms, that 'the work offers different handles, and one ought to try and grasp them all', but rather that Sterne is mocking those who take the work by the 'wrong' handles. With a touch of mock-deconstructive humour New claimed that Iser's own approach pays only 'lip service to multiple readings', his own critique being typically 'monolithic and decisive'.[3]

These two objections have much in common. They both depend on the assumption of an ironic intention in Sterne's text. According to New's own 'monolithic and decisive' reading of *Tristram Shandy* in his important book *Laurence Sterne as Satirist*, Tristram is continually the object of Sterne's satiric attack, an ironic persona in the tradition of Jonathan Swift. According to Keymer, the narrator's invitation to the reader to 'fill the gaps', in Sterne as in Fielding, is part of a tradi-tional ironic humour which mocks the narrative voice. Such arguments involve a move towards an author-centred text, protecting the authorial intention from the wanton relativism of reader-response criticism. Sterne has an ironic and/or satiric intention which it is the right reader's responsibility to recognize.

The problem here is that Sterne's text resists monolithic readings of all kinds, particularly with respect to the issue of narrative voice. Tristram presents us with an extreme form of the problem of *all* first-person fictional autobiographies: how far is he 'reliable' or 'unreliable'? What is the implied distance between the views of the author and the 'opinions' of the narrator? Is Tristram derided or celebrated by his 'own' account? Is he himself an ironist? All attempts to determine Sterne's intentions depend on highly ambiguous textual information. (Unlike Swift's manifestly naïve ironic personae, Tristram is never made to propose the eating of babies or the abolition of Christianity, which would allow us to settle the issue.) Certainly Sterne's book has been read as 'satire', but it has also been read as sentiment, philosophy and learned wit; it has been called a comic novel; an anti-novel; not a novel at all; and, famously, 'the most typical novel of world literature'.[4] Even those who do consider *Tristram Shandy* to be a satire do not agree on the terms. So New's view of Tristram as naïve persona is very different from De Porte's argument concerning notions of rationality and common sense: 'the intention is to show that they, not Tristram, are inadequate'.[5] And John Traugott, in the book which New has called 'the single work that has most dominated criticism of *Tristram* over the past four decades',[6] makes a distinction between Swift and Sterne on the grounds of the satirist's moral idealism:

> If any one form shapes Sterne's work, it must be his sense of contrast, not the contrast of the world's affairs with a devoutly held moral conception, as with Swift, but a sense that can discover exceptions to any proposition.[7]

This is an astute comment. The history of the reception of *Tristram Shandy* confirms that whereas any number of 'single handles' have been taken, there have always been others to take: the propositions always have equally obvious exceptions.

To return to the opening quotations: the main issue is how *determined* by the text our readings are. New even argues that Tristram's invitation for us to 'paint' Widow Wadman for ourselves, leaving us a

blank space in which to do so, does not evoke a sense of textual indeterminacy, appearing in a fixed context which 'limits readerly participation'[8] by reference to the central textual conflict between 'desire'
and 'conscience' ('paint her [. . .] as like your mistress as you can ——
as unlike your wife as your conscience will let you'). Furthermore,
New believes that our respect for the authorial intention here is borne
out by our unwillingness literally to inscribe the page with 'our'
description:

> Yet, despite Sterne's encouragement of readerly fecundity, I have
> never come across a copy of the work in which someone has written
> or even sketched on the blank page. One reason for this creative
> failure is simply that the blank page is so highly determined, so inca-
> pable of significant division.[9]

This version of New's claim is taken from his published version of the
lecture, which appeared in print the year following the conference.
But, significantly, it does not record the exchange that took place at
this point in the original paper. Prior to his lecture New had asked
Kenneth Monkman, curator of Shandy Hall and bibliographical
expert, to confirm that all the 'blank' pages he had seen had indeed
remained blank. Unfortunately Monkman had come across one
edition where the reader *had* filled the space with remarks. Another
proposition; another exception. *Tristram Shandy* seems so to anticipate the openness of postmodernist theories that, ironically, to
attempt to read it 'against the grain' can obviously lead to the paradoxically conservative claim that its voids are eloquently determined.
But, however we might seek to fill such voids, their determination
must testify to the formative nature of the reader's response, and
New's interpretation is just one form of possible inscription (which
could, of course, have been noted in the space provided by Sterne,
thus, in a sense, literally reconstituting 'the text').

   Actually, to do justice to the subtlety of New's argument, it should
be pointed out that he is ready to acknowledge that his reading is
merely one of any number of readings – given Sterne's own recognition that 'the art of reading' involves 'hovering among alternatives'.[10]
However, he also asserts that Sterne 'had no delusions about the
strength of the reader's need to falsify the "facts" in order to establish
meaning'.[11] The reader's interpretation, then, is always 'prejudiced'
(though New does not use the word to imply the connection between

reading and pre-judging, as we will in the next chapter). Sterne is right to complain that we take whichever handle suits us, twisting the textual 'facts' as we please. We are biased in favour of our own hobby-horsical interpretations. But it is 'Tartuffery' to pretend that the meanings we find are not really the ones we believe to be there: 'Our interpretations are our lives, and we invest enormous stakes of psychic pleasure and security in their well-being.'[12] This is a rather strained argument. Really, New himself is paying lip service to multiple readings, albeit with a degree of self-consciousness. The text is 'richly determined' and correct readers will understand its determinations, and so proclaim their readings in the name of truth. The problem is that the determination can never be separated from the act of reading (it is the reader who takes a particular handle, and twists it) and therefore suggestions that there are right, intended, and determined meanings in the *text* are neither the result of textual facts nor authorial intentions but of reading strategies. The inverted commas around the 'facts' (and similar inverted commas will be an issue in Chapter 7) are therefore revealing. We are to judge our readings against the 'facts' that our readings create!

Whatever we do with the blank left for the widow Wadman's description, its presence acknowledges the freedom of the reader's imagination. The reader is indeed free to claim that other readers are not free and that the space is already 'highly determined' for them. But that would be to prefer a particular reading; other readers, however perverse it might seem to the determined critic, are still free to fill the space in their own way.

But, equally, the refusal to describe the character implies the limitations of language either to determine a complete 'picture', or fully to determine our response. So we can return to our first example from Volume II, Chapter 11, and discover a similar acknowledgement. The instruction 'let the reader imagine' is not diminished or disenabled by the details then given as to the nature of what we should imagine. A 'wash'd', 'condoled with', 'felicitated', 'bepumped' Dr Slop is hardly the determined mimetic representation of a full human presence. The reader still has everything to do to imagine Dr Slop. Of course, there are other details throughout the novel which might be said to add to our picture of Slop. Hogarth, certainly, could draw him. So might we, and depending on our imaginative responses we would all end up with different pictures (even admitting an equal level of draughts-manship), full of details to be found nowhere in Sterne's pages. It is surely not a commitment to the clichéd analogy *ut pictura poesis* (originally Horace's casual comparison – 'as it is in painting, so it is in poetry') that leads Sterne to use so many pictorial metaphors in *Tristram Shandy*. It is rather a comic acceptance that what we might be able to *see* can never be equally determined by the words we have to use to describe it. So, when Tristram tries most exhaustively to determine a description, he tries to compensate for the hilarious inexactitudes of words by mock reference to the exactitudes of art and science. Here is Trim about to read his sermon:

> He stood before them with his body swayed, and bent forwards just so far, as to make an angle of 85 degrees and a half upon the plain of the horizon; —— which sound orators, to whom I address this, know very well, to be the true persuasive angle of incidence [. . .]
>
> He stood, — for I repeat it, to take the picture of him in at one view, with his body sway'd, and somewhat bent forwards, — his right leg firm under him, sustaining seven-eighths of his whole weight, — the foot of his left leg, the defect of which was no disadvantage to his attitude, advanced a little, — not laterally, nor forwards, but in a line betwixt them; his knee bent, but that not violently, — but so as to fall within the limits of the line of beauty; — and I add, of the line of science too; — for consider, it had one eighth part of his body to bear up; — so that in this case the position of the leg is determined, — because the foot could be no further advanced, or the knee more bent, than what would allow him, mechanically, to receive an eighth part of his whole weight under it, — and to carry it too. (p. 98)

The language of science seems, indeed, to echo Tristram's word, to be the most 'determined' of languages, but the humour here depends on the impossibility of crediting such accuracy and precision. The $85\frac{1}{2}°$ angle and the exact division of eighths incongruously meets the vaguely 'swayed' body, 'somewhat' bent forward, the left foot advanced 'a little'. The painterly analogy of the passage again suggests the relative indeterminacy of language. The needful recapitulation – 'He stood . . . with his body sway'd' – as Tristram's syntax, typically, runs away with him, emphasizes that words *cannot* 'take' Trim 'at *one* view'. Also, the kind of determinacy implied by the geometry conflicts with the idea of pictorial representation. How can a weight ratio of exactly one eighth to seven eighths be 'pictured'? Far from facilitating our accurate 'view' of the commonplace idea of a human posture, the

passage rather defamiliarizes poor Trim. Perversely, the more determined the description tries to make him, the less determined he
becomes, eventually disappearing in the abstractions of angles, fields,
and forces. If this is 'pictorial' it is closer to the dynamics of futurism
than to simple representation. Finally, the reader is overwhelmed by
the mechanics, but they lend a bizarre, estranging humour to our
imagination of a comically incongruous, portentous Trim, hardly the
apt exemplar of a pious conscience, dramatizing his performance.

Such a passage testifies to Iser's claim concerning Sterne's 'awareness of the ineradicable difference between the given object and its
representation'.[13] And, interestingly, this observation recalls Mikhail
Bakhtin's comments on Rabelais (who, primarily through Ozell's
edition of Urquhart and Motteux's translation of *Gargantua and
Pantagruel*, provided the most important of Sterne's stylistic influences):[14]

> In Rabelais ... a parodic attitude toward almost all forms of ideolog-
> ical discourse – philosophical, moral, scholarly, rhetorical, poetic ...
> was intensified to the point where it became a parody of the very act
> of conceptualizing anything in language . . . Turning away from
> language (by means of language, of course), discrediting any direct or
> unmediated intentionality and expressive excess ... presuming that
> all language is conventional and false, maliciously inadequate to
> reality – all this achieves in Rabelais almost the maximum purity
> possible in prose.[15]

No textual statement can exhaust its 'subject': for everything 'said'
there is something 'unsaid'. The text is full of gaps and indeterminacies which promote the mediating involvement of the reader.

But there is a further problem here which returns us to the debate
of Chapter 1. If language is 'inadequate to reality' then the object to be
described is never really Iser's 'given' object. Here arises a criticism of
Iser very different from that offered by Keymer and New. As we have
seen, it is Stanley Fish who argues that Iser's model of indeterminacy
tends to depend on an unworkable notion of 'determinacy'. We can
briefly rehearse the kind of claim made by Iser which Fish finds objec-
tionable:

> How can we describe the status of a literary text? The first point is
> that it differs from any text presenting an object that exists indepen-

dently of the text. If a piece of writing describes an object that exists with equal determinacy outside it, then the text is simply an exposition of the object.[16]

The issue here is not the literary *text*, but an idea of literary *language* which makes the text definable as 'literature'. But the idea of any 'language' that can describe the world with an 'equal determinacy' is not only untenable, but also meaningless, implying that language can totally 'say' or (by a kind of word-magic) 'constitute' the thing it describes, and imagining an impossible 'equivalence' (whatever that means) between words and things.

To return to Bakhtin's summary of Rabelais's position, he claims that: '*all* language is conventional and false, maliciously inadequate to reality'. So Sterne and Rabelais make a point of parodying those very languages which most pretend to determine and exhaust their subjects (hence the use of vocabularies associated with mathematics and law). Particularly relevant, here, is Fish's argument, discussed in Chapter 1, that scientific language – 'talk of angles and ratios and velocities' – is no more 'determined' than non-scientific language, and that all languages are equally the subject of a mediating response. Developing this point in his essay 'Why No One's Afraid of Wolfgang Iser', Fish gives the example of a hand raised in a classroom: we see it because it belongs to a 'conventional system of purposes, goals, and understood practices'. He then imagines, as Sterne does with Trim's stance, the most seemingly determinate of languages which might describe such a hand:

> Even if one had recourse to a supposedly neutral vocabulary and described the action in terms of angles, movements, tendons, and joints, that description would itself be possible only under a *theory* of movement, ligatures, etc., and therefore would be descriptive only of what the theory (that is, the interpretation) prestipulates as available for description.[17]

Fish does not share Bakhtin's acute sense of the *problem* of language as he feels he can dispense with the notion of a 'true' reality. There are *only* mediated responses. We will return to this debate in Chapter 7, but we can note here that Fish's extreme position too conveniently avoids our problem that no language seems adequate to grasp a world we sense outside of us. To return to Bakhtin:

Any concrete discourse (utterance) finds the object at which it was directed already as it were overlain with qualifications, open to dispute, charged with value, already enveloped in an obscuring mist – or, on the contrary, by the 'light' of alien words that have already been spoken about it.[18]

Bakhtin's second metaphor does not disqualify the first. Language obscures as it enlightens. Its reference to an external reality is as indeterminate as the black and marbled pages of *Tristram Shandy*, and this indeterminacy suggests that 'reality' may be profoundly unknowable:

> —— And pray who was *Tickletoby*'s mare? — 'tis just as discreditable and unscholar-like a question, Sir, as to have asked what year (*ab. urb. con.*) the second Punic war broke out. — Who was *Tickletoby*'s mare! — Read, read, read, read, my unlearned reader! read, — or by the knowledge of the great saint *Paraleipomenon* — I tell you before-hand, you had better throw down the book at once; for without *much reading*, by which your reverence knows, I mean *much knowledge*, you will no more be able to penetrate the moral of the next marbled page (motly emblem of my work!) than the world with all its sagacity has been able to unraval the many opinions, transactions and truths which still lie mystically hid under the dark veil of the black one. (p. 184)

The black and marbled pages of *Tristram Shandy* dramatize the impossibility of single, determined meanings. Even if readers limit the play of possibilities by taking the black page to signify death and the marbled page to signify the protean eccentricity of Tristram's narrative, this will not constrict their subjective responses. Indeed, the very fact that in the first edition every marbled page is unique – marbled by hand – suggests the uniqueness of each individual's imaginative 'reading'. Such pages are evidently inexhaustible; hence Tristram's playful mockery of the failure of the 'world' to determine the meaning. The passage gives good evidence for Geoffrey Hartman's idea, introduced in Chapter 1, of 'the resistance of art to the meanings it provokes'. But it also suggests the intertextual nature of reading, Bakhtin's 'alien' words already overlying Tristram's subject. Actually our lack of reading here, conveniently considering the reference to Bakhtin, is, partly, a lack of reading Rabelais, where the reference to Friar Tickletoby's frisking filly is to be found. The allusion is first prompted by Tristram's fear that Satan will get astride the reader's imagination and aim *'to frisk it, to squirt it, to jump it, to rear it, to bound it, — and to kick it'* (p. 184). The reference serves as a shorthand for further proliferation, as Rabelais's horse also 'funks it', 'trots it', 'farts it', 'gallops it', 'spurns it', 'calcitrates it', 'winses it', 'leaps it', and 'curvets it'!

Obviously the reader's imagination has remarkable resources, encouraged rather than limited by the nature of Tristram's warning. Aptly, Tristram's Saint Paraleipomenon is the saint of 'things omitted'. Tristram's text needs Rabelais's 'supplement', which only the reader can supply. The 'knowledge' is deferred – we must read elsewhere if we are to 'fill in' the omissions. And this is not the only point in Sterne's novel where proliferation and omission are associated with Rabelais. When Tristram fears abuse for his previous omission of two whole chapters – 'I look upon a chapter which has, *only nothing in it*, with respect' (p. 530) – it is Rabelais who again comes to mind:

> —— Why then was it left so? And here, without staying for my reply, shall I be call'd as many blockheads, numsculs, doddypoles, dunderheads, ninnyhammers, goosecaps, joltheads, nicompoops, and sh--t-a-beds —— and other unsavory appellations, as ever the cake-bakers of Lernè, cast in the teeth of King Gargantua's shepherds. (pp. 530–1)

Here the reference is to an even greater proliferation – one of Rabelais's astonishing collections of invectives:

> The Cake-bakers were in nothing inclinable to their Request; but (which was worse) did injure them most outrageously, calling them *prating Gabblers, lickorous Gluttons, freckled Bittors, mangy Rascals, shite-abed Scoundrels, drunken Roysters, sly Knaves, drowsy Loiterers, slapsauce Fellows, slabber-degullion Druggels, lubbardly Louts, cousening Foxes, ruffian Rogues, paultry Customers, sychophant Varlets*...[19]

The list continues with another twenty-six terms of abuse, and then, as if innocently, adds: 'and other such defamatory Epithets'.

Here, then, are two extremes: on the one hand, Rabelais's verbal proliferation (which acts as an appendix to Sterne's); on the other, Sterne's verbal reduction (marbled and black pages, and missing chapters). It is revealing that Sterne should refer to Rabelais at such points, because proliferation and reduction are two sides of the same problem. For Bakhtin, Rabelais typifies the spirit of the 'carniva-lesque' which is 'hostile to all that was immortalized and completed'.[20] There is no end to the number of words which may be used to describe a horse's movement (especially as both Rabelais and his translators demonstrate a boundless capacity for neologism), as there is no end to the abuse which Tristram deserves – no formula of abuse that will exhaust or determine his depravity. Even the monu-mentally inclusive 'curse' of Ernulphus cannot exhaust the list of cursable aspects. Rabelais's own remarkable linguistic catalogues all imply infinite extension. Indeed, the translators of Rabelais, as Bakhtin notes, have exercised an appropriate freedom of response. To the 217 different games that Gargantua played, a Dutch version added 63 purely Dutch games, and the first German translator added no fewer than 372 items to Rabelais's original list. If we have to read Rabelais to become a 'learned' reader of *Tristram Shandy*, then we find that Rabelais extends rather than forecloses the potential for creative participation. We have not been referred, for the acquiring of 'much knowledge', to the external world, but to other texts.

The other main sources influencing Sterne confirm the sense of intertextual proliferation. When Tristram inveighs against plagiarism, asking 'Shall we for ever make new books, as apothecaries make new mixtures, by pouring only out of one vessel into another?' (p. 283), the answer, hilariously, must be yes, as the passage is plagiarized from the preface of that most remarkable collection of others' learning, Robert Burton's *The Anatomy of Melancholy* (1621). (Sterne even gives the reader a clue, as the borrowing follows the epigraph '*non Ego, sed Democritus dixit*' – 'not I, but Democritus said it' – Burton having styled himself 'Democritus Junior'.) The reading experience is inter-textual (a point we shall explore further when we come to Byatt's postmodernist novel, *Possession*) and there is no end to the reading that we need to do to fathom the mysteries of Tristram's dark veil.

The last two quotations from *Tristram Shandy* have both, typically, dramatized the active involvement of readerly responses. First, 'Sir' was reprimanded for asking 'And pray who was *Tickletoby*'s mare?'. Then the conservative reader's bafflement at Tristram's blank chap-ters was 'voiced': 'Why then was it left so?' Such devices not only textualize the importance of reader response, they also encourage in the 'real' reader a problematic questioning of his or her status as the 'implied' reader. Iser, at times, rather overlooks this problem, as when he disregards the perplexity of the male reader in commenting: 'When [Tristram] wants to do his reader a special favour, his invitation is to "step with me, Madam, behind the curtain . . .".'[21] Sterne's novel is full of such references to narratees, who have loosely defined characteristics. 'Sir' is generally consulted on matters of interpretation and knowledge; 'Madam' has a rather salubrious imagination and her 'presence' encourages innuendoes and appeals to delicacy and decorum. Some of the problems attendant on the use of narratees are tellingly suggested by Gene Moore.[22] He quotes the following famous passage:

> —— How could you, Madam, be so inattentive in reading the last chapter? I told you in it, *That my mother was not a papist.* —— Papist! You told me no such thing, Sir. Madam, I beg leave to repeat it over again, That I told you as plain, at least, as words, by direct inference, could tell you such a thing. — Then, Sir, I must have miss'd a page. - - No, Madam, — you have not miss'd a word. —— Then I was asleep, Sir. — My pride, Madam, cannot allow you that refuge. —— Then, I declare, I know nothing at all about the matter. — That, Madam, is the very fault I lay to your charge; and as a punishment for it, I do insist upon it, that you immediately turn back, that is, as soon as you get to the next full stop, and read the whole chapter over again. (p. 48)

'Where', asks Moore, 'does this exchange take place?':

> . . . and in what sense can Madam be said to have been (mis)reading? How, given the privacy of the act of reading, can the narrator *know* that she has failed to draw a particular inference? The narrative is presented here simultaneously as something written (or printed; in any case, something to which one can return); as an ongoing oral performance which continues in Madam's absence; and as a text to be (re)read.[23]

Tristram's 'read, read, read, read, my unlearned reader' is echoed in numerous such passages, proving that 'the act of reading is . . . firmly embedded in Tristram's text'.[24] But Moore notes that the above passage conflates a complicated range of 'diegetic' levels – hence the question concerning narrative levels: 'where does this exchange take place?' ('Diegesis' is the narratological term for 'story' or 'narrated events'.) It blurs the distinctions between writing, reading and speech. But we can also add that the position of the 'real' reader is almost as odd as 'Madam's'. The real reader, after all, has the same freedom to re-read, the same tendency to misread, and the same licence to return to the narrative at a different point. And 'Madam's' specific problem of response, here, is almost certainly the same as the reader's. It would be the sign of a remarkable astuteness in the 'real' reader not to have missed the esoteric information that upsets 'Madam'. Tristram had 'told' her, he claims, that his mother was not a Papist by the sentence 'It was *necessary* I should be born before I was christen'd.' This, of course, precedes the very learned debate by the *Docteurs de Sorbonne* on the possibility of baptizing the Catholic foetus by an injected 'squirt'. Similarly, to return to one of our earlier examples, any reader who has not read Rabelais (and many who *have*) will not know who Tickletoby's mare is, and will therefore be, to some extent, in the same position of ignorance as 'Sir'. Consequently the 'real' reader *is*, and *is not*, the 'Sir' and the 'Madam', both constructing and being constructed by the text. Hence *Tristram Shandy* dramatizes the dynamic act of reading as it simultaneously challenges the reader's reading identity.

Such methods also allow Sterne to raise all the central issues of the reading process. Rebuking 'Madam' in her 'absence' for 'reading straight forwards' in search of adventures, Tristram has made comic use of the linear process of reading and the difficulties associated with it. We are always, in a sense, improperly 'inattentive', as we lack the future textual information at any reading moment to know properly what we ought to be attending *to*. Sterne reflects this situation in his comic use of syntax. 'Madam' is imagined responding to an instruction before knowing *how* to respond, and *when* to respond. If she turned back 'immediately' ('I do insist upon it, that you immediately turn back . . .') she would not know that she had to read the whole chapter again. Since the full sentence is marked by a full stop, she is told to wait for it before responding to the demand ('. . . that is, as soon as you get to the next full stop, and read the whole chapter over again').

It is not simply the reader's experience of the words which interests Sterne, but also the experience of their sequence. 'What then', comments Tristram, 'do you think must the terror and hydrophobia of Dr. *Slop* have been, when you read, (which you are just going to do) that he was advancing thus warily along . . .' (pp. 85–6). We know that Slop is terrified and hydrophobic, but we do not know why and we do not know what to think until we have been given more information, until we have read further. The parenthesis is there simply to point out this aspect of our reading experience, and, comically, to further delay our fuller understanding of the words we have just read. The reader thinks before knowing what to think, and is victimized by Sterne's syntax. At times he or she has only to read the opening of a sentence to realize that any expectations of a straightforward development represent a misplaced optimism:

> Here, —— but why here, —— rather than in any other part of my story, —— I am not able to tell; —— but here it is, —— my heart stops me to pay to thee, my dear uncle *Toby*, once for all, the tribute I owe thy goodness. — Here let me thrust my chair aside . . . (p. 182)

The 'here', a point in the narrative, interrupted and stressed in this way, becomes the 'here' of a moment in the text, the 'here' of a place on the page. The interruption makes it clear that the 'here and now' of discourse always displaces itself and is always deferred. It does not mean 'here'; it means 'in what follows'. (It is interesting to note that there is another 'unreadable' 'here' of discourse in *Great Expectations* – see Chapter 4.) And if it is normal to wait for the full stop before assuming a completed phase of discourse, then the reader of *Tristram Shandy* often has to wait a very long time. The proliferation of material demands an extreme degree of structural, syntactic, displacement. Here is a typical example:

> THE abbess of Andoüillets, which if you look into the large set of provincial maps now publishing at Paris, you will find situated amongst the hills which divide Burgundy from Savoy, being in danger of an *Anchylosis* or stiff joint (the *sinovia* of her knee becoming hard by long matins) and having tried every remedy —— first, prayers and thanksgiving; then invocations to all the saints in heaven promiscuously —— then particularly to every saint who had ever had a stiff leg before her —— then touching it with all the reliques of the convent, principally with the thigh-bone of the man of Lystra, who had been impotent from his youth —— then wrapping it up in her veil when she went to bed —— then cross-wise her rosary —— then bringing in to her aid the secular arm, and anointing it with oils and hot fat of animals —— then treating it with emollient and resolving fomentations —— then with poultices of marsh-mallows, mallows, bonus Henricus, white lillies and fenugreek —— then taking the woods, I

mean the smoak of 'em, holding her scapulary across her lap —— then decoctions of wild chicory, water cresses, chervil, sweet cecily and cochlearia —— and nothing all this while answering, was prevailed on at last to try the hot baths of Bourbon . . . (p. 416)

The full sentence is still incomplete, and the full stop many words away yet. So far the main sentence fragment, about which the whole passage is built, reads: 'The abbess of Andoüillets . . . being in danger of an *Anchylosis* . . . and having tried every remedy . . . was prevailed on at last to try the hot baths of Bourbon.' The rest is amplification concerning the whereabouts of Andoüillets, the kind of knee problem, and the various remedies. It results in the verb 'was' being separated from its person by 196 other words, and nine 'then' clauses. The description of remedies is implicitly a list, but the comedy is heightened by including it within the prose structure and so disrupting the syntax. The sequence gains a momentum which becomes wilder and wilder, seeking to escape the burden of syntax entirely in its amassing of words: 'then decoctions of wild chicory, water cresses, chervil, sweet cecily and cochlearia . . .' The humour depends as much on the form as the content, the repeated 'then' clauses conveying the excess that defeats the conventional syntactic development of the sentence. Obviously the amassing technique results in the lengthening of the period. The 'sentence' which completes this passage is, in all, 306 words long. There are many others in *Tristram Shandy* of similar length. A. S. Byatt's comment, quoted below in Chapter 8 ('All my heroes . . . wrote long sentences') should have made Sterne one of her heroes. Such syntactic delay, in complicating the reading experience, makes the reader self-conscious about the process of making sense of sentences. The more complicated the syntactic convolution, the more likely the reader is to get lost, an experience comically parodied by Tristram himself, when he loses the sense of his own digressive sentence and has to begin it all over again (p. 383). Of course, in Fishian terms (as we shall see) the reader 'prematurely hazards' an interpretation while reading a sentence, and this leads to more localized problems of misinterpretation:

> I was five years old. —— *Susannah* did not consider that nothing was well hung in our family, —— so slap came the sash down like lightening upon us; — Nothing is left, — cried *Susannah*, — nothing is left — for me, but to run my country. —— (p. 310)

This, the unfortunate 'circumcision' of Tristram, could be described as syntactic ambiguity. The phrase 'nothing is left' seems to be a completed expression embracing the awful possibility that Tristram has been entirely dismembered, a sense encouraged by the sexual overtones of the phrase 'well hung' (referring to the sash window). The reader then discovers that the full exclamation was suspended, but this discovery does not entirely supplant the first suggestion. Indeed, if nothing of Tristram's sensitive part were left, then Susannah would have very good cause to emigrate. Later the reader learns that the harm was reportedly only superficial, but then a family which already has one serious groinal injury (Uncle Toby's war-wound) would want to secure the reputation for wholeness of its youngest 'member'. In any case the insinuation that Tristram has been fully castrated is rumoured for the rest of his life:

> — And FAME, who loves to double every thing, — in three days more, had sworn positively she saw it, — and all the world, as usual, gave credit to her evidence ——— "That the nursery window had not only
> *
> * *; —— but that * * * * * * * * * * * * * *
> * * * * * * * *'s also." (p. 359)

Here the responsibility for the rumour is again passed on to the reader, appropriately for she/he has already contemplated the possibility. It is interesting that so many textual blanks surround the question of what is 'left' of Tristram's and Toby's vital organs of generation. As Iser comments:

> Sexuality, in the words of R. Alter, 'energizes the reader's imagination, invites it to free and rapid play . . . The effect . . . of this elaborate rhetorical strategy is to make the reader Sterne's accomplice' [. . .] The complicity between author and reader lies in the communication of what decorum forbids to be communicated. This circumvention is meant to goad the reader's imagination into giving substance to what has been adumbrated.[25]

Innuendo, then, offers one of the most obvious of all invitations to the reader's imagination. So active in this sense is the reader that asterisks suffice. We find the same asterisks attending the awful possibilities of Tristram's difficult delivery:

Sir, if the hip is mistaken for the head, — there is a possibility (if it is a boy) that the forceps *26

Somehow the use of 27 consecutive asterisks suggests the gravity of such a possibility. Of course, it is Tristram's nose that suffers the blow of Dr Slop's obstetrical fervour. But the association is now formed that will link nose and phallus throughout the novel, despite (and indeed partly because of) Tristram's protests about the determinate meaning of 'nose':

> For by the word *Nose*, throughout all this long chapter of noses, and in every other part of my work, where the word *Nose* occurs, — I declare, by that word I mean a Nose, and nothing more, or less. (p. 178)

There follows, in Volume IV, Slawkenbergius's Tale, with its sustained pattern of innuendo. The reader is left to enjoy the many possible salacious parallels affecting the stranger's prodigious nose. But the Tale also acts as a satire on nosiness, an allegory of our thirst for narrative 'outcomes' (an issue which will be developed in Chapter 3). The stranger has made a vow that his ridiculous nose shall not be touched by those who wish to satisfy themselves of its genuineness:

> It never shall be touched, said he, clasping his hands and bringing them close to his breast, till that hour —— What hour? cried the inn-keeper's wife. —— Never! — never! said the stranger, never till I am got — For heaven sake into what place? said she. — The stranger rode away without saying a word. (pp. 205, 207)

This citizen of Strasbourg is frustrated by the kind of syntactic delay we have already noted. But here, of course, the crucial sentence remains uncompleted and typifies the whole narrative method of *Tristram Shandy*. Sterne was just as hostile as Rabelais to all that is completed. 'Of all restless desires', notes the Tale, 'curiosity' is 'the strongest' (p. 221). It is a kind of curiosity that compels all readers to read on in anticipation of development and denouement. The inhabitants of Strasbourg suffer the same frustration as 'Madam' in her 'straight forwards' search for narrative adventure.

This brings us, finally (and not before time you may think), to the digressive tendency of Sterne's novel. In a sense this central feature of

Tristram Shandy has almost inevitably been anticipated by most of the points raised so far in this chapter. The sense that there must be an exception to every proposition (and therefore another view, another 'opinion'); the interruptions of 'Sir' and 'Madam'; the appeal to the reader's response; the blanks, gaps and misplaced chapters; the rows of asterisks; the intertextual allusions (and the interpolation of 'other' texts such as Slawkenbergius's Tale); the doomed attempts to exhaust a subject; the verbal proliferation; the polysemantic ambiguity of language which encourages puns and innuendo; the syntactic delay and retardation – all these point to the most pervasive aspect of the reader's experience of *Tristram Shandy.*

> Digressions, incontestably, are the sun-shine; —— they are the life, the soul of reading; - - - take them out of this book for instance, - - you might as well take the book along with them . . . (p. 58)

To return, here, to the matter of Sterne's syntax, the principle of digression radically affects the sentence structures of *Tristram Shandy.*

> I Told the Christian reader —— I say *Christian* —— hoping he is one —— and if he is not, I am sorry for it —— and only beg he will consider the matter with himself, and not lay the blame entirely upon this book, ——
> I told him, Sir —— for in good truth, when a man is telling a story in the strange way I do mine, he is obliged continually to be going backwards and forwards to keep all tight together in the reader's fancy —— which, for my own part, if I did not take heed to do more than at first, there is so much unfixed and equivocal matter starting up, with so many breaks and gaps in it, — and so little service do the stars afford, which, nevertheless, I hang up in some of the darkest passages, knowing that the world is apt to lose its way, with all the lights the sun itself at noon day can give it —— and now, you see, I am lost myself! —— (p. 383)

Stylistically the passage, with its numerous connectives, conjunctions and Shandean 'dashes', offers an excellent example of syntactic digression, and there is a perfect consonance between style and subject. The digressive material which interrupts the proposed sentence 'I told the Christian reader [that] . . .' directly concerns the nature of narrative digression – Tristram's 'strange way of telling a story'. The example offers a kind of linguistic 'embedding' where many subordinate clauses interrupt the main sentence. This feature has its exact corollary in what we can call narrative embedding. 'So', writes John Stedmond,

> we have the Chinese box effect of the story within the story, the digression within the digression, so characteristic of Tristram's narrative style. In this comic world, stories simply do not get told, though in a sense this is the point of the whole 'story': one of the main themes of this 'story' is the frustrating impossibility of humans ever getting a story told, of their ever being able to tell 'all' about anything.[27]

The same analogy, of the Chinese boxes, is used again and again in Sterne criticism. Here is A. A. Mendilow:

> These tales offer interesting examples of the technique of 'Chinese boxes'. Sterne writes a book about Tristram Shandy writing his life in which he, in the year 1760, relates how Trim in 1723 tells the story of Le Fever's death in 1706; or how Walter Shandy translated for the benefit of his brother the work of Slawkenbergius on noses in the course of which there is given the story of Julia and Diego.[28]

The structuralist and narratologist Tzvetan Todorov, in *The Poetics of Prose*, gives other examples of the same technique. One is taken from *The Arabian Nights*, and concerns the story of the 'bloody chest'. Here, writes Todorov:

> Scheherazade tells that
>   Jaafer tells that
>   the tailor tells that
>   the barber tells that
>   his brother (and he has six brothers) tells that . . .
> The last story is a story to the fifth degree; but it is true that the two first degrees are entirely forgotten and no longer have any role to play. Which is not the case in one of the stories of *The Saragossa Manuscript*, where
> Alfonso tells that
>   Avadoro tells that
>   Don Lope tells that
>   Busqueros tells that

> Frasquetta tells that . . .
>
> and where all the degrees, except for the first, are closely linked and incomprehensible if isolated from one another.[29]

The examples here come in a section headed 'Digression and Embedding', where Todorov applies the term from linguistics to narrative structures. The linguistic analogy is explicit, with Todorov giving the example of a German sentence which reads: 'Whoever identifies the one who upset the post which was placed on the bridge which is on the road which goes to Worms will get a reward.' Todorov comments:

> In the German sentence, the appearance of a noun immediately provokes a subordinate clause which, so to speak, tells its story; but since the second clause also contains a noun, it requires in its turn a subordinate clause, and so on, until an arbitrary interruption, at which point each of the interrupted clauses is completed one after the other. The narrative of embedding has precisely the same structure.[30]

Tristram's problem, though, is one of almost infinite deferral and regression. Every piece of information requires further subordinate information. The more you say, the more you have to say. Also, the longer a sentence continues, the more it delays the following sentence, and so the more it contributes to the narrative digression. Northrop Frye makes the point: 'As grammar may be called the art of ordering words, there is a sense – a literal sense – in which grammar and narrative are the same thing.'[31] The unfolding of the narrative is conveyed by the unfolding of the sentences. Convoluted syntax makes for convoluted stories. Tristram discovers, in a sense, that his life is embedded in the stories of others, and that they each have stories to account for themselves. Sterne's syntax expresses perfectly the endless sequences of cause and effect in people's lives and in the stories of their lives.

But, to return to Tristram's 'lost' sentence, we have to ask what is the subordinate information embedded *in*? The idea of embedding implies a completed utterance *within* which other statements are embedded. As it is, Tristram does not get beyond his 'I Told the Christian reader . . . '. So the stylistic problem further mirrors the narrative problem. In *Tristram Shandy*, as digression becomes the main subject, then, in a sense, it can no longer be called 'digression', which, like 'embedding', requires a subject to be digressed from, returned to, and supposedly completed. Fish, discussing a sentence which begins with the word 'that', comments:

> 'That' is a demonstrative, a word that points *out*, and as one takes it *in*, a sense of the referent (yet unidentified) is established. Whatever 'that' is, it is outside, at a distance from the observer-reader; it is 'pointable to' (pointing is what the word 'that' does), something of substance and solidity. In terms of the reader's response, 'that' generates an expectation of finding out *what* 'that' is.[32]

What if, then, we never get to a 'what'? What if the referent is forever deferred by an infinite series of 'thats', never finally to be identified? To the extent that Tristram's narrative promises are broken, and his life remains untold, the question becomes a necessary one for the reader.

We could, of course, adopt a stylistic approach to the relationship between style and subject to 'account' for *Tristram Shandy*. We could even count the number of conjunctions, connectives and marks of punctuation to prove the relationship between sentence structure and narrative digression. But we would do well to remember Fish's call for an 'affective stylistics':

> I am calling not for the end of stylistics but for a new stylistics, what I have termed elsewhere an 'affective' stylistics, in which the focus of attention is shifted from the spatial context of a page and its observable regularities to the temporal context of a mind and its experiences.[33]

The most important aspect of deferral, delay, interruption and indeterminacy in *Tristram Shandy* concerns the reading *experience*, for, unless experienced, these conditions have no meaning. They each posit a 'what' that compels the reader forwards. In fact, 'forward movement' itself becomes the issue because of the power of the digressive tendency to threaten all conclusions. It is not surprising, then, that Tristram's narrative should so consistently concern itself with the reader's response. Tristram's opening gambit, 'I Told the Christian reader', leaves the reader waiting for a 'what', only to discourse, digressively, on the impossibility of providing one. The 'unfixed and equivocal matter'; the 'blanks and gaps'; the difficulty of 'following' so 'strange' a story (itself reflected in the difficulty of following Tristram's sentence); the dark obscurity that leaves us 'unenlightened' (despite Tristram's 'stars', or asterisks, which *we* might say rather add to the problem); and the tendency of the world (including Tristram) to 'lose its way' – the passage provides a catalogue of these aspects of the reading experience which make the search for meaning, truth and finality so comically the *reader's* discovery of ambiguity, relativism and regression.

3 The Process of Reading: *Pride and Prejudice*

To move from a novel as explicitly transgressive as *Tristram Shandy* to the proprieties of *Pride and Prejudice* (1813) might seem no easy transition. Yet, as we ended Chapter 2 with 'blanks' and 'gaps', so too can we begin our consideration of Jane Austen's second novel. No less than *Tristram Shandy* does *Pride and Prejudice* offer rich pickings for a reception theorist like Wolfgang Iser. Indeed he quotes Virginia Woolf's comment on Jane Austen to show 'the extent to which the "unwritten" part of a text stimulates the reader's creative participation':

> 'Jane Austen is thus a mistress of much deeper emotion than appears upon the surface. She stimulates us to supply what is not there. What she offers is, apparently, a trifle, yet is composed of something that expands in the reader's mind and endows with the most enduring form of life scenes which are outwardly trivial . . . The turns and twists of the dialogue keep us on the tenterhooks of suspense. Our attention is half upon the present moment, half upon the future . . . Here, indeed . . . are all the elements of Jane Austen's greatness.'[1]

Before examining in detail the process of reading *Pride and Prejudice*, it is interesting to dwell on the implications of this idea that Jane Austen 'stimulates us to supply what is not there'. The expression anticipates the debate about the source of textual meaning; if we supply what is not there then we must be creating the text, but in what way is the text the stimulus? Does it force us to supply what we supply? Iser's gloss on this passage reads:

> The unwritten aspects of apparently trivial scenes, and the unspoken dialogue within the 'turns and twists', not only draw the reader into the action, but also lead him to shade in the many outlines suggested

by the given situations, so that these take on a reality of their own. But as the reader's imagination animates these 'outlines', they in turn will influence the effect of the written part of the text. Thus begins a whole dynamic process: the written text imposes certain limits on its unwritten implications in order to prevent these from becoming too blurred and hazy, but at the same time these implications, worked out by the reader's imagination, set the given situation against a background which endows it with far greater significance than it might have seemed to possess on its own. In this way, trivial scenes suddenly take on the shape of an 'enduring form of life'. What constitutes this form is never named, let alone explained, in the text, although in fact it is the end product of the interaction between text and reader.[2]

As the confusion of metaphors might indicate, there are problems with this description. The 'unwritten aspects' and 'unspoken dialogue' act as the constraining subject of Iser's expression – they 'draw the reader into the action' and 'lead him' to 'shade in the outlines' of the 'given' (and we have seen what Fish makes of Iser's idea of the 'given' in the first two chapters). Or, if we prefer the organic to the artistic, readers 'animate' the outlines. What is described as the effect of interaction between text and reader seems rather to be a textual imposition. The 'given' parts of the text do not seem to be substantially different from the 'ungiven': it is as if the text that is *not* there is as much there as the text that *is*. The reader becomes the illustrator's assistant, providing the shading for a pre-existent drawing in line with the master's instructions (which are *given* either by the text or by its silences – the silences are 'aspects' of the text). We can apply Iser's shading metaphor, perversely, to his idea that the reader is 'drawn into' the action. In this theory the text draws the reader; the reader cannot draw the text. Indeed, in a later version of this idea, Iser changes the expression to 'the reader . . . is drawn into *events*', the amendment reminding us that the 'action' meant is not an action of reading, but 'the action of the novel' – the reader is precisely *not* drawn into 'action'. Iser obviously finds Woolf's comment particularly useful to his theory as a whole, and the subtle variations in the later reworking of this material (for instance in *The Act of Reading* in 1978 and, 11 years later, in *Prospecting*) merit close attention. Here is the revised passage, from *Prospecting: From Reader Response to Literary Anthropology* (1989):

What is missing from the apparently trivial scenes, the gaps arising out of the dialogue - this is what stimulates the reader into filling the blanks with projections. He is drawn into the events and made to supply what is meant from what is not said. What is said only appears to take on significance as a reference to what is not said; it is the implications and not the statements that give shape and weight to the meaning. But as the unsaid comes to life in the reader's imagination, so the said 'expands' to take on greater significance than might have been supposed: even trivial scenes can seem surprisingly profound. The 'enduring form of life' which Virginia Woolf speaks of is not manifested on the printed page; it is a product arising out of the interaction between text and reader.[3]

The revisions here all point to the problems with the previous passage, although they do not resolve them. There are not, now, 'unwritten *aspects*' (which would imply, according to the etymology of 'aspect', something to look at, as if the 'unwritten' were 'written'). Now we have a something 'missing' – there are 'blanks' which the reader projects into. Gone is the rather bizarre 'unspoken dialogue' (an oxymoron conveying Iser's sense that even the 'unspoken' is 'spoken' by the text). Now we have 'gaps *arising* out of the dialogue' which the reader fills. The ideas of 'animation' and 'shading' have gone – now we have the more abstract metaphors of 'shaping' and 'giving weight'. These changes seem to give the reader a more active role, at least to an extent 'supplying' meaning. Crucially, though, it is a meaning the reader is '*made* to supply'. The revision of the passage, on one level, tries to give the reader more to do, but continues, essentially, to restrain and constrain ideas of creative response. Iser's claims here, as in the discussion of Sterne, invite the kind of critique offered generally by Fish. Iser's problem is the distinction between the 'said' and the 'not said', and the idea (central to his whole theory) of an 'interaction between text and reader'. The second passage reveals readily enough the rather tortured logic: the 'said' only has significance in relation to the 'not said', which 'comes to life in the reader's imagination', allowing the 'said' to expand. Logically, then, the 'said' has not been said either. In fact the 'said' is as much the reader's creation as the 'not said', subject to the same reading strategies for it to have any meaning at all. As Fish notes:

If the 'textual signs' do not announce their shape but appear in a variety of shapes according to the differing expectations and assumptions of different readers, and if gaps are not built into the text, but appear (or do not appear) as a consequence of particular interpretive strategies, then there is no distinction between what the text gives and what the reader supplies; he supplies *everything*.[4]

The emphasis of Fish's critique can be applied usefully to Woolf's comment on Austen. It is not some disembodied idealized authority – 'Jane Austen' – that masters (or 'mistresses') 'much deeper emotion than appears on the surface'. It is rather that we *as readers* have the emotions. Our ability to discover 'implications' allows us to reject the notion of 'triviality'. Further, we determine what should count as trivial in order, then, to retroactively pronounce it 'of greater significance'. This may lead us to the conclusion 'Jane Austen is a great novelist because she invests the apparently trivial with great significance', but our admiration of her authorial achievement will rather be a testimony to the skills, pleasures and emotions of the reading process.

But we can easily see why Iser has problems, and the problems are themselves revealing. We can apply some of his terms to a passage from *Pride and Prejudice* and see why the idea of a two-way interaction is superficially convincing. We have selected here an unremarkable (or, to echo Woolf, a 'trivial') passage which narrates no crisis or turning point, and which can be treated as generally representative:

> DURING dinner, Mr. Bennet scarcely spoke at all; but when the servants were withdrawn, he thought it time to have some conversation with his guest, and therefore started a subject in which he expected him to shine, by observing that he seemed very fortunate in his patroness. Lady Catherine de Bourgh's attention to his wishes, and consideration for his comfort, appeared very remarkable. Mr. Bennet could not have chosen better. Mr. Collins was eloquent in her praise. The subject elevated him to more than usual solemnity of manner, and with a most important aspect he protested that he had never in his life witnessed such behaviour in a person of rank — such affability and condescension, as he had himself experienced from Lady Catherine. (p. 58)

Our experience of this passage seems readily translatable into Iser's and Woolf's terms. We feel that a range of things are 'unspoken' here; that the irony and humour depend on 'unwritten aspects'; that 'gaps' are 'arising out of dialogue' (here in indirect speech). Not only can we supply some of them, but we also feel stimulated to supply them: we do not feel we have a free choice in the matter. It is impolite of Mr Bennet not to speak throughout dinner; he still does not want to speak to Collins; he is belatedly observing a propriety; it is not that he expects Collins to 'shine': he expects him to *think* he shines; he starts the subject partly because he is humoured by absurd vanity and partly so that he will not have to contribute much to the conversation; he does not think Collins is truly 'fortunate' in Lady Catherine's 'condescension'; 'condescension' means both 'affability to one's inferiors' (for Collins) and 'stooping from a position of pride to someone unworthy' (for Bennet); a 'more than usual solemnity of manner' for Collins means a truly ridiculous degree of solemnity . . . the possibilities of 'projecting' into the 'gaps' seem endless. And this is the main point: they are endless. Though we feel bound to come up with such readings, they are not, therefore, simply *there*. None of the possibilities mentioned in this list is stated. Perhaps none of the possibilities would bring a clear agreement between readers. For readers untrained in this kind of teasing none of the possibilities might even be read (teenagers reading Austen often find it difficult to see *anything* beyond the trivial, and wonder what all the fuss is about). Our response has (literally) to do with what it is to be a literate reader of literary novels. We supply the projections not because the text demands it but because it is a convention of reading so to do. However, our undoubted feeling that the text is partly responsible for these readings is genuinely a part of this process of reading, and therefore the idea of an 'interaction' continues to seem reasonable. But we are never interacting with something that is *not* already constructed by our response. There is no simple external 'truth' in the statement 'Mr. Bennet scarcely spoke at all' : we cannot interact with it – we can only 'create' what it means.

It is hardly surprising that Iser should wish to re-use Woolf's comment, as it touches on four of the most important general claims made by reader-response theorists. First, we 'supply what is not there', so, whatever our view of the Iser/Fish debate, the reader at least participates in creating the 'text', which cannot be said to be simply contained in the words on the page. Secondly, the 'reader's mind' discovers profound meaning beneath the trivial appearance, so the text is meaningful only in relation to the reader's imaginative involvement. Thirdly, reading is dynamic, a matter of 'turns', 'twists' and the 'tenterhooks of suspense'. Finally, and implicit in this last idea, the reader's experience is temporal, and the excitement of reading depends on the difference between our present 'knowledge' at any given moment and our expectations for the future. Such claims lie at the centre of theories of the reader's response and deserve elaboration.

Whether we side with Iser in accepting the influencing role of the text, or with Fish in celebrating reading *as* text, we can at least agree that what we refer to as 'the text', implying that it has an autonomous existence beyond ourselves, does not, in an important sense, exist outside our reading of it. It does not simply 'contain' meaning (as was evident in the extreme case of Sterne's marbled, black, and blank pages); meaning is in the experience of the reader. Since we are to consider a novel which depends for its effects on the 'unsaid', it is worth proving this point by referring to the effect of irony itself. An ironic statement is only meaningful if the reader can supply a 'real', or 'intended' meaning, unstated or perhaps even contradicted by other readings. When we say that *Pride and Prejudice* is an ironic novel we imply that the text does not make explicit what it means, and that we have to invert or supplement its statements. For an appearance we substitute a truth, and in this sense we can be said to 'perform' the text. *Pride and Prejudice* is not a 'text', it is an 'experience'.

But the reader's response to particular ironies is, in practice, much more complicated than these generalizations might imply. The 'truth' we might want to discover is often elusive and ambiguous. In fact the famous opening of *Pride and Prejudice* proves the point even in its direct reference to 'a truth':

> IT is a truth universally acknowledged, that a single man in posses-
> sion of a good fortune, must be in want of a wife. (p. 5)

What, exactly, are we to make of this? Our response is certainly not a matter of simple substitution or inversion. It *is* a truth that is *generally* acknowledged that such a man *probably* does want a wife. That the general view is so prejudiced about this tends to encourage conformity and makes it certain that such a man will know it is expected of him to find a wife. And we, too, expect it of him. The irony does not cancel out the intimation of plot (particularly for those readers who know that Austen's novels tend to end with marriages); this novel will indeed be concerned with such a man's marital future. The irony rather draws attention to what will be one of the novel's most impor-tant themes – the difference between public opinion and private experience. As Austen continues:

> However little known the feelings or views of such a man may be on his first entering a neighbourhood, this truth is so well fixed in the minds of the surrounding families, that he is considered as the right-ful property of some one or other of their daughters. (p. 5)

Ironically, then, it does not matter what one's private views are: public opinion is prejudiced on the matter. For the public it is a matter of course that such a man will want to marry (particularly for those members of the public who have marriageable daughters). For an individual, should the marriage prophecy become true, it will be a matter of crisis. The intimate and private details that will lead to marriage will only become a public concern if they are scandalous (as they certainly threaten to become in this novel through the activities of the eloping Lydia). But the act of marriage, personal as the circum-stances that lead to it may be, is a public concern. Marriage, then, evokes a subtle and complicated relationship between our private feelings and our public professions. The exaggeration revealed by the ironic reading of the opening passages serves as a kind of warning about public conduct. Such a man will be watched, his behaviour will be predicted, and, more importantly, judged.

Note that the reader's response depends also on an imagined authorial view, influenced by historical perspective. The reader does *not* assume that the irony of the opening intends a condemnation of a homophobic society (why should a man not want a man?) or a condemnation of the institution of marriage (why should he not wish to live with a woman rather than marry her?). This does not mean that we cannot deduce that the author's society is both homophobic and intolerant of non-marital sexual relationships, but we do not attribute such possible readings to the irony of the passage.

Austen's use of irony depends on the reader's ability to imagine an authorial perspective which will be said to represent her view. In this sense it is not only the text which is recreated by the reader, but the author as well. 'Jane Austen' is the reader's projection; an authorial 'presence' (though always 'non-present') to whom we will attribute the intentions that we ourselves discover, and which are 'censored' to satisfy our idea of 'her'. As Matei Calinescu suggests, 'imagining or inventing the author is actually one of the most complicated and interesting aspects of the game'.[5] In the process we also recreate ourselves, playing the role of the hypothetical reader we imagine being addressed (a point we shall develop further in Chapter 4). But note that our creation of an 'authorial' point of view, however it might be sanctioned by one of Fish's 'interpretive communities', will still reveal the partiality of our own perspectives. How far, for instance, will we be influenced by the historical fact of Jane Austen's gender to infer particular ironies in the passage's confident distinction between 'a man of fortune' and a dependent 'wife'? And how far will the reader's own gender influence the reading? The struggle for independence within relationships in a context of financial dependency is a crucial issue in *Pride and Prejudice*, but our response must be influenced by our gendered prejudices – a point to which we shall return in Chapter 5. It is far from true, then, that the reading of this opening 'leaves the reader passive and subject to a monolithic unfolding of a tale'.[6] The comment comes from Lennard J. Davis, who has been giving his own reading of the opening of *Pride and Prejudice*:

> Although Austen's statement is said to be 'universally acknowledged', the point Austen really wishes to make is that most people are quite foolish and that their views on marriage are equally contemptible. And the reader is immediately included in a circle of people who do not really believe what is universally acknowledged. The primary belief of the new possessive individualism of the middle class is that their individuality is sacrosanct and guaranteed . . .[7]

According to our view of the passage this would be a misreading of the irony. But we cannot really point to the text to refute Davis. He is doing what we are doing – supplying something that is not there. The ironic meaning is not *in* the text, and any reading will use contextual information to create rhetorical support for its claims (here Davis evokes the ideology of middle-class individualism). But we *can* refute Davis's idea of reading passivity. His own reading, like ours, is a testimony to his reading activity. His claim that computer technology might improve *Pride and Prejudice* by allowing the reader to plug in 'yes' or 'no' to the question as to 'whether Elizabeth should go to the dance at which she first meets Darcy', though intentionally perverse, sacrifices profound involvement to trivial intervention. It should not come as a revelation, at the end of a critique which proposes that we must 'resist' novels, that 'the text is only part of the transaction' and that 'changing the reader can change the text':[8] it is the very precondition of his or anyone's idea of the 'text' that the reader has already changed it.

Irony is a specialized and especially complicated evidence of 'indeterminacy'. In *Tristram Shandy* the 'gaps', 'blanks' and 'vacancies' were themselves the issue, explicit in the typography. Any attempt to determine them could only be made by acknowledging the quasi-arbitrary imposition of our interpretations. Since the point was this very acknowledgement there was no urgency about the nature of the possibilities. But an ironic reading strategy involves a positing of particular determinations which, inevitably and paradoxically, will reveal partiality in both senses of the word. We *have* to supply the 'something missing', but can do so only in part, and in a way which reveals our prejudice. The reading of *Tristram Shandy*, which to Viktor Shklovsky and the Russian Formalists typified the laying bare of artistic devices, allowed a kind of impersonality: however we might determine Widow Wadman to ourselves, the *point* of the blank page was beyond such particularities. But reading *Pride and Prejudice* is a deeply personal, implicating experience, as our filling of its silences rather lays bare ourselves.

Crucially, this experience is temporal, an idea central to the achievements of textual response, and one which should not be lost to holistic ideologies of reading. We read one word before another, one sentence before the next, page one before page two. Both authors and readers can subvert this general pattern: we can actually read the pages in any order we choose, and our urgent desire for the denouement may prompt us to read the end before we have actually reached it; and novelists can disrupt the conventions in any way they choose – Sterne, as we have seen, 'omits' pages, and places a Chapter 25 before a Chapter 18. But such perversities are a confirmation rather than a denial of the temporal nature of the act of reading. If, then, we are to talk meaningfully about the reader's participation in the text we must talk about the effect of this sequential aspect of the reading process. At any given moment, as we read, we have a memory of what we have read thus far and expectations concerning what we might read thereafter. So vital to our experience are the processes of what Iser calls 'retention' and 'protension'. We are always looking back or looking forward, and each new piece of information we are given will force us to revise our expectations and 'rewrite' our memories. (The idea of 'modified expectations' will prove particularly resonant in Chapter 4, where the title of Dickens's novel reveals the thematic importance of all 'Expectations'.)

In *Is There a Text in This Class?* Fish claims that approaches which consider the text as a completed whole are misleading in that they do not take this aspect of our experience into consideration, transforming something 'temporal' into something 'spatial'. Such an approach 'steps back and in a single glance takes in a whole . . . which the reader knows (if at all) only bit by bit, moment by moment'.[9] The result is to discount important aspects of the reading process. As we read we continually make decisions on the basis of what we have read thus far. Our guesses, our predictions, our forethinkings, are all part of our reading of any text and should not be simply dismissed if what follows does not exactly fulfil them. Fish makes the following claim for his account of the reading experience:

> The getting throughs, the figuring outs, the false starts, the interpreta-
> tions (as it turns out) prematurely hazarded are not in my analyses
> regarded as the disposable machinery of extraction; rather, they are
> the acts of structuring and restructuring, hypothesizing and dehy-
> pothesizing, stance taking and stance revising, the succession of
> which is the structure of the reader's experience.[10]

It is interesting that Fish uses the kind of Sternean parenthesis discussed in Chapter 2 to exemplify his point even on a syntactic level. The 'interpretations' of his sentence are '(as it turns out)' – *will* turn out to have been, with the next words of the sentence – 'prematurely hazarded'! At any point in the process of reading we are making judgements on the basis of insufficient information. In one sense all our interpretations while reading are 'prematurely hazarded'. Paradoxically, vital to our pleasure in reading novels is that we do not know how to read them until we have read them.

To sum up, Iser describes the act of reading in these terms:

> We look forward, we look back, we decide, we change our decisions,
> we form expectations, we are shocked by their nonfulfillment, we
> question, we muse, we accept, we reject; this is the dynamic process
> of recreation.[11]

An acceptance of the importance of the reader in determining the text gives a special significance to what Fish calls 'a whole new set of facts':

> These include patterns of expectation and disappointment, reversals of direction, traps, invitations to premature conclusions, textual gaps, delayed revelations, temptations, all of which are related to a corresponding set of authors' intentions.[12]

Obviously such 'facts' can be discussed in relation to any text, but it will be the argument of the rest of this chapter that we can only really make sense of the experience of reading Austen's novels if we concentrate on such issues.

As in all of Austen's novels, in *Pride and Prejudice* the elements of expectation aroused by the relationship between the heroine and the (as it turns out) hero form one of the main complications of plot for the reader. The questions: does he/does he not love her?; is he/is he not to be thought well of?; and does she/does she not love him? form a pattern of anticipations and reversals. The reader is all the time thinking 'what is the present evidence?'. This happens, it could be claimed, even if the reader is particularly astute and an experienced reader of Austen's other novels. If the reader predicts early on that Elizabeth will come to love Darcy then expectations are aroused for the growing confirmation of that prediction. It would be fair to say we do not read Austen for the pleasure of the outcome, but for the process of discovery.

The evidence concerning this main relationship forms a pattern of oppositions. Elizabeth and Darcy first meet at the ball in Chapter 3. Here Elizabeth overhears Darcy turning down his friend's suggestion that he ask Elizabeth to dance: ' "She is tolerable; but not handsome enough to tempt *me*" ' (p. 13). In terms of a potential relationship this would in any circumstances be damning. Here its negative effect is threefold: he does not find her attractive; she overhears his judgement and so is not likely to think highly of him; it makes him seem an unworthy candidate for our heroine and confirms the general report that Darcy was discovered 'to be proud, to be above his company, and above being pleased' (p. 12). On the positive side, he is very good-looking and rich, and the reader may suspect that statements of dislike are a prelude to liking (what we might call '*The Changeling* principle'), and that Austen enjoys giving false impressions.

At their next meeting Darcy experiences a shift of interest in

Elizabeth, and the reader a consequent shift of interest in *him*: 'no sooner had he made it clear to himself and his friends that she had hardly a good feature in her face, than he began to find it was rendered uncommonly intelligent by the beautiful expression of her dark eyes' (p. 23). This represents the clearest possible turning point as far as his interest in her is concerned. But Elizabeth is not aware of his new view (although she sees, and is confused by, his interest in her). From this point onwards we see Darcy becoming more and more interested in her as she is correspondingly more and more offended by him. The two most crucial factors for Elizabeth are Wickham's bad report of Darcy, and Darcy's reported interference in the potential match between Bingley and her sister Jane (' "there were some very strong objections against the lady" ' [p. 154]). This is the worst evidence of all. When the reader hears of it there are various possibilities, as, for instance:

   (i)   yes, he did interfere, and perversely;

   (ii)   yes, he did interfere, but his reasons were not perverse;

   (iii)   no, it was not quite like that; there must have been some misunderstanding;

   (iv)   no, the report is false; he did not interfere.

Elizabeth believes the first of these possibilities to be the truth and so the evidence mounts against a possible involvement with Darcy. Against this developing view Elizabeth has of him, there are the conflicting views of other characters. Miss Bingley, for instance, tells Elizabeth that Wickham's account of Darcy is a false one: ' "as to Mr. Darcy's using him ill, it is perfectly false; for, on the contrary, he has been always remarkably kind to him, though George Wickham has treated Mr. Darcy in a most infamous manner" ' (p. 80). If the reader feels able to trust the speaker then this would provide an important counterbalance to Wickham's report. But the fact that the deplorable Miss Bingley says this complicates things and tends, if anything, to support the bad view of Darcy. (It is an interesting sign of the complexity of Austen's irony that it is often the most blinded or narrow characters who reveal the 'truth'.) Against Elizabeth's view of Darcy we have Bingley's very high view, as reported by Jane, but Bingley does not know Wickham and is prejudiced by friendship. Then again we have Jane's own high view of Darcy, but Jane is ready to believe the best of everyone.

    There is no end to this kind of analysis, and only some of the most obvious points have been selected here. Suffice it to say that the reader builds up a series of probabilities and possibilities, and that the reading process involves, at any given moment, juggling the evidence.

One of the key pieces of evidence noted above as affecting the relationship between Darcy and Elizabeth is the true nature of the relationship between Darcy and Wickham. Here lies, for the reader, one of the main mysteries to be unravelled. The first meeting in the novel between the two men poses the whole problem of the mystery:

> [Darcy] was beginning to determine not to fix his eyes on Elizabeth, when they were suddenly arrested by the sight of the stranger, and Elizabeth happening to see the countenance of both as they looked at each other, was all astonishment at the effect of the meeting. Both changed colour, one looked white, the other red. Mr. Wickham, after a few moments, touched his hat — a salutation which Mr. Darcy just deigned to return. What could be the meaning of it? — It was impossible to imagine; it was impossible not to long to know. (p. 63)

Here, in a nutshell, we have both the problem and the pleasure of the reading experience. It is always, in a sense, impossible to imagine – we do not have the vital clues at any given point in the mystery; we are lacking the vital information. And yet it is impossible not to long to know. You might say that in narrative this is the essential aspect of our response to plot. It is the essence of intrigue, suspense, mystery, and anticipation – Woolf's 'tenterhooks', the very stuff of novels. The context might change the nature of the question posed – who committed the murder? What is the skeleton in the cupboard? Who is the madwoman in the attic? What is the truth about Darcy and Wickham? But the reader's situation is similar in each case. Moreover, as Frank Kermode in *The Sense of an Ending* suggests, the urgency of our yearning to know is particularly a condition of fiction. In normal adult life, he argues, we sensibly guess 'how long we shall have to wait for some desire to be gratified' and moderate our anticipation accordingly. Children, juvenile delinquents and the emotionally disturbed, he adds, are much less able to do this, and a similar state applies to readers, who 'seem to partake of some of these abnormally acute appetites. We hunger for ends and for crises.'[13] So strong is this demand, at times, that we will read all night to satisfy the need and reach the denouement. (This human yearning for ends, this need to know, so vital to our reading experience, will be explicitly an issue in Chapter 8; indeed, Byatt's formulation of the idea is strikingly similar to Kermode's – ' "We are driven/By endings as by hunger" ', writes Ash in *Possession* [p. 476].)

Elizabeth, then, wants to know more and obtains the knowledge in a vital interview with Wickham. The subject of their discussion is Darcy, and Elizabeth is speaking:

> 'Upon my word I say no more *here* than I might say in any house in the neighbourhood, except Netherfield. He is not at all liked in Hertfordshire. Every body is disgusted with his pride. You will not find him more favourably spoken of by any one.'
>
> 'I cannot pretend to be sorry,' said Wickham, after a short interruption, 'that he or that any man should not be estimated beyond their deserts; but with *him* I believe it does not often happen. The world is blinded by his fortune and consequence, or frightened by his high and imposing manners, and sees him only as he chuses to be seen.' (p. 67)

We cannot fail to struggle with the convolution of Wickham's expression here. 'I cannot pretend to be sorry' is a complicated opening as it leaves the possible pretence uncertain; it might be a matter of pride or regret that the speaker is not sorry. But 'sorry' about what? The syntax is interrupted here by the apparently innocent 'said Wickham, after a short interruption'. (*What* interruption?) This itself is a short interruption which further complicates the sentence structure, lending a slight uncertainty to the pronouns which follow: 'that he or that any man should not be estimated beyond their deserts'. The convolution continues: 'but with *him* I believe it does not often happen'. We could paraphrase this along the lines: 'I'm not saying that it's not right that he's not overestimated, but it's not usually the case.' This is hardly plain speaking, and its indirectness becomes particularly revealing on a second reading when we can see how replete with irony the whole passage is. As Wickham is telling Elizabeth that the world is 'blinded' by Darcy and sees him 'only as he chuses to be seen', so Elizabeth is being blinded by Wickham and seeing *him* only as *he* chooses to be seen. Just as Wickham is not 'sorry that he or that any man should not be estimated beyond their deserts', so Elizabeth is already estimating *him* beyond his deserts and underestimating Darcy.

Considering such an exact pattern of 'reversals' it is hardly surprising, as Kermode notes, that Aristotle's peripeteia (an unexpected reversal in a character's fortunes) has been compared with irony:

The story that proceeded very simply to its obviously predestined end would be nearer myth than novel or drama. Peripeteia, which has been called the equivalent, in narrative, of irony in rhetoric, is present in every story of the least structural sophistication. Now peripeteia depends on our confidence of the end; it is a disconfirmation followed by a consonance; the interest of having our expectations falsified is obviously related to our wish to reach the discovery or recognition by an unexpected and instructive route.[14]

The reference to Aristotle, though, is a reminder of a distinction to be made between some forms of tragic irony and the ironies of the proto-realist novel. In Sophocles (who provides Aristotle with much of his material) our 'confidence of the end' is *certain*: the cruel reversals affecting Oedipus are known in advance by reputation, and confirmed by recurrent prophecy. The future of the hero's fate is explicitly predetermined. When Oedipus publicly curses the killer of the King, the ironic reversal reveals him to be cursing himself. When he mocks the blindness of Tiresias he is himself most blind. But we know the truth *as* he speaks. Kermode's point holds, in that the method of disclosure in Sophocles is compelling, but the revelations themselves conceal no mystery. Much more uncertainty attends the past and future of the characters in *Pride and Prejudice*, whose destinies are not subject to the external forces of fate. Though the reader may be suspicious about Wickham's speech she/he is not in a position to assess the full irony (or potential for peripeteia) when it is *first* read. Here, then, is a crucial example of retrospective irony, the kind of irony most affected by the process of reading. We do not know that in the novel's 'past' Wickham had tried to elope with Darcy's young sister. We do not know that in the novel's 'future' he will elope with Elizabeth's sister. We are not yet in a position properly to judge his words. And neither is Elizabeth.

Typically, such ironies make the second readings of novels very different experiences from first readings. A second reading confounds Tristram Shandy's assertion that 'if I thought you was able to form the least judgment or probable conjecture to yourself, of what was to come in the next page, — I would tear it out of my book' (*Tristram Shandy*, p. 64). It is interesting, in this sense, that all first readings depend on deferral, whether or not the desire for ends is fulfilled (whether we have the marriages of *Pride and Prejudice* or the 'cock and bull story' of Sterne). Second readings have a different psychology. Henry Fielding, another master of retrospective irony, makes both aspects of the reading experience clear in his advertisement to one of the chapters of *Joseph Andrews*: 'in which we prophesy there are some Strokes which every one will not truly comprehend at the first Reading'.[15] It is not only that we will come to comprehend through the process of reading and re-reading, but the measure of our former ignorance in the example from *Pride and Prejudice* becomes the measure of Wickham's deception. It is not difficult to see why irony should be the tool of the social critic or the satirist, since it works to reverse the processes of propaganda and hypocrisy. Where they would claim no disparity between the 'truth' and what is said, irony depends upon such a distinction. Re-reading Wickham's comments, after completing the novel, allows us the omniscient privilege of ironic prophecy which we had with *King Oedipus*. This is our compensation for the loss of the thrill of uncertainty. The reversals that at the moment of our first reading lie in the 'future' and may surprise us, on second reading are coterminous with our reading present, and give us a sense of justice. We see the hypocrisy, but look forward to its unmasking. The usefulness of the idea of peripeteia, then, is particularly relevant to our re-reading, which is why Calinescu, whose subject *is* re-reading, is drawn to quote C. S. Lewis's comment on 'ideal surprisingness':

> The re-reader is looking not for actual surprises (which come only once) but for a certain ideal surprisingness . . . In the only sense that matters the surprise works as well the twentieth time [as] the first. It is the *quality* of unexpectedness not the *fact* that delights us. It is even better the second time . . . We do not enjoy a story fully at the first reading. Not till the curiosity, the sheer narrative lust, has been given its sop and laid asleep, are we at leisure to savor the real beauties . . . [C]hildren understand this well when they ask for the same story over and over again, and in the same words . . . It is better when you know it is coming: free from one shock of actual surprise you can better attend to the intrinsic surprisingness of the *peripeteia*.[16]

We ought to add that we should not underestimate, or marginalize the 'sheer narrative lust' of first readings, and that both the surprises and the anticipated pleasures of reversal are essential to the pleasure of reading.

Since Elizabeth assures herself that Darcy cannot be interested in her, and, more importantly, that she could never be interested in Darcy, a tension arises in the novel. He is obviously interested in her, and the reader finds her protesting too much her lack of interest in him (' "Heaven forbid! — *That* would be the greatest misfortune of all! — To find a man agreeable whom one is determined to hate!" ' [p. 77] – the 'determined' is very suggestive). Having put out of mind the possibility that Darcy might be in love with her, his behaviour is constantly surprising to her, though not to the reader. The reader is now in a privileged position, and Austen uses subtle syntactic skills to help the reader enjoy the privilege:

> ELIZABETH was sitting by herself the next morning, and writing to Jane, while Mrs. Collins and Maria were gone on business into the village, when she was startled by a ring at the door, the certain signal of a visitor. As she had heard no carriage, she thought it not unlikely to be Lady Catherine, and under that apprehension was putting away her half-finished letter that she might escape all impertinent questions, when the door opened, and to her very great surprise, Mr. Darcy, and Mr. Darcy only, entered the room. (p. 147)

It is instructive to consider the way in which this revelation is delayed – so much indeed that it *does* seem like a revelation rather than someone just visiting! By the time he arrives in the second sentence Darcy's presence is invested with significance. There are two processes of elimination at work: Elizabeth's and the reader's. She is writing to Jane, so it is unlikely to be her sister calling; Mrs Collins and Maria are out, so it cannot be them. Notice the effect of the words 'she was startled by a ring at the door, the certain signal of a visitor'; this last phrase is redundant in meaning; of course if someone rings the bell they are visiting (even if the 'visit' is a more formal idea for Austen); its main purpose is to delay and suspend the discovery further. Elizabeth thinks it must be Lady Catherine, but for the reader the mere fact of her supposition works against the idea. By the end of the paragraph the reader is prepared for Darcy, but Elizabeth is not, and her surprise is emphasized by the repetition 'Mr. Darcy, and Mr. Darcy only, entered the room'. There is a pattern of such surprises. A few pages later Elizabeth is thinking with pleasure that Darcy is to leave, after the suffering he has caused her sister:

> While settling this point, she was suddenly roused by the sound of the

> door bell, and her spirits were a little fluttered by the idea of its being
> Colonel Fitzwilliam himself, who had once before called late in the
> evening, and might now come to enquire particularly after her. But
> this idea was soon banished, and her spirits were very differently
> affected, when, to her utter amazement, she saw Mr. Darcy walk into
> the room. (p. 156)

Austen, we might say, is rewarding the reader's sagacity with delayed
disclosures.

By this point Austen has exhausted the suspense of Elizabeth's
ignorance. In the paragraph following this last example of delay Darcy
makes the 'discovery' himself: ' "You must allow me to tell you how
ardently I admire and love you" '. Now the nature of the suspense will
change. In the following chapter Darcy's revelations will continue
with the crucial letter explaining his behaviour and his version of the
past. If the ruling motif of Elizabeth's attitude to Darcy was disappro-
bation, it now becomes embarrassment and humiliation, and will be
increasingly mingled with a feeling of vaguely acknowledged personal
interest. When Mrs Gardiner proposes an excursion to Darcy's seat,
Pemberley, with the advertisement ' "Wickham passed all his youth
there, you know" ', it is not Wickham whom Elizabeth dreads to meet.
But, reassured by the chambermaid that Darcy is abroad, Elizabeth
looks forward to the scheme. There follows a piece of sustained delay
which acts as a preparation for the new tone of Elizabeth's relationship with Darcy. Elizabeth admires the taste of Darcy's house and
grounds, and hears an impressive character witness from his housekeeper. After six pages or so of such measured preamble, we read:

> As they walked across the lawn towards the river, Elizabeth turned
> back to look again; her uncle and aunt stopped also, and while the
> former was conjecturing as to the date of the building, the owner of it
> himself suddenly came forward from the road, which led behind it to
> the stables. (p. 205)

Note, here, the indirectness. It is not ostensibly Elizabeth's thought-
process which is interrupted by this appearance, but Mr Gardiner's.
And it is not 'Mr. Darcy' who appears, but 'the owner', which for the
reader acts as a moment of hesitation equivalent to Elizabeth's
moment of recognition. The sense of 'suddenness' is typical of
Elizabeth's encounters with Darcy, their impact implying a panic of

emotions. There is an embarrassed exchange of compliments before Darcy takes his polite leave. But the moment of suspense is almost immediately repeated, as the walk continues:

> Whilst wandering on in this slow manner, they were again surprised, and Elizabeth's astonishment was quite equal to what it had been at first, by the sight of Mr. Darcy approaching them, and at no great distance. The walk being here less sheltered than on the other side, allowed them to see him before they met. Elizabeth, however astonished, was at least more prepared for an interview than before, and resolved to appear and to speak with calmness, if he really intended to meet them. For a few moments, indeed, she felt that he would probably strike into some other path. This idea lasted while a turning in the walk concealed him from their view; the turning past, he was immediately before them. (p. 208)

Elizabeth is 'equally' surprised here because she assumes Darcy would have withdrawn and made another 'chance' encounter impossible. The reader, of course, knows better. Even now, despite the evidence before her, she expects him to turn aside, so there is a further slight delay before the re-encounter. So, when he is known to be approaching a few minutes away, his appearance still manages to surprise with its immediacy. Elizabeth never seems to have quite enough time, to adapt a line from T. S. Eliot, 'to prepare a face to meet the one face she must meet', and the meetings are invested with tension, expectancy and emotion.

The reader's prediction of a marriage between the two now finds its necessary conditions, as objections to Darcy are supplanted by obligations and, more importantly, affection. And as one thematic pattern is reversed, so is another. When Darcy was the unknown lover it was Darcy's appearance at the door and Darcy's letter which provided the moments of revelation. Now, as the reader expects Darcy's concluding addresses, it falls to others to promote the denouement. Here, then, is the revised formula for the unexpected arrival:

> ONE morning, about a week after Bingley's engagement with Jane had been formed, as he and the females of the family were sitting together in the dining room, their attention was suddenly drawn to the window, by the sound of a carriage; and they perceived a chaise and four driving up the lawn. It was too early in the morning for visitors, and besides, the equipage did not answer to that of any of their

neighbours. The horses were post; and neither the carriage, nor the livery of the servant who preceded it, were familiar to them. As it was certain, however, that somebody was coming, Bingley instantly prevailed on Miss Bennet to avoid the confinement of such an intrusion, and walk away with him into the shrubbery. They both set off, and the conjectures of the remaining three continued, though with little satisfaction, till the door was thrown open, and their visitor entered. It was lady Catherine de Bourgh. (p. 283)

Lady Catherine, here, acts as the unwilling emissary for Darcy, informing Elizabeth of his marrying intentions in the process of warning her off. There soon follows another letter:

> The next morning, as [Elizabeth] was going down stairs, she was met by her father, who came out of his library with a letter in his hand. (p. 291)

Letters, as we know by now, are one of the most important means of disclosure. It was Darcy's letter that reversed the tendency of Elizabeth's former opinions. This new letter is full of portent. ' "Lizzy," ' says her father, ' "I was going to look for you; come into my room" ' (p. 291). Elizabeth can hardly bear the suspense and, as usual, she begins to form expectations along with the reader:

> She followed him thither; and her curiosity to know what he had to tell her, was heightened by the supposition of its being in some manner connected with the letter he held. It suddenly struck her that it might be from lady Catherine; and she anticipated with dismay all the consequent explanations. (p. 291)

That Elizabeth expects the letter to be from Lady Catherine rather militates against the possibility, as the reader has been so thoroughly prepared for her continually to be surprised. Surely, then, the letter must be from Darcy:

> She followed her father to the fire place, and they both sat down. He then said,
> 'I have received a letter this morning that has astonished me exceedingly. As it principally concerns yourself, you ought to know its contents. I did not know before, that I had *two* daughters on the brink of matrimony. Let me congratulate you, on a very important conquest.'

The colour now rushed into Elizabeth's cheeks in the instanta-
neous conviction of its being a letter from the nephew, instead of the
aunt; and she was undetermined whether most to be pleased that he
explained himself at all, or offended that his letter was not rather
addressed to herself . . . (p. 291)

So, one step behind the reader, Elizabeth realizes the letter must be
from Darcy. But, for the reader, no sooner does it become an
acknowledged possibility than it becomes less likely. Elizabeth's
possible offence would, after all, be justified by an impropriety which
asked her father for her hand before formally asking her. Her father
now enjoys overtly the kind of ironic power the reader has often exercised privately but cannot now, on first reading, immediately share:

'You look conscious. Young ladies have great penetration in such
matters as these; but I think I may defy even *your* sagacity, to discover
the name of your admirer. This letter is from Mr. Collins.' (p. 291)

With typical pretentious allusiveness Collins, of course, has related
the gossip about a forthcoming liaison between Elizabeth and a
'young gentleman' of 'splendid property, noble kindred, and exten-
sive patronage'. It is amusing that Collins, 'author' of the first
proposal to Elizabeth, but so inconsequential to her main relationship, should provide the final evidence. His letter makes public the
most private of possibilities and concludes the phase of speculation
first fixed by that earlier momentous letter from Darcy to Elizabeth, a
letter much more worthy of the concluding remarks of this chapter.

Significant in each of the seven novels discussed in this book is the
explicit acknowledgement of the importance of reading, often
supported with detailed description of the act of reading itself. In all
cases, reading always 'functions', always has some profound consequence for the reader's personal destiny, from the unfortunate filial
implications of Walter Shandy's obscure tracts on names and noses to
the irrepressible patterns linking readers with their textual subjects in
Possession. Despite the diversity of the seven novels there is the
common assumption that reading and living are inseparable. They all
intensify our sense of reading as experience by giving us examples of
formative experiences of reading. It is certainly convenient for the
purpose of this discussion that the major turning point of *Pride and
Prejudice* should come in a letter. We have been considering the expe-

rience of the reader, and the effects of the reading process. Now we find, almost exactly at the pivotal centre of this novel (pages 162–7 out of 308 pages in the Penguin edition), *Elizabeth's* experience as reader. First we are given the letter and read it with *our* sense of discovery. Then Austen recounts Elizabeth's response, but not to the finished letter. Since *discovery* is the vital issue we are told about the *developing* response of the reader:

> IF Elizabeth, when Mr. Darcy gave her the letter, did not *expect* it to contain a renewal of his offers, she had formed *no expectation at all* of its contents. But such as they were, it may be well supposed *how eagerly she went through them*, and what a contrariety of emotion they excited. Her feelings *as she read* were scarcely to be defined. With amazement did she *first* understand that he believed any apology to be in his power; and stedfastly was she persuaded that he could have no explanation to give, which a just sense of shame would not conceal. With a strong prejudice against every thing he might say, she *began* his account of what had happened at Netherfield. *She read, with an eagerness* which hardly left her power of comprehension, and *from impatience of knowing what the next sentence might bring, was incapable of attending to the sense of the one before her eyes.* (p. 168; our italics)

The italics above show how explicit is the concern with the reading process as a process. Like the real reader, Elizabeth is forced to revise her views in the light of new evidence. Like Sterne's 'inattentive' reader she must go back and re-read: 'in half a minute the letter was unfolded again'. And as for the real reader to whom new information is given, a re-reading is a different experience altogether: 'Widely different was the effect of a second perusal' (p. 171). So Austen is making central to her novel the kind of experience that we have been discussing, and directly invoking the aspects of the reading experience that are the result of its process.

But the interests of this novel as a perfect paradigm for reader-response theorists should not end here. It is crucial to the thematic structure of the novel that Elizabeth should first read Darcy's letter '[w]ith a strong *prejudice* against every thing he might say' (p. 168; our italics). The experience of re-reading brings with it the painful acknowledgement 'that she had been blind, partial, *prejudiced*' (p.171; our italics). This is partly, of course, due to an honest reflection on her past experience, against which she tries the testimony of Darcy. Importantly, though, the letter and future events will not allow the dropping of prejudice, only its re-direction. Elizabeth will learn to be prejudiced in favour of her future lover and husband. She does not have the choice of *not* being prejudiced, because there is not an *un*prejudiced 'truth' about Darcy (or anyone else). So, important to Elizabeth's change of view of Darcy (what we might call her new partiality) is the account given of him by his housekeeper, Mrs Reynolds: 'He is the best landlord, and the best master . . . that ever lived' (p. 204). Elizabeth's companion, Mr Gardiner, is 'highly amused by the kind of family prejudice, to which he attributed her excessive commendation of her master' (p. 204). 'Family prejudice', here, must be seen as a kind of positive discrimination, and it certainly does not lead to the invalidation of Mrs Reynolds's opinions. Mrs Reynolds has what we can call a 'natural prejudice' (we would rightly be thought inhuman if we were not naturally biased where our affections are concerned).

Equally, the same kind of prejudice can be negative. Lady Catherine's affections and sense of family are certainly concerned in her continued prejudice against Darcy's alliance at the very end of the novel. Hers is a prejudice before and after the event. But there is another kind of prejudice vital to Elizabeth's experience, which uncovers another, often forgotten, meaning of the word. When Darcy (with a natural prejudice) claims that Elizabeth's 'retrospections must be . . . totally void of reproach' he justifies the point with reference to her previous 'ignorance' (p. 297). Vivien Jones, in a note on this word, reminds us that 'in Cassandra Austen's copy of the novel, "ignorance" is corrected to "innocence" ', but she is right to prefer the text's 'ignorance'.[17] In temporal terms Elizabeth has made a presupposition: she has judged Darcy and formed preconceptions about him in *ignorance*. Her self-recriminations have depended on the benefit of hindsight, absent at the time of first judgement.

Prejudices, preconceptions, presuppositions: such habitual attitudes of mind are necessarily inherent in all processes of reading, as Austen's novel abundantly makes plain. Not only do we read novels, we 'read' (make sense of) the world. Perhaps it is not so surprising, therefore, that such ideas are important in philosophical debates seemingly far removed from the nuances of Jane Austen's novels. Robert Holub, in his survey of reception theory, gives this account of the importance of 'preconceptions' to 'our interpretations and understandings':

While previous theory had advocated a purging of preconceptions, Heidegger claims that it is precisely our being-in-the-world with its prejudices and presuppositions that makes understanding possible. As he writes in *Being and Time*: 'Whenever something is interpreted as something, the interpretation will be founded essentially upon fore-having [*Vorhabe*], fore-sight [*Vorsicht*], and fore-conception [*Vorgriff*]. An interpretation is never a presuppositionless apprehending of something presented to us' . . .

Gadamer takes up this issue most thoroughly in his discussion of prejudice (*Vorurteil*). The word in German, like its English equivalent, although etymologically related to pre-judging or merely forming a judgement about something beforehand, has come to mean a negative bias or a quality that excludes accurate judgement. The enlightenment, Gadamer claims, is responsible for the discrediting of the notion of prejudice . . . Prejudice, because it belongs to historical reality itself, is not a hindrance to understanding, but rather a condition of the possibility of understanding. 'What is necessary is a fundamental rehabilitation of the concept of prejudice and a recognition of the fact that there are legitimate prejudices, if we want to do justice to man's finite, historical mode of being.'[18]

Holub revisits these points in his later chapter for *The Cambridge History of Literary Criticism* (1995), where he concedes that 'despite its problems, the notion that one's prejudices and preconceptions are a fundamental part of the hermeneutic situation has been extremely suggestive'.[19] It is an idea particularly suggestive for the hermeneutics of response. 'Prejudice', in this sense, evokes the inevitability of interpreting the world from within its context. As Holub goes on to note: 'one's "prejudices" and preconceptions are a fundamental part of any hermeneutic situation'. To interpret *is* to preconceive, and it is one of the pleasures of reading, as of life, to have one's preconceptions challenged or confirmed. Elizabeth Bennet, like us as readers of Austen's novel, has an interpretative 'horizon' – in Gadamer's terms 'a standpoint that limits the possibility of vision'.[20] She learns to read better by broadening the context from within which she judges the world around her.

Reading involves the imaginative assimilation of other possible contexts, other perspectives, and these, in turn, change the nature of our own hermeneutic position. So, *Pride and Prejudice* – the title is apt in a profound sense. To have a prejudice, as Holub's point about the etymology of the word reminds us, is, in one sense, to *pre-judge*, or 'to influence the mind or judgement of something beforehand' (*OED*). We, as readers, all suffer, or rather 'enjoy', Elizabeth Bennet's problem. We always judge things before we know properly how to judge of them. It is a condition of the reading process, as indeed it is a condition of life.

4 The Experience of Reading: *Great Expectations*

Although 'reading' and 'interpretation' are not exact synonyms, each activity may obviously be said to overlap with the other to a very considerable extent. Indeed, the fourth definition of 'read' in the *OED* is 'the act of interpreting or expounding', and etymologically the word 'read' derives from the Old English *rǣdan* – advise, consider, discern. The process of considering or deliberating sometimes entails 'putting to the test' or 'an experiment' (part of the first *OED* definition of 'experience'). But, as the *OED*'s definitions indicate, 'experience', like 'expectation', has a personal, subjective dimension to it ('being consciously affected by an event') as well as an impersonal, objective dimension ('actual observation of fact or event'). To read, to interpret, to experience, – these are all 'acts' (or 'actions') performed by individual human beings, whether alone or with others. 'Acts' suggests 'acting', and 'active', and yet there is clearly a 're-active' (if not passive, exactly) aspect to reading, interpretation, and experience. *Something* is being read, interpreted, experienced. Repeated acts become a 'practice', the second *OED* definition of which word reads:

> the habitual doing or carrying on *of* something; usual, customary or constant action; action as distinguishable from profession, theory, knowledge, etc.; conduct . . .

So, to attempt to discuss 'the experience of reading' in a book entitled *The Practice of Reading: Interpreting the Novel* might appear to be a foolhardy enterprise. For not only do individual practices and experiences of reading and interpretation inevitably vary from individual to individual, the very phrase 'the experience of reading' is read, interpreted, experienced differently from one person to the next. What hope can there be, then, for discussing *some*thing if we cannot even be sure that what we are discussing is the *same* thing?

That the phrase 'the experience of reading' is used differently by various writers, critics and theorists becomes apparent once we consider specific instances of its usage. Take the following statements, for example:

> . . . the interest in the present volume concerns reading in retrospect; with the attempt to make a coherent account out of the immediacies of our reading experience . . . (Ian Gregor)[1]

> . . . all poems (and novels and plays) [are], in some sense, about their readers, and . . . therefore the experience of the reader, rather than the 'text itself,' [is] the proper object of analysis. (Stanley Fish)[2]

> To read is to play the role of a reader and to interpret is to posit an experience of reading. (Jonathan Culler)[3]

There is nothing especially new about stressing the importance of the experience of reading; the attention paid by reader-response critics, reception aestheticians, and reader theorists in general, to what readers actually *do* to literary texts, and to what really *happens* when a text is read, has been a marked feature of the international academic literary-critical scene since the mid-1960s. Variants of the collocation 'the experience of reading' are to be found almost everywhere in published scholarship and criticism. But it is a phrase which covers a multitude of sins. On the one hand, it is used by those critics (such as Jonathan Culler, quoted above) who make it their business to draw explicitly and systematically upon recent developments in contemporary literary theory in proffering their readings of texts. On the other hand, the phrase is also used by those rather more traditional critics who are sceptical about some of the claims advanced in the name of theoretical abstractions, objecting to the dreary, pretentious and alienating modes of obscurantist critical discourse which more fashionable colleagues specialize in producing. Thus, Philip Davis, who takes his cue from Charles Dickens's David Copperfield, 'reading as if for life', is interested in opening up the study of the nineteenth-century realist novel to 'ordinary serious readers', to show such readers 'how reading [can be] personal' and 'a part of the way we try to think about ourselves'; there is, insists Davis, 'some vital relation between the two, the reading and the living, the living and the reading'.[4]

This emphasis upon the experiential dimension of reading takes us back to our comment in Chapter 3, where we argued that '*Pride and Prejudice* is not a "text", it is an "experience"'. Exactly what is involved in the process of reading a novel was investigated in that chapter, using Austen's novel for illustrative purposes (the point being that with such an ironic novel, the reader was called upon to be extremely actively involved in the reading process). In this chapter we take our investigation into the actual thought-and-felt experience of reading further, in relation to a later and very different novel, Dickens's *Great Expectations*, first published in weekly instalments, under Dickens's own editorship, in *All the Year Round* from 1 December 1860 to 3 August 1861.

Returning to the three critical quotations above, it is instructive to compare and contrast how each writer refers to the experience of reading. Ian Gregor, for example, refers to 'reading in retrospect', to the notion of readers looking back on their experience of reading a novel and trying to make some kind of sense of the whole event: he does not seem particularly interested here in the concept of the reading experience as a dynamic, ongoing, temporal process (though elsewhere he does attend to 'the feeling of what it is actually like to read a novel').[5] He also writes of 'our' reading experience, which indicates his concern with what (he presumes) readers have in common, as opposed to what differentiates particular reading experiences.

Compare Gregor's usage with Fish's phrase, 'the experience of the reader', which probably sounds more objective, more neutral in tone, though this might be a rhetorical strategy for presenting his own (subjective) readings as normative. That would hardly be proper: the word which springs to mind here is its French cognate *propre*, for it is his *own* readings which Fish quite brilliantly presents as 'the informed reader's' in his writings. But Fish knows this, and his ironic gloss on 'Literature in the Reader: Affective Stylistics' indicates as much.[6] (It also hints at his subsequent abandonment of the text-reader dualism, a matter we discussed in Chapter 1.) Notice the foundation for his claim that we should analyse the reader's experience rather than the text: all texts are 'in some sense, about their readers'. What can this mean? *All* texts? It is obviously true of a novel like *Tristram Shandy*, but how could it apply to novels outside the self-conscious tradition such as *Pride and Prejudice* or *Great Expectations*? Fish's claim is not a perverse generalization, and it needs careful consideration: we shall deal below with the some of the issues it raises.

Finally, we might usefully consider Culler's proposition (which, as it happens, arises out of a witty discussion of Fish's work) that 'to interpret is to posit an experience of reading' – an experience which involves playing 'the role of a reader'. Culler is no less emphatic than Fish – he writes definitively – but he is fonder of the *in*definite article. In relating various 'stories of reading' he reveals how fraught with problems most accounts of the experience of reading are: his argument that reading involves acting, playing the role of a hypothetical reader, is certainly provoking, and one which will be explored further in relation to *Great Expectations*.

In his magisterial essay on *Great Expectations* Christopher Ricks writes that 'the most important things' about the novel 'are also the most obvious – a fact that is fortunate for the book, but unfortunate for the critic', and he instances 'convincing and often profound characterization, a moving and exciting story, and a world observed with both literal and moral fidelity'; referring to the scene where Pip receives Magwitch on his return to England, Ricks comments: 'tears such as Magwitch weeps leave us moved and shamed'.[7] Ricks's account of how many readers find themselves reacting to the experience of reading the novel is deft, persuasive and confirmatory. His references to Magwitch's tears and to how moving the novel is must not be passed over in silence here. For to neglect altogether to mention the emotional dimension of the reading experience would be to misrepresent fundamentally the experience.

It is worth pausing at this point to consider why it is that, in practice, relatively little stress is laid on a novel's humour or pathos, in critical descriptions and analyses of reading experiences. Various explanations spring to mind: there is no point in stating the obvious (so 'take it as read'); the subjects are difficult to do justice to (the psychology of emotional states being a complex area); it would be murdering to dissect (a joke explained is no joke at all). But each of these excuses leaves something to be desired. At the heart (one might say) of the reluctance of critics to dwell on the emotional components of the reading experience is the sense that readers, like people generally, are different: what moves one reader to laughter or tears may not have the same effect on another, so to attempt to deal with such empirical matters theoretically would be, to say the least, a complicated business. Wimsatt and Beardsley raised this problem in their discussion of what they termed the 'affective fallacy', which they defined as a confusion between a text and its results ('what it *is* and what it *does*'); in their view, such an approach leads inexorably to impressionism and relativism.[8] But although Fish, among others, has exposed the argument of Wimsatt and Beardsley as itself fallacious,[9] feeling continues to be the poor relation of thought. This may have something to do with the fear of a slide towards subjectivism – a worry Fish confronts in putting forward his theory of 'the authority of interpretive communities'. But it must be axiomatic that no two readings can be identical (whether by two different people, or by the same person at different times): if only in very minute particulars each actual reading experience is bound to be a unique, unrepeatable process. So a measure of subjectivism would seem to be inevitable, a 'given' with which one can do little other than accept.

There are, inevitably, those theorists and critics who seek to make a virtue out of this necessity, arguing in favour of 'subjective criticism' on the grounds that the reading experience is primarily psychological in nature: readers read in order to understand themselves better, responding to literary texts by a process of assimilation and projection; the work of Norman Holland is relevant here.[10] David Bleich formulates a distinction between a reader's initial spontaneous felt response to (say) a novel, and the attempt of that reader to state objectively what the novel means; the latter can only be understood in terms of the former, he argues: hence, in his view, the importance of understanding the psychology of individual readers (and critics).[11] Bleich's distinction is of interest because it sheds more light on the question posed earlier: why *are* the emotional aspects of the reading experience so often underplayed in accounts of reading? A cynical response would be that of John Reichert, who claims that 'critics often argue on behalf of a response that no reader ever had'.[12] (Not all critics though. Q. D. Leavis, whose chapter on Dickens's novel is entitled, 'How we must read *Great Expectations*', sets out a prescriptive agenda, on the assumption that there is only one 'correct' response possible!)[13] A more sophisticated rationale, perhaps, is hinted at by Culler, above: 'to read is to play the role of a reader and to interpret is to posit an experience of reading'. When we read we play one role; when we comment on what we have read (or on what we think we have read) we play another, discrete role. (Hence, incidentally, Culler's deconstructive emphasis on what he refers to as the 'gap or division within reading'.)[14]

Which brings us, rather usefully, back to *Great Expectations* – a novel with an ironic title which could so easily be substituted for the titles of many Victorian novels (from *Wuthering Heights*, through *Middlemarch*, to *Jude the Obscure*). Dickens's *Bildungsroman* about a painful education of the heart and head is a novel with much to say about reading, about role-play, and about the split or divided self. Above all, *Great Expectations* is a novel which illustrates perfectly what happens when we try to interpret the meaning of a past experience, using the complex medium of language to construct a history of the self for others to experience vicariously through a reading of the narrative.[15]

That *Great Expectations* has to do, to a marked extent, with readers and reading – both literally and metaphorically – has been noted before now.[16] From the moment of Pip's appearance on the first page of the novel, reading his parents' tombstone(s), to the final chapter in which Pip revisits the churchyard and gazes at the same inscriptions with young Pip for company, the novel is replete with descriptions of reading experiences of various kinds. (In this respect it is strikingly similar to *Pride and Prejudice*.) Peter Brooks makes this point effectively in his important study, *Reading for the Plot: Design and Intention in Narrative*, when he comments on how the reader 'must mime Pip's acts of reading but do them better'. He continues:

> Both using and subverting the systems of meaning discovered or postulated by its hero, *Great Expectations* exposes for its reader the very reading process itself: the way the reader goes about finding meaning in the narrative text, and the limits of that meaning as the limits of narrative.[17]

Brooks is right. Illustrative references to and quotations from letters, notes, books and newspapers fill the novel, from Joe's fumbling attempt at reading Pip's writing ('how interesting reading is!', p. 46), to the dramatic communication which concludes the twenty-seventh instalment:

> 'Here's a note, sir. The messenger that brought it, said would you be so good as read it by my lantern?'
>   Much surprised by the request, I took the note. It was directed to Philip Pip, Esquire, and on the top of the superscription were the words, 'PLEASE READ THIS, HERE.' I opened it, the watchman

holding up his light, and read inside, in Wemmick's writing:
'DON'T GO HOME.' (pp. 365–6)

Dickens skilfully keeps the reader in suspense until the very end of the chapter, and the (delayed) appearance of the three crucial final words. Dickens's first readers, of course, would have had to wait a week for the next two chapters. It is not an unrepresentative passage, and it is worth staying with, for it attends most precisely to an act of reading on the part of Pip. The word 'act' is used advisedly here, for it is the account of an act (of what Pip did, of what Pip read) which is given to us, and not the account of what Pip 'experienced' as he acted, as he read. That information is *not* given to us: there is very clearly, here, a gap which we are invited to fill; we can only speculate about the significance of Wemmick's note, and what Pip was actually thinking and feeling as he read the note. Our role as readers is plain enough: it is to provide what is lacking in the text itself, on the basis of what is present in the text itself or, to be more strictly accurate in Iserian terms, on the basis of our retrospection and projection, combining our memory of the preceding text with our predictions for its future. But what does our experience as readers amount to, in so far as it is possible to say? What else is involved in this act of reading? The passage above affords us a clue. For Pip's reading performance – as it is given – is intensely self-conscious: Pip reads in front of the watchman, and if not exactly 'in the limelight' (a phrase more applicable to Orlick's letter to Pip, suggesting that he *return* home) then certainly under the light of the watchman's lantern. (The illustration, 'DON'T GO HOME!', by the artist Marcus Stone, which is one of eight plates commissioned by Dickens for the Library edition of 1864, foregrounds Pip's self-conscious reading performance dramatically.)[18] What Pip reads is Wemmick's version of his own name, 'Philip Pip, Esquire', the peculiar, suggestive force of which amalgam, it might be supposed, has struck Pip (since he includes that particular written detail in his narrative), followed by two instructions, the first of which, 'PLEASE READ THIS, HERE', is read by both Pip and the reader simultaneously, as it were. The word 'THIS' is readable enough in one sense: it refers to the note, and in particular to the next three unenlightening words, 'DON'T GO HOME'. In another sense it is radically unreadable, or unfollowable, since it refers, at least by implication, to the words 'PLEASE READ THIS, HERE' themselves, and the request/command is asking/ordering Pip – and the reader – to do something which has already been done in the very act of reading about what one should do in some near-instantaneous future. The 'THIS, HERE' (future) becomes a 'THAT, THERE' (past) in a split-second readerly present. The result is a moment, therefore, of extraordinarily heightened self-consciousness on our part as readers as we watch ourselves reading Pip's words describing his (also self-conscious) reading of Wemmick's words in front of the watchman with the lantern.

The experience of reading *Great Expectations*, then, is profoundly self-conscious, because of the way in which the novel draws our attention to what we are doing in the very act of doing it. This is not to say that the novel is systematically self-conscious in the way that *Tristram Shandy* is, however. Dickens's novel clearly lacks the many formal literary devices of Sterne's novel which are self-evidently there specifically to heighten the reader's awareness of the complex relationship between fictional artifice and reality. The later novel's tendency to return readers to themselves is, in part, a consequence of the point of view and narrative method adopted (a sustained, subtle and intermittently ironic, first-person account) and its (chronologically linear) structure. And, obviously, it is a novel which has for its subject the central character's developing self-consciousness. Most readers of *Great Expectations* – from Dickens's time to the present (and irrespective of age, gender, race, class or ideology) – in the process of reading the novel, identify to some extent with Pip, reading *as if* Pip, acting out an imaginary role as the (anti-)hero of this novel. But just as there is a part of Pip's self (the older, more experienced narrator) which is linked to and yet divided from another part (the younger, inexperienced subject of much of the narrative), so too with the reader. We may sympathize with Pip-the-young-victim, we may identify with Pip-the-mature-adult as he confesses his shame and embarrassment at his earlier behaviour; but there is a part of ourselves which engages in no role-play other than that of self-conscious readerly reflection. The experience of reading *Great Expectations* involves division and projection, then: we hear Pip speaking about himself (using that most problematical of pronouns, 'I'),[19] and we see Pip reading his own name (as if alienated from it, as in the letter quoted above), just as we witness the behaviour of the other divided selves among the novel's dramatis personae such as Wemmick, Magwitch, and Miss Havisham, along with the many examples of role-play and acting in the novel.[20] (Is there any character in the novel who does not role-play at some stage?) But, at the same time, it is difficult to avoid listening to ourselves, witnessing our own behaviour as active, role-playing readers, inside an experience (looking out) and outside it (looking in). (The word 'expectation', incidentally, derives from the Latin *ex + spectare* – 'to look out'.)

That the experience of reading *Great Expectations* involves a sense of self-division is apparent if we return to thinking as we did in Chapter 3 about reading as a crucially temporal activity. Self-division can only take place within and across time. Fish, for example, refers to the text's 'patterns of expectation and disappointment, reversals of direction, traps, invitations to premature conclusions, textual gaps, delayed revelations, temptations . . .'[21] and the challenges and opportunities these features can present to the active reader. *Great Expectations* is abnormally well-stocked with such features, so that Iser's description of the creative, self-corrective reading process as 'a continual interplay between modified expectations and transformed memories',[22] taken together with his resonant argument that 'expectations are scarcely ever fulfilled in truly literary texts',[23] has a particular bearing on this novel. For to read Dickens's novel is indeed to experience, time and again, with Pip and on one's own account as reader, the frustrating non-fulfilment of expectations. This is true both on the level of individual sentences, and on the level of the novel taken as a whole.

To illustrate these points about the experience of reading in time, it might be helpful to consider an example drawn from the novel itself. Take the case of Chapter 29, which comes about midway through the novel. Pip has returned to the town of his childhood on a brief visit. This is how the chapter (which begins the seventeenth instalment) opens:

> Betimes in the morning I was up and out. It was too early yet to go to Miss Havisham's, so I loitered into the country on Miss Havisham's side of town — which was not Joe's side; I could go there to-morrow — thinking about my patroness, and painting brilliant pictures of her plans for me.
>
> She had adopted Estella, she had as good as adopted me, and it could not fail to be her intention to bring us together. (p. 231)

A point which needs to be made at once is that the experience of reading *Great Expectations* first time around is very different in kind

and degree from subsequent readings. (Again, a comparison with
Pride and Prejudice suggests itself.) On re-reading the novel, because
one is familiar with the plot and the novel's ending(s), the experience
of being kept in suspense is obviously much diminished; the hints
and clues which lace the narrative, some of which would have been
missed on an initial reading, are more readily picked up; and the
novel's many ironies (especially dramatic ironies) are more easily
recognized. The previous chapter ended with Pip's arrival at the Blue
Boar, having overheard a disturbing conversation between two
convicts in the coach on his journey there:

> I could not have said what I was afraid of, for my fear was alto-
> gether undefined and vague, but there was great fear upon me. As I
> walked on to the hotel, I felt that a dread, much exceeding the mere
> apprehension of a painful or disagreeable recognition, made me
> tremble. I am confident that it took no distinctness of shape, and that
> it was the revival for a few minutes of the terror of childhood. (p. 230)

The experience of reading this paragraph for the first time must
involve a dim sense that there is something significant (but not yet
revealed) about Pip's childhood experience with the (not yet named)
convict. The alert reader will probably identify with Pip's apprehen-
siveness to some degree, yet will also be expecting a clarifying revelation at some point. But a closer reading of the above sentences, in
order, is itself revealing. The first two clauses are tautologous: Pip,
looking back, is telling us that he was afraid. The third clause emphasizes the magnitude of his fear. The second sentence must intensify
the reader's impression that Pip's 'dread' is no idle fear but a powerful
foreboding: it is strong enough to actually make him tremble. And
then comes the final throw-away sentence, apparently dismissing the
fears which had been made so much of: the final declaration is
emphatic and authoritative, coming as it does from the older Pip. But
it is hard to imagine any reader regarding this sentence as an
adequate explanation of Pip's fear and dread, for it flies in the face of
the narrative expectations which the detailed account of the preceding episode had set up. The reader is led up a path only to be turned
around again: in thinking Pip's fear was indeed a *fore*boding – in other
words, related to some future development – the reader has ostensibly been corrected by the text, and informed that it really relates to
Pip's past (and is therefore not so significant after all). The novel

sends out the message, 'entertain no expectations about what might happen to Pip, or about what Pip's true situation might turn out to be, on the basis of what you have just read'; the reader decodes the message as, 'it is justifiable to build up expectations based on this passage, because its implications outweigh in significance the dubious explanation tendered'. So the temporal experience of reading these sentences successively gives the attentive reader the self-conscious sense of expectations being played around with, and in an experienced reader is likely to leave a suspicion of the narrator protesting too much about the lack of significance of the experience just related. These sentences effectively form the temporal context for reading the opening words of Chapter 29, quoted at the beginning of this paragraph. Re-reading them, in the light of the above discussion, we interpret Pip's behaviour in the morning as illustrating not so much his fears about an indefinite future, so much as an anxiety about his imminent visit to Miss Havisham and Estella, coupled with a certain amount of guilt (which Pip rationalizes) about not visiting Joe. But Pip's references to Miss Havisham would give any observant reader of Chapter 28 pause for thought. Pip's quite casual mention of her at first as his 'patroness' might pass unnoticed – might even momentarily confirm the reader's sense, shared with Pip, that she will in the end turn out to be his anonymous benefactress. But Pip's portrayal of himself 'painting brilliant pictures of her plans for me', together with the unimpressive attempt at a syllogism which comprises the opening sentence of paragraph two ('She had adopted Estella, she had as good as adopted me, and [therefore] it could not fail to be her intention to bring us together.') – a sentence which ushers in a typical Pip fantasy, in which he 'was the hero', aiming to 'do all the shining deeds of the young Knight of romance' (p. 231) – can only make the reader suspect the legitimacy of Pip's expectations. This readerly suspicion is in part founded on the sense of the fallibility of expectations, itself a product of the experience of reading the previous chapter, and it finds confirmation in what follows; see, for example, a later reference in the same chapter to Pip's credulity concerning Miss Havisham: 'at the height of the assurance I felt that our patroness had chosen us for one another. Wretched boy!' (p. 239). The 'I felt' is weak enough; the exclamation needs no comment. So Iser's description of the reading experience as involving 'modified expectations' and 'transformed memories' is amply borne out by reflecting on the experience of reading these two chapters. Our memory of reading Chapter 28 is transformed by what we read in Chapter 29: and our expectations concerning Pip's own expectations are modified correspondingly.

The reader then, like Pip, is continually forced to revise expectations formulated at an earlier interpretative stage. The cautious reader will form expectations tentatively, recognizing their provisionality quite self-consciously. How speculative the temporal experience of constructing working hypotheses and filling the narrative gaps is, will vary from reader to reader, and is less a matter of temperament, perhaps, than of the degree of creative autonomy readers award themselves. In order to fill some textual holes first time round, a healthy disrespect for the text is as likely to produce results as an undue reverence for it. To return to Chapter 29: three times in this chapter, Pip poses the question, 'what *was* it that was borne in upon my mind when [Estella] stood still and looked attentively at me?' – a question no first-time reader is likely to be able to answer satisfactorily, on the basis of what has been read thus far.

But consider the following three examples of readers' interpretations, which depend (to varying degrees) on the notion of reading 'in time', and lead to questionable conclusions. The first is from Christopher Ricks, commenting on Pip's refusal of financial help for himself from Miss Havisham in Chapter 49. In response to Miss Havisham's question, 'is there nothing I can do for you yourself?', Pip answers: 'Nothing. I thank you for the question. I thank you even more for the tone of the question. But, there is nothing' (p. 397). Ricks observes: 'That comma after "But" must be the least careless comma in Dickens – the decent mystery of leaving the rest unsaid.'[24] Ricks interprets the comma as betokening a pause or silence, a moment's hesitation on Pip's part as he struggles with his conscience, eventually coming through the temptation, all the more noble for not having beaten his breast about it to the reader. The gap is certainly there, and Ricks has equally certainly filled it. But in filling it, Ricks, whether he is aware of it or not, is exhibiting a reader's delight in the free play of interpretation rather than adhering to such strictly 'textual' evidence as there is. For although the comma does look unusual, taking the passage out of context, the fact is that the entire novel, like other Dickens novels, is crowded with such idiosyncratic forms of punctuation. Many sentences begin with the word 'But' followed by a comma in *Great Expectations*: indeed they occur with monotonous regularity, and are, for the most part, utterly innocuous. But, the gap is there and Ricks has filled it.

The second example is from John Schad, who quotes the passage where Pip watches Estella leave the brewery during his first visit to Satis House:

> I saw her pass among the extinguished fires, and *ascend some light* iron stairs, and go out by a gallery high overhead, as if she were going out into the sky. (p. 64; Schad's italics)

Schad's comment reads as follows:

> In reading this sentence we are . . . tempted, by the following words – 'and ascend some light' – with a vision of her climbing some ladder of light, a vision no sooner entertained than negated by the adjective 'iron' and the 'stairs' it modifies. In other words, the reader must reject as a misreading the very ascent of the sky that, in the final clause of the sentence, Pip himself imagines . . .[25]

Schad's temptation as a reader may be no less real than Pip's in Ricks's example, but it is unfortunate that, unlike Pip, Schad gives in to his. The gap between 'light' and 'iron' is wholly of Schad's making, and it is highly improbable, to say the least, that any 'in tempo' experience of reading in time would lead to the commission of the error that Schad refers to by the word 'misreading'. (Schad's commentary here is pseudo-Fishian: compare Fish's brilliant reading of Milton's line in *Paradise Lost*, 'Nor did they not perceive the evil plight', where he stresses the reader's experience of the syntax.)[26]

Our final example actually made the front page of the *Observer* on 12 January 1997, under the headline, 'Coded erotica of "filthy" Dickens'. Barry Hugill was reporting to the newspaper's readers on the publication of a critical work by an American academic – William A. Cohen's *Sex Scandals: The Private Parts of Victorian Fiction*. In his book, Cohen argues that, reading between the lines, *Great Expectations* has much to say about sex and sexuality in general, and about masturbation and paedophilia in particular. Thus, after his first meeting with Magwitch, Pip hides his slice of 'bread-and-butter' down his trouser-leg, where it becomes a 'secret burden' until he is able to 'deposit that part of my conscience in my garret bedroom' (pp. 11–13). The inference is predictable: for 'butter' read 'semen'. Here is an instance of a Victorian novelist writing about the unwritable in the only way then possible – by subterfuge, in code. Dickens's very

Victorian guilt about masturbation (Pip, we recall, was brought up 'by hand') thus emerges obliquely. The reporter in the *Observer* was – or pretended to be – shocked. John Sutherland, Lord Northcliffe Professor of Modern English Literature at University College London was quoted on the 'chasm between common sense and the further shores of literary theory: "Any ordinary Dickens fan reading Cohen will think he's a Martian"'. How far can you go? Cohen, in filling one particular kind of textual gap in *Great Expectations* has clearly gone further than Schad, and much further than Ricks. Sutherland is presumably of the view that Cohen has arrogated to himself too much 'creative autonomy', having approached Dickens's novel with an '*un*healthy disrespect' for the text. Butter, for Sutherland, remains butter, even if it does 'trickle down [Pip's] leg', as the *Observer* has it. (One is reminded of a butter-substitute spread, much advertised in the 1990s, with the unlikely name, I Can't Believe It's Not Butter!) Cohen's reading of *Great Expectations* is intemperate in so far as it is insufficiently constrained by the *in*trinsic, *ex*plicit textual evidence. Because what is *not* said is accorded much greater significance than what *is* said, a critical reading is arrived at which, for the average purchaser of the *Observer*, defies the experience of the (millions?) of readers of Dickens's novel (whether they constitute an 'interpretive community' or not). And so it is that any reading, if it lacks firm, explicit textual support and flies in the face of the experience of most readers of the text, will always be liable to be dismissed as a wilful *mis*reading, off the wall.

So much for experiences of reading – and misreading – in time. But there is another context in which reading takes place, as a number of reception theorists have been at pains to point out, and that is the problematical context of history. For, as Hans-Georg Gadamer has argued, in speaking of 'the reader' it makes sense to emphasize the 'historical situatedness' of the reader.[27] The experience of reading *Great Expectations*, the attempt to interpret and understand this novel, can only take place within a specific historical context, from a particular vantage-point in history. In other words, it is not just that the past to some extent conditions and determines the present; the past itself is only graspable from the limited perspective of the present. Therefore, to write of the experience of reading Dickens's novel is to write of the experience of reading Dickens's novel from a particular point in history (the present). Moreover, not only is it impossible to read outside a framework into which is built an interpretation of the past, it is similarly impossible to read in some vacuum as a 'solitary reader': one reads as a member of the reading public, and the reading experience will be affected by the various factors which influence the knowledge, assumptions and attitudes of that wider readership. Jauss's renowned phrase for the dominant set of cultural presuppositions, norms, values and conventions, which govern the 'transsubjective' practice (and therefore the experience) of reading at any one stage in history, is the 'horizon of expectations'.[28] The concept is not without its difficulties, as various writers have indicated,[29] but it does form the basis of one kind of explanation as to why later readings of a text frequently differ quite markedly from earlier readings, and, secondly, it does provide us with an alternative way into thinking about the experience of reading *Great Expectations*.

Take the second point first. One way of summing up *Great Expectations* would be to describe it as a novel in which Pip (re)writes his past history from his (present) perspective as a more experienced 'reader' of his life and the lives of those whose destinies crossed his. Looked at from this point of view, Pip's narrative stresses the superiority of his later perspective over and above the limited perspectives of his erring past, with all the latter's moral, psychological and social blind spots. There is nothing relativistic about this; if anything, it accords well with Victorian meliorist thinking – 'Let knowledge grow from more to more', as Tennyson's line from *In Memoriam* has it (though the word 'meliorism' was actually coined by George Eliot). Pip's narrative, in other words, is structured around the duplex notion that to understand the present one must look at the past, and that to look at the past is to look with the eyes of the present. *Great Expectations*, throughout, enacts a dialogue between past and present in this sense, contrasting strikingly with those Victorian first-person novels which do this only minimally (think of *Jane Eyre*, for example). Pip's account of the first time he kissed Estella bears this out:

> I kissed her cheek as she turned it to me. I think I would have gone through a great deal to kiss her cheek. But, I felt that the kiss was given to the coarse common boy as a piece of money might have been, and that it was worth nothing. (p. 93)

(Note the comma after 'But'.) Past and present are mixed up here, and it is not wholly clear to what extent the Pip of the present is *actually* present: the simile 'as a piece of money' is richly suggestive, but is more likely to come from the older Pip who has learnt, in the terms of his narrative, the true worth of money and wealth. That the past and the present can be so easily confused, and ultimately perhaps never completely disentangled, is indicative. The experience of the reader, trying to work out the balance between past and present, younger Pip and older Pip, earlier response and later interpretation, can be taken as an illustration of what is involved in reading in history: the attempt to fuse past and present perspectives is, arguably, as fraught as the attempt to separate them; but that there *is* a two-way relationship between a 'textual' past and a 'readerly' present is difficult to gainsay. The end of Chapter 9 offers a different metaphor:

> That was a memorable day to me, for it made great changes in me. But, it is the same with any life. Imagine one selected day struck out of it, and think how different its course would have been. Pause you who read this, and think for a moment of the long chain of iron or gold, of thorns or flowers, that would never have bound you, but for the formation of the first link on one memorable day. (p. 72)

More George Eliot than Wordsworth, the appeal is to the reader's present: and what the reader is being invited to do is rather more than filling a gap in the text. If you wish to make sense of reality, if you wish to construct a narrative whose shapely logic will satisfy, then (the advice runs) read the present in terms of the past, and the past in terms of the present.

In the light of all this, what can be said about the difference between the experiences of earlier readers of the novel, and the experiences of late-twentieth-century readers? And, more particularly, putting on one side the vastly different cultural situation of Dickens's readers of the 1860s, what can usefully be added about the experience of what might be termed reading-in-time-in-history, that is, reading *Great Expectations* in the form of weekly instalments, as originally published?

Paul Pickrel describes *Great Expectations* thus:

> It is a fantasy of a beneficent if unpredictable universe that will someday shower us with gold without any effort or indeed any merit on our part.

He comments: 'anyone who buys a chance on a Cadillac or a

sweepstakes ticket shares it, and probably it plays a larger part in the fantasy life of adults than most of us would care to admit'.[30] His essay dates from 1960. Compare the remarks of an anonymous reviewer of one hundred years earlier:

> Pip . . . is low-born, fatherless and motherless, and he rises out of the cheerless degradation of his childhood into quite another sphere . . . [and] through some unaccountable caprice of fortune, the puny son of poverty suddenly finds himself the child of affluence.[31]

On the surface, the same point is being registered by readers writing a century apart: the story of Pip does indeed revolve around the sudden, mysterious acquisition of considerable personal wealth, with all that that entails. But the element of fantasy to which Pickrel refers is, on the whole, rather more of a twentieth-century phenomenon. This is not to say that Dickens's Victorian readers did not fantasize about suddenly becoming enormously rich through inheriting money, gambling or crime; they undoubtedly did. (After all, such occurrences had a long enough history, as a glance at Hogarth's satiri-cal engraving, *The Lottery*, of 1724, makes plain.) But it would have been an unrealistic dream for many people, and recognized for what it was. Whereas twentieth-century readers of Dickens's novel, with twice-weekly national lottery tickets or with football pools coupons, might well be used to thinking of themselves as potential lucky winners: the media feed the dreams of those who cherish the possibil-ity that they too (one day) could become several million pounds better off – 'it could be you!' This is not a negligible point to make: the *actual* expectations of readers – whether in terms of what they imagine might happen next as they read the novel, or in terms of how they conceive of their own financial prospects – exert considerable influence on the reading experience. The dominant myth of the nine-teenth century was not of the lottery ticket variety, but that of Samuel Smiles: by sheer hard work and individual merit riches could be (and should be) well-earned. Pip's windfall must have struck many a reader of 1861 as ill-gotten and ill-deserved – its true, tainted origin (the criminal Magwitch), and Pip's associated guilt, would surely have struck a chord. The older Pip who, at the end, describes himself as working 'pretty hard for a sufficient living' (p. 484) would have undoubtedly seemed a more admirable figure to the Victorians.

The point should not be laboured, and it is worth reminding

ourselves that Jauss's project also involves looking at the specifically literary assumptions and conventions which influence the experience of readers in different historical periods. Today's readers, for example, are quite likely to be familiar with the basic story-line of *Great Expectations* before even reading the first page, perhaps having already seen a film version of the novel (such as David Lean's classic adaptation); in such cases, the ensuing reading experience is bound to be significantly at variance with that of those Victorian readers who came to Dickens's novel fresh (whether they read the novel by themselves, or heard it read aloud in the family circle).

But what can the experience of reading the novel as it first came out, have been like? The first point to note, in historical terms, is that Dickens's contemporary readers would have had a strong sense of being addressed in the reading 'present', even though the novel is set back in time (a king is on the throne, and a further dating clue puts the action of the novel at the time of Pip's London phase at around the 1820s: see p. 291). An observation such as 'At that time, the steam-traffic on the Thames was far below its present extent' (p. 435) would come across as a friendly concession to the reader of 1861. Other topical and literary (especially biblical) allusions would have had a similarly reassuring effect on those readers in a position to identify them.[32]

Less reassuring for readers then would have been the many teasing deferrals and delays built into the narrative as delivered in its serial form in 36 instalments in *All the Year Round*. Not all of these occur at the ends of instalments. An example is to be found in Chapter 55, in which Pip puts off deciding whether to accept Herbert's invitation to live with Clara and him, explaining his thinking to the reader thus:

> Firstly, my mind was too preoccupied to be able to take in the subject clearly. Secondly —— Yes! Secondly, there was a vague something lingering in my thoughts that will come out very near the end of this slight narrative. (p. 450)

The reader has to wait until Chapter 57 (in the penultimate instalment) to learn what 'that Secondly, not yet arrived at' (p. 471) is – his decision to propose to Biddy. This is more than the stock-in-trade of a novelist who deals in suspense. For the effect is to transfuse into the reader's thoughts the 'vague something', and raise in the reader an expectation of a metafictional kind as 'the end of this slight narrative' approaches, so that when Pip learns that Biddy is already married to Joe, and reflects on 'this last baffled hope' (p. 479), the familiar pattern of expectations frustrated is underwritten once more. Dickens's original readers, forced as they were to read by instalments (or by numbers), would have experienced a readerly equivalent of expectation and frustration in a way which it is difficult (if not impossible) to replicate unartificially today.

But, as might be expected, it was the endings of a number of instalments which presented Dickens's first readers with the most demanding reading and interpretational challenges. Some of the endings must have encouraged the tendency to speculate as to where the plot was heading: a case in point is the melodramatic end of the ninth instalment, which concludes with the picture of Pip's sister lying senseless on the kitchen floor, 'destined never to be on the Rampage again, while she was wife of Joe' (p. 119). The reader-as-detective comes into play at such moments – and, odd though it may seem, such moments are playful. The two instalments which mark the end of the first and second stages of Pip's expectations (instalments 12 and 24) call upon the reader to do more than hazard guesses and attempt to fill a few narrative holes. Here is the end of the twelfth instalment; Pip has left home, and is on his way by coach to London:

> We changed again, and yet again, and it was now too late and too far to go back, and I went on. And the mists had all solemnly risen now, and the world lay spread before me.

THIS IS THE END OF THE FIRST STAGE OF PIP'S EXPECTATIONS (p. 160)

The experienced reader may pick up on the masked quotation from *Paradise Lost*, a text that is alluded to on several key occasions (including the ending as published) and reflect on its significance, but even if that were missed (and many Victorian readers would have been more familiar than today's readers with Milton's epic poem), a perceptive reader with a good memory should have been able to refer back to those earlier sections of the novel where the 'marsh mists' were in evidence. It would have been difficult for those early readers to make some of the textual connections waiting to be made, notwithstanding the longer time available to read the novel, but in essence the detecting and forging of such connections across the gaps – both spatial and temporal – would have constituted a large part of the reading experience then, as it still does today.

In *On Deconstruction*, Jonathan Culler comments:

> A reader who creates everything learns nothing, but one who is continually encountering the unexpected can make momentous, unsettling findings.[33]

The experience of reading *Great Expectations*, as we have seen, is one which involves the constant, if provisional, formulation of expectations only to have many of those expectations frustrated and denied, so that the reader is continually forced to abandon or revise some of them in the light of various encounters with the unexpected. The experience of reading Dickens's novel involves reflecting self-consciously on, and actively attending to, the (in part, subjective) act of reading itself – to the thoughts and the feelings which arise in the individual reader in the process. It involves self-projection and self-division, reading 'as if', role-play, acting out the part of a reader – here on the inside (looking out), there on the outside (looking in), as we attempt to bring what we read into some kind of relation with our own lives, and as we reflect upon how our experience – like Pip's – is made and remade. It involves reading in time, moving backwards and forwards, filling the narrative blanks. It involves reading in history, aware of the 'horizon of expectations' which, since it includes how others have read in the past, provides a defining context. Finally, the experience of reading the novel involves confronting the unreadable, the contradictory, the paradoxical, in the never-ending quest of interpretation.

This last point has been deliberately underplayed in this chapter. It implies a model of reading which directs the reader back, still more closely, to the text itself. It is to this model – the model of deconstruction – that we now turn our attention, and to one of the strangest of all Victorian novels: George Eliot's *Daniel Deronda*.

5   Deconstruction and Reading: *Daniel Deronda*

For good and for ill, the fortunes of deconstruction from the late 1980s through the 1990s were mixed. Certainly, by 1989, when revelations about the late Paul de Man's allegedly pro-Nazi past broke upon the critical scene, the concept had already been under attack from two opposite, if not equal, camps. On the one hand, entrenched conservatives continued to pour scorn on what they considered to be an absurd, self-refuting, even nihilistic approach to reading and criticism.[1] On the other hand, born-again historicists and cultural materialists were beginning to react vigorously against the emergence of what they saw as a disturbingly ahistorical, apolitical critical wisdom.[2] The rearguard actions fought since then by some of deconstruction's proponents and exemplars, however, have varied enormously in terms of their effectiveness, ranging from the embarrassingly inept to the impressively astute.[3] And battle is still joined, despite apocalyptic predictions of literary theory's imminent demise.[4] Reports of the death of deconstruction, at any rate, would appear to have been somewhat exaggerated.

But when we speak of 'deconstruction', whether as a philosophical or theoretical concept, or whether as a practical literary-critical operation, what do we actually 'mean'? Is whatever is 'referred' to or 'represented' by the term deconstruction even definable, let alone defensible? And how might a defence of '*reading* deconstructively' be mounted without distorting or neutering the process? As the inverted commas signal, the very questions as framed beg further questions, given deconstruction's emphasis on the 'problematics' of 'meaning', 'interpretation', 'representation', and the complex nature of human communication more generally. But a good place to begin to answer these questions is Barbara Johnson's influential study, *The Critical Difference*. Johnson explains deconstruction thus:

Deconstruction is not synonymous with *destruction* . . . It is in fact much closer to the original meaning of the word *analysis*, which etymologically means 'to undo' – a virtual synonym for 'to de-construct'. The de-construction of a text does not proceed by random doubt or arbitrary subversion, but by the careful teasing out of warring forces of signification within the text itself. If anything is destroyed in a deconstructive reading, it is not the text, but the claim to unequivocal domination of one mode of signifying over another. A deconstructive reading is a reading that analyzes the specificity of a text's critical difference from itself.[5]

Christopher Norris, erstwhile revisionist disciple of Derrida, makes a related point about the importance of the reader's attentiveness to the text when he writes that deconstruction is 'an activity of reading which remains closely tied to the texts it interrogates'.[6] Jonathan Culler, one of deconstruction's most lucid exponents, describes it as 'a style of reading'; he comments: 'Deconstruction . . . is a practice of reading and writing attuned to the aporias that arise in attempts to tell us the truth.'[7] While Hillis Miller, perhaps the most flexible and nimble-minded theorist and critic of the so-called Yale School, is rather more forthright when he equates the 'rhetorical analysis of works of literature' (which, for him, is *one* way of defining deconstruc-tion) with 'good reading'.[8]

So one way in which deconstruction can be understood is to see it as a particular kind of theorized praxis, as a reflective *practice of reading* which attends as closely as possible to the text itself, and which proceeds by careful, vigilant analysis. This may sound remark-ably like a summary of the methodology of early- to mid-twentieth-century New Criticism. But compared with the earlier Anglo-American orthodoxy, its latterday Franco-American develop-ment puts forward a model of close reading which is more fundamen-tally questioning and sceptical, and suspicious of easy assumptions. It is unafraid to 'problematize' (inelegant though the word is) the appar-ently straightforward, always seeking to expose the hidden, the repressed 'unconscious' of the language-tissue of the text's discourse(s). This may seem – flatly – perverse, as if the principle of Occam's razor (do not multiply entities unnecessarily) had never been stated. Does not this approach needlessly over-complicate texts, inventing problems where none exists?

The answer, for once, is simple: no. Texts – especially highly self-conscious literary texts, such as the novels explored in this study – *are* complex, *do* contain contradictions, and *can* mislead. So, rather like those reader-response theorists and critics who, as we have seen, conceive of the reader's role in terms of filling the textual gaps or lacunae, the deconstructive reader also reads 'between the lines' or 'against the grain', to use two common metaphors. And what such a reader searches for are those moments (we are back to the temporal nature of the reading process) when the text appears to unwittingly transgress its own laws of construction. Typically, the deconstructive reader seeks to unpack those oppositions which make up the text's ideological baggage. The privileging of one term over its antithesis is picked out and undone: the underprivileged, antithetical term may be shown to inhere in the 'original' thesis (perhaps as its enabling precondition), so that the dichotomy under investigation in effect collapses. This kind of resistant reading exercise may be thought to be – on the face of it – a negative strategy. The very tropes which deconstructive readers and critics use (and some of the metaphors are *very* mixed) have a distinctly reactive ring to them: a novel's hierarchies are 'upset', 'overturned', 'subverted', 'undermined', 'unravelled', 'untangled', 'challenged', 'reversed', 'displaced', 'dislodged', 'dislocated', and so on. Reading begins to sound like an act of warfare (rather like our account of the deconstruction controversy at the beginning of this chapter). Sometimes, on a different figurative tack, one term is referred to as 'contaminating' or 'cross-infecting' another. The discussion is frequently of deferral and *différance*, absence and trace, blindness and misreading, self-contradiction and paradox, unreadability and indeterminacy. As David Lodge's Professor Morris Zapp muses: 'Literature was never about what it appeared to be about, though in the case of the novel considerable ingenuity and perception were needed to crack the code of realistic illusion.'[9] But to read deconstructively is not to read wilfully, in a spirit of captious destructiveness, like some kind of critical vandal keen to deface and deform a text's much-cherished traditional features. Rather, as Barbara Johnson suggests above, it is a matter of carefully opening up what is really already *there* in the text itself. However, as Hillis Miller has observed, since all great texts explicitly anticipate the critic's attempts at deconstruction, the reader who is intent upon doing the utmost justice to such a text in effect *collaborates* with it to produce a deconstructive reading. So, to return to Derrida's own metaphor (encountered in Chapter 1), reading becomes 'transformational'.[10]

Now a transformative, collaborative, deconstructive reading of a novel will be found to have various dimensions. It involves attending to detail, to the apparently trivial, to the 'marginal' and the 'supplementary'. It involves examining particularly closely those moments of *aporia* where the novel seems in danger of becoming unstuck. It involves identifying the novel's priorities, questioning its dominant values, assumptions and arguments, and unearthing its problems and contradictions. It is especially alive to the potentially disruptive, destabilizing, alogical properties of the novel's rhetoric. It is arguably more different in degree than in kind from the models of reading discussed in relation to *Great Expectations* in the previous chapter. It is *more* radically uncertain, *more* provisional, *more* closely attuned to the novel's complex linguistic texture. But it remains an open activity of reading, which, while eschewing finality, neatness and completion, is – ideally – circumspect, observant, curious and (endlessly) patient.

To attempt to read George Eliot's *Daniel Deronda* (1876), her final, most ambitious, most experimental novel – and on any reckoning an unusual novel by Victorian standards – is to be called upon to exercise the faculties of circumspection, observation, curiosity and (certainly) patience in no small measure. It has been claimed before now that Eliot 'can be seen as a deconstructionist *avant la lettre*',[11] while the argument that 'an essential feature of any comprehensive world-view in George Eliot's fiction is the inevitability of its self-deconstruction'[12] is not difficult to sustain in the case of this particular novel. Evidence might be adduced in support of such an argument by pointing in the first instance to the many critics – including Henry James, F. R. Leavis, U. C. Knoepflmacher, and Sally Shuttleworth – who, notwithstanding Eliot's own assertion in a letter that 'I meant everything in the book to be related to everything else there',[13] claim that *Daniel Deronda*, far from being a coherent unity, is essentially a novel split two ways into a psychologically and socially observant account of the Gwendolen/Grandcourt relationship and its context, and a rather melodramatic, didactic narrative, full of improbable coincidences, revolving around Deronda's discovery of his Jewish inheritance.

Critics who stress *Daniel Deronda*'s structural bifurcation tend to write of its contrasting discourses in 'either/or' terms (using, for example, the realism/romance opposition), though usually conceding the 'both/and' nature of the novel's ostensible design. Leavis's influential reading, which explores the relationship of what he calls the 'good half' of *Daniel Deronda* – (re)christened by him *Gwendolen*

Harleth – to Henry James's *The Portrait of a Lady* (1881), goes further still:

> In no other of [Eliot's] works is the association of the strength with the weakness so remarkable or so unfortunate as in *Daniel Deronda*. It is so peculiarly unfortunate, not because the weakness spoils the strength – the two stand apart, on a large scale, in fairly neatly separable masses – but because the mass of fervid and wordy unreality seems to have absorbed most of the attention the book has ever had . . .[14]

It is regrettable that Leavis makes so little of the (interesting) structural division itself, opting instead for a largely evaluative critique in which the split is taken as read and so, in effect, dismissed. Furthermore, it is fascinating to read of 'an extraordinary and revealing reversal, fifty years in advance, of Leavis's position' in Terence Cave's introduction to *Daniel Deronda*. Cave is quoting from an account of Mordecai Ben Hillel Hacohen's essay, 'Israel and Its Land in Fiction', which dates from 1899–1900:

> Half of the story of Daniel Deronda does not derive from the visions and life of the Jews . . . If someone were to excise from this story all the chapters which tell of these Gentiles who have almost nothing to do with its main theme and basic idea . . . the story would lack almost nothing.[15]

Neither Leavis nor Hacohen, with their opposite interests, is in any doubt about the novel's split, and each favours the construction of a new novel by a destruction of that half of the text which each considers to be inferior. A deconstructive reading should seek to move beyond such limited ways of proceeding which ultimately falsify the whole novel that is *Daniel Deronda*.

But any approach constructed on either/or terms runs the risk of playing down, or ignoring altogether, the notion that all texts consist of incompatibilities, being not homogeneous but heterogeneous. A deconstructive reading of *Daniel Deronda*, on the other hand, allows for that aspect of its textuality to be given its due. As Barbara Johnson observes:

> Instead of a simple 'either/or' structure, deconstruction attempts to

elaborate a discourse that says *neither* 'either/or' *nor* 'both/and' nor even 'neither/nor', while at the same time not totally abandoning these logics either. The very word 'deconstruction' is meant to under-mine the either/or logic of the opposition 'construction/destruction'.[16]

From this perspective, to conceive of the novel as little more than the sum of so many 'binary oppositions' looks less than adequate. Retrospectively, it may well be convenient to analyse *Daniel Deronda* in terms of polarities such as individual/society, egoism/altruism, judgement/tolerance, freedom/determinism, but any such analysis runs the not negligible risk of falsifying the activity of reading it purports to be based upon if it permits itself to be subject to the very categories it offers as the objects of its scrutiny in the first place. For, as we have seen, reading is a dynamic process of constant adjustment and negotiation with a text which, far from being static, is protean, slippery and frequently elusive. So to argue over whether, for example, the circumcision of Daniel Deronda is a presence or an absence in the novel as some critics have done (reading, as the late Roland Barthes might have put it in *S/Z*, 'against the groin'),[17] is to seek to impose an interpretation upon a text which, ironically enough, is partly about the problems of interpretation and the intricacies of interpretative and hermeneutic processes. The temptation to reduce, to oversimplify, is one which must be resisted in a deconstructive reading if a sense of the text as complex and heterogeneous is to be preserved.

Some idea of the complexity and heterogeneity of *Daniel Deronda* can be gained by a deconstructive reading of part of the novel's 'para-text' – the title-page of the first four-volume edition – immediately prior to the opening chapter. This innocent-looking page, which says so little compared with (say) the original title-page of Daniel Defoe's *Moll Flanders* (1722), reads as follows:

DANIEL DERONDA

BY

GEORGE ELIOT

VOL. I.

WILLIAM BLACKWOOD AND SONS
EDINBURGH AND LONDON
MDCCCLXXVI

The page is fairly conventionally laid out, and the seeming obviousness of its presentation probably masks for many readers that very weight of self-contradiction which a deconstructive reader would find so telling. Consider the hierarchization implied by the order of the words and the (steadily diminishing) size of the print face: novel title/author's name/publisher's firm/place and date of publication. What is 'naturally' given pride of place – the novel title – is a supreme fiction; the publication details (mere factual impedimenta) are relegated to the bottom of the page. The title doubly misleads: first, as a guide to the novel's subject-matter it gives no hint that at least half of it will be concerned not with the eponymous male protagonist but with a (the) female protagonist – Gwendolen Harleth (later Gwendolen Grandcourt); secondly, Daniel's name as given is, in the novel's own terms, a fiction – his true name (he was not christened) is Daniel Charisi (though neither he nor the reader is aware of this 'fact' as the novel's first scene unfolds).

Literally and metaphorically the first words of this novel are full of holes: the sign (or, more precisely, 'the signifier') claims to be what it is not – it is, in two senses, an 'assumed' name, and the assumption made by the reader will – like so many assumptions in the reading process – subsequently turn out to be false. It is not the only assumed name on the page, of course. Mary Ann Evans's own assumption of the male pseudonym 'George Eliot' complements nicely the novel's title; 'nicely' because if (the arguably feminized) Deronda represents a partial self-portrait of Eliot herself (and Deronda's frame of mind as depicted in Chapter 32 might be adduced in support of this notion) then we have here a classic instance of the second term inhering in the first, but by a kind of subterfuge. So what is foregrounded, signalled as important on this page, is both fictitious and factitious. Far more authoritative (because it is the product of 'authorization' rather than of 'authoring') is the smaller type of the publisher's imprint at the foot of the page: convention dictates that commercial (and thus patriarchal) reality should make an appearance here, and it does, underwriting, as it were, the preceding fiction, though not without introducing (again, conventionally) an ideological fiction of its own in the form of the Western/Christian year-dating method employed, complete with Roman numerals (the equivalent Jewish 'year' to AD MDCCCLXXVI would be, in Arabic numerals, 5636 or 5637).

The title-page, then, seems to promise the first-time reader a conventional (fictional) biography, and as a bill of fare this is inaccurate enough, as anyone re-reading the novel would appreciate. But to go further and read this page deconstructively is to recognize, returning to Barbara Johnson's phrase at the beginning of this chapter, 'the specificity of a text's critical difference from itself'. Not only is the page replete with contradiction; not only does the page defer anything like full meaning (reasonably enough for a title page); it also offers a spurious order in which dubious concepts of the self (with the feminine masquerading as the masculine in this all-male page) are writ large over the novel's own genealogy (which contains its own fictive construct of history). The novel's title-page in effect announces Eliot's idealistic agenda, with the signifier 'Daniel Deronda' standing for a 'signified' of psychological and moral health; but a probing deconstructive reading allows the novel's alternative agenda to be unveiled – an agenda which, it will be seen, points to a scathing critique of reality noticeably at odds with Eliot's fictional idealism.

A deconstructive reading of the opening paragraphs of the first chapter confirms that this is to be a novel riddled with oppositions which collapse under close scrutiny. The epigraph (to begin there) opposes inaccurate grandmother Poetry to accurate grandson Science: each term, initially, defines the other – it is the difference between them, it is suggested, which is significant. But by the end of the epigraph the opposition has collapsed: there is no real distinction between them, strictly speaking; both begin *in medias res*, though Science pretends not to. Poetry is as accurate, or as inaccurate, as Science, Science as arbitrary as Poetry: both Poetry and Science hypothesize, 'make-believe', providing orderly fictions. Any system of time- or date-measurement is arbitrary, it is implied (shades of the date on the title-page). The note struck is important: it *is* a deconstructive note; the emphasis is on the falsity of hierarchical oppositions, and on the arbitrariness and fictiveness of certain ways of thinking. Either/or ways of thinking, in particular, are exposed as limited, and the very nature of causality is called into question in the epigraph's final sentence:

> No retrospect will take us to the true beginning; and whether our prologue be in heaven or on earth, it is but a fraction of that all-presupposing fact with which our story sets out. (p. 7)

The opening which then unfolds as the 'story sets out' is indeed *in medias res* chronologically speaking, but the moment at which the reader enters the narrative is far from arbitrary; on the contrary, the reader is made privy to a scene which is delicate in its balance and subtle in its poise. The first paragraph presents a series of five questions, as an unnamed male subject surveys an unnamed female object:

> Was she beautiful or not beautiful? and what was the secret of form or expression which gave the dynamic quality to her glance? Was the good or the evil genius dominant in those beams? Probably the evil; else why was the effect that of unrest rather than of undisturbed charm? Why was the wish to look again felt as coercion and not as a longing in which the whole being consents? (p. 7)

Four of the five questions are explicitly of the 'either/or' variety. The list of apparent oppositions runs thus (the privileged term is on the left in each case):

beautiful/not beautiful;
good/evil;
charm/unrest;
consent/coercion.

The stereotypical, aporetic mode of thinking of the male subject (named a few lines later – before his female 'object' – and so identified as the novel's titular subject) could obviously be read as Daniel Deronda's attempt to rationalize, and so control, the sexual attraction he feels towards Gwendolen. (Compare Deronda's very definite reply to his mother's question as to whether he thinks Mirah beautiful, much later on in the novel, p. 664.) When the opening is read in this way, Deronda himself becomes the object of the reader's attention and scrutiny; and it is not until the second paragraph, with the intervention of the omniscient narrator, that the focus switches to Gwendolen and to another opposition – nature/civilization. The fascination which Gwendolen begins to feel for Deronda in turn is kept from the reader until near the end of the chapter. There is something going on here more than the sexual attraction of opposites – such as Eliot had explored in Chapter 6, 'Illustrating the Laws of Attraction' of the sixth book ('The Great Temptation') of her second full-length novel, *The Mill on the Floss* (1860). The 'attraction' is not so much of opposites in terms of the novel's personalities, but of oppositions in terms of the novel's ideological polarities, which may be seen to collapse subsequently in the text.[18]

Take the male/female opposition – probably the most striking opposition in the opening chapter. As far as the act of reading is concerned, the oppositional relationship would seem to run thus:

READER reads NARRATOR reads DERONDA reads GWENDOLEN

and:

READER reads NARRATOR reads GWENDOLEN reads DERONDA

(a rough balance – in terms of space – is struck between giving us Deronda's view of Gwendolen, and Gwendolen's view of Deronda). The filtering of female through male, and male through female, is far from straightforward, even putting aside the roles of narrator and reader, for Gwendolen is depicted as possessing some masculine qualities, and Deronda is at least implicitly presented as having certain feminine characteristics. The dissolution of the line dividing male and female (in conventional thinking) is underlined (not undermined) by the generally fairly consistently androgynous narrator (who is obviously not to be simple-mindedly identified as Mary Ann Evans writing as George Eliot) with her/his references both to 'weak females' and to 'the unscrupulous male' (p. 41), throughout the entire novel. Indeed, the only 'slip', if slip it be (and the sentence is ambiguous in its context), occurs much later in the text, when the narrator observes that 'It is a little hard upon some men that they appear to sink for us in becoming lovers' (p. 653). It is left up to readers – female and male – to complete the deconstruction of this most 'natural' of oppositions by acting out the differently gendered roles the text offers. The acute reader will not only be aware of the different kinds of roles being offered but will act out the roles with a large measure of self-consciousness (the word 'act' seems apposite here). The activity of reading, according to this interpretation, is seen to be improvisatory and experimental. (Readers can easily test this claim by noting their reactions to those passages where the narrator interposes the words 'feminine' or 'womanly': see, for instance, pages 31, 39, 86, 100, 276, 407, 604 and 608.)

That *Daniel Deronda* is a novel replete with paradox and self-contradiction, then, should be apparent on even a first reading. In order to make sense of specific 'obvious' instances of self-contradiction (for example, where Gwendolen is described as engaging in an 'unconscious kind of acting', p. 316) the reader has perhaps only to make use of the usual critical skills and tools. Of greater interest to the deconstructive reader are those moments in the text whose problematical nature is not immediately striking and which, therefore, present a special kind of challenge. Such moments often take the form of asides, parentheses, or illustrative analogies. The challenge, which tends to arise retrospectively (perhaps on a subsequent reading of particular passages), is essentially interpretational in nature. More often than not, it takes the form of the question: 'How should I read this?' A not overly difficult example is to be found in Chapter 33:

> In most other trades you find generous men who are anxious to sell you their wares for your own welfare; but even a Jew will not urge Simson's Euclid on you with an affectionate assurance that you will have pleasure in reading it, and that he wishes he had twenty more of the article, so much is it in request. (p. 385)

This apparently innocent, humorous generalization about human behaviour (with a suggestive aside on 'pleasure in reading') forms part of a series of reflections offered by the narrator to the reader in the episode in which Deronda, searching for relatives of Mirah, enters a second-hand bookshop and catches his first glimpse (did he but know it) of Mirah's brother, Mordecai (otherwise known as Ezra) Cohen. The tricky phrase takes the form of a caveat or qualification: 'even a Jew'. How is this to be read? As a (pre-Freudian) slip by the otherwise circumspect author? As a (rhetorical) concession to many of the novel's contemporary readers, given their latent (or not so latent) anti-Semitism? Neither possibility seems very likely, given the way in which the novel as a whole is geared to produce a greater degree of understanding of, and sympathy for, the Jewish people. The phrase could be read ironically, of course, but in that case what is the reader to make of the narrator's glowing reference earlier in the same paragraph to 'that wonderful bit of autobiography, the life of the Polish Jew, Salomon Maimon' – a reference which throws the casual, implied racism of 'even a Jew' into yet starker relief? Perhaps some clue is afforded by a much earlier passage, which reads: 'Deronda could not escape (who can?) knowing ugly stories of Jewish characteristics and occupations . . .' (p. 206). The rhetorical question in parenthesis constitutes an appeal to the reader's experience and knowledge similar in kind, though diametrically opposed in substance, to that framed in the words 'even a Jew'. The latter phrase draws on, but does not deny the truth of, 'ugly stories of Jewish characteristics and occupations'; the question, 'who can [escape knowing such ugly stories]?', on the other hand, while excusing Deronda's (and the reader's) familiarity with such 'stories', implies a condemnation of the stories themselves on three counts: (i) they are merely 'stories' (and – therefore! – false); (ii) they are 'ugly'; and (iii) it is worth trying to 'escape' from them. The appeal to the reader in both cases is an appeal to authority – a rhetorical device, it would seem, designed to strengthen the reader's (un?)conscious sense of the authority of the narrative voice itself.

This is a strategy followed throughout the novel: on relatively few occasions does the narrator use the give-away, first-person pronoun 'I'. Commonly, the narrator uses passive constructions (as in 'One is led to fear . . .', later in the paragraph on Salomon Maimon, p. 385), or invokes the reader's agreement more directly (as in 'In most other trades you find . . .', quoted above). Instances of special pleading ('Surely a young creature is pitiable . . .', p. 273) are noticeably less common in this novel than in its immediate predecessor, *Middlemarch* (1871–2), which abounds in exclamations of the 'Poor Dorothea!', 'Poor Casaubon!' variety (in the later novel, the phrase 'Poor Gwendolen!' occurs a few times, but 'Poor Grandcourt!' is nowhere to be found).

In *Daniel Deronda*, then, the reader is appealed to on numerous occasions; in some instances she/he is flattered for (apparently) ulterior motives. But the deconstructive reader will be aware of these attempts, some more subtle than others, at ideological manœuvring – for that is what they are. The question, 'How should I read this?' can then be translated as 'on what basis am I being appealed to here?' or 'upon what premises is the implied argument constructed?'. Occasionally the attempt to manipulate will self-deconstruct almost before it has got under way: signs of linguistic strain and slippage are usually in evidence in such instances. Thus, just before his 'chance meeting' with Mordecai in Chapter 40, Deronda muses:

> Not that there is any likelihood of a peculiar tie between me and this poor fellow . . . But I wonder whether there is much of that momentous mutual missing between people who interchange blank looks . . . (p. 492)

The awkwardness of the phraseology in this instance, with the excessive degree of alliteration – Deronda is supposed to be *thinking* these words – offers one example among many of the novel's realist enterprise being deconstructed by its idealistic agenda. The language here shows the text 'striving' too hard, to use one of Deronda's favourite words (a word which Grandcourt, notably, does *not* tend to use – though he manages 'stiving', p. 675).

More felicitous as an aside is Mab's comment on Deronda:

> 'No woman ought to want him to marry her,' said Mab, with indignation. '*I* never should. Fancy finding out that he had a tailor's bill, and used boot-hooks, like Hans. Who ever thought of his marrying?'
> (p. 656)

The reference to 'boot-hooks' here might seem trivial – one of those moments where the text demonstrates, for all its metaphysical concerns, its realism. Deronda does, after all, live in a world where such items as boot-hooks exist. But, equally, it implies the novel's copious silences on matters personal, supporting an idealism whereby heroes should not (really!) be discovered in the act of putting their boots on. More references to Deronda's 'boot-hooks', as it were, would perhaps have made for a still more realist novel (though not approaching the naturalism of Zola, much less the modernism of Joyce).

That the reading process is one which involves the filling of gaps and blanks (inevitably there in any narrative) has been stressed often enough earlier in this study: reading this novel is no exception. When Gwendolen and Grandcourt first meet, we are given their dialogue in some detail, with all the pauses indicated (rather as in a play by Beckett or Pinter); we are told how Gwendolen fills them, but the reader is left to work out what Grandcourt, for his part, may be thinking or feeling during them (pp. 112–14). Much later, when they are together on Grandcourt's yacht, the conversation is rather different:

> 'Oh dear, no!' said Gwendolen, letting out her scorn in a flute-like tone. 'I never expect you to give way.'
> 'Why should I?' said Grandcourt, with his inward voice, looking at her, and then choosing an orange – for they were at table. (p. 675)

The reader is here confined to speculating on the degree of

Grandcourt's egoism: it would appear to stop short of solipsism, but not by much; the act of choosing an orange at that precise point (from a bowl of assorted fruit or – worse – from a bowl containing *only* oranges?) is a detail peculiarly suggestive in its force.

More challenging than filling such gaps are the decisions readers have to make about the different kinds of silences in the novel. Every reader will agree that there is no clear, unambivalent, explicit statement as to whether or not Deronda was circumcised – indeed, the word 'circumcision' (unlike the word 'boot-hooks') is never used; but as mentioned earlier, critics continue to disagree over whether the novel contains oblique, implicit references to the subject. Silences are ambiguous, and demand interpretation; gaps come in various shapes and sizes, and readers fill them accordingly.

Consider the broad issue of sexuality in this novel. Barbara Hardy asserts quite emphatically that one of the novel's 'profound and original' features, compared with many other Victorian novels, is that it does deal with the sexual aspects of human relationships.[19] But, in so far as it does this, it does so, for reasons which hardly need explaining, largely by implication. 'By implication' is another way of stressing how much work the reader has to do. The reader knows about Grandcourt's sexual relationship with Lydia Glasher, and about the children she has had by him. But what of Deronda's sexual feelings towards Gwendolen – or Gwendolen's towards Deronda? And what does the reader make of the relationship between Gwendolen and Grandcourt, in sexual terms? A close reading of the language used affords a number of hints: behind various statements there is considerable sexual excitement. We are told that there were 'many less passionate men' than Deronda, and that he felt 'the fascination of [Gwendolen's] womanhood. He was very open to that sort of charm . . .'. Later in the same paragraph, the narrator generalizes about how 'one man differs from another', according to the 'variety of needs, spiritual or other' (p. 324). The phrase 'or other', coming where it does – Deronda is thinking of the relative attractions of Mirah and Gwendolen – is telling. It could be interpreted, in retrospect, as foreshadowing the 'choice' Deronda eventually has to make between an essentially spiritual love (Mirah) and an essentially sexual attraction (Gwendolen). His choice of the spiritual over and above the sexual, in as much as it appears to be authoritatively underwritten by the novel's ideology, would seem to point to a very definite hierarchy, where spiritual commitment is clearly privileged above sexual inclination.

But is the opposition as stark as this, on a considered reading? It should be re-emphasized here that in this text – as in other Eliot texts – any 'either/or' opposition is likely to self-deconstruct once it is examined with due care and attention. (And, note, this is not because of what the deconstructive reader expects to see happen – a point to which we shall return later.) Nothing, in Eliot's novels, is completely anything. Deronda finds Mirah spiritually *and* sexually attractive, and his interest in Gwendolen's spiritual and moral welfare is *more* than a mere transmutation or projection of his sexual desires. Perhaps the clearest instance of the spiritual/sexual hierarchy collapsing is to be found in Chapter 50; Deronda is musing on what the future may hold in store for him (just before his meeting with his mother), hoping

> that the very best of human possibilities might befall him – the blend-ing of a complete personal love in one current with a larger duty . . .
> (p. 623)

In this passage of free indirect style, it is not clear whether the words given are the narrator's or Deronda's, but either way they are most emphatically stamped with authority. In hierarchical terms the ideal – the *very* best possibility – is where duty and desire coincide. In reality such 'coincidences' may be considered rare. It is only in the pages of a romantic novel, and *Jane Eyre* is the classic example, that both the hero and the heroine are, as it were, allowed to have their cake and eat it.

Daniel Deronda is a realist novel, but with romance (and Romantic) features: Eliot, to the disgruntlement of many critics, is driven to contrive all manner of coincidences to bring about *her* desired end, which sees the novel's central male character completely fulfilled – spiritually, morally, socially and sexually. Furthermore, the sexual dimension, far from being the icing on the Deronda's (wedding) 'cake', is central. Reading the above quotation, it is observable that what is claimed as 'best' is 'the blending . . . in one current' of 'a complete personal love'. The physicality of the metaphor, apart from its consonance with patterns of imagery running all the way through the novel, is much stronger in the impression it makes on the reader than the rather limp 'a larger duty'. And in the phrase, 'a complete personal love', every word counts: this is what Deronda wants, and this is (interestingly) what he is rewarded with at the end of the novel.

The word 'personal' needs glossing here, and an attentive reader will have noticed other significant occurrences of the word, in its adverbial form, which may be taken as evidence to reinforce the argument being made about the deconstruction of the opposition spiritual/sexual – but this time in connection with the relationship between Gwendolen and Grandcourt. Consider the following two examples. In the first, Mr Gascoigne is quizzing Gwendolen in an attempt to establish why she has been discouraging Grandcourt's advances:

> 'I suppose I hesitate without grounds.' Gwendolen spoke rather poutingly, and her uncle grew suspicious.
> 'Is he disagreeable to you personally?'
> 'No.' (p. 142)

At which point the Rector asks whether she has heard anything which has affected her estimation of Grandcourt (to which the answer is also 'no'). In the second example, the reader is given an insight into Grandcourt's thinking about Gwendolen, after her acceptance of his proposal of marriage:

> She had been brought to accept him in spite of everything – brought to kneel down like a horse under training for the arena . . . On the whole, Grandcourt got more pleasure out of this notion than he could have done out of winning a girl of whom he was sure that she had a strong inclination for him personally. (p. 320)

The meaning of the word 'person' relevant to the above use of 'personally' is given by the *OED* as the

> living body of a human being; either (*a*) the actual body as distinct from clothing, etc., or from the mind or soul, or (*b*) the body with its clothing and adornment as presented to the sight of others; bodily frame or figure.

In this sense, we read of Gascoigne himself that 'One of his advantages was a fine person' (p. 30 – this very quotation is given in the above entry in the *OED* to illustrate that precise definition). Compare the description of Laura Fairlie in Wilkie Collins's novel of sensation, *The Woman in White* (1859–60): 'She is a sweet, lovable girl, as amiable and attentive to everyone about her as her excellent mother used to be – though, personally speaking, she takes after her father.'[20] Gwendolen, to begin with, is quite taken with Grandcourt's personality, behaviour and general demeanour; and she considers him a 'splendid specimen' (p. 137); by contrast she has a 'physical antipath[y]' towards Lush (p. 122). Her initial doubts about marrying Grandcourt spring from a wish to preserve her independence, and a corresponding distaste for the state of marriage – thoughts of which she does not apprise her uncle in the above interview. Hence his puzzlement: here is a man of wealth and rank, whom Gwendolen finds 'personally' attractive: why will she not undertake to accept him? Later, as a consequence of her meeting with Lydia Glasher, Gwendolen does develop a physical disgust for Grandcourt alongside her moral distaste: it is this sense of physical repulsion that Grandcourt detects, and which the sexual sadist in him relishes. The incident where Grandcourt kisses Gwendolen under her ear is instructive:

> . . . Gwendolen, taken by surprise, had started up with a marked agitation which made him rise too and say, 'I beg your pardon – did I annoy you?' 'Oh, it was nothing,' said Gwendolen, rather afraid of herself, 'only I cannot bear – to be kissed under my ear.' She sat down again with a little playful laugh, but all the while she felt her heart beating with a vague fear . . . (p. 327)

The pause (signalled by a dash) after 'I cannot bear' is a telling silence: how often has Gwendolen been kissed under the ear in the past that she can tender such an excuse with any degree of conviction? Grandcourt finds her behaviour 'particularly fascinating' (p. 327) on this occasion. It is interesting to note that when writing *Daniel Deronda* Eliot wrote to Frederic Harrison, positivist and professor of jurisprudence, for legal advice about its plot: she was toying with the idea of giving Gwendolen a son by Grandcourt.[21] The notion was rejected, and nowhere is it made plain to what extent the Gwendolen/Grandcourt marriage was sexually active. The silence, here, is unsurprising. Perhaps the closest the novel comes to giving any indication about the topic is in Chapter 54, when the reader is told that Gwendolen

> was reduced to dread lest she should become a mother. It was not the image of a new sweetly-budding life that came as a vision of deliver-

ance from the monotony of distaste: it was an image of another sort. (pp. 672–3)

Gwendolen's sense of guilt and self-disgust may not spring solely from her notion of the wrong she has done Lydia Glasher: the above lines suggest that there may be an important sexual dimension to her feelings about both herself and her husband. In the novel as a whole, the reader might be inclined to think, sexual issues underwrite the spiritual and moral preoccupations around which the text appears to be principally constructed.

So much for the novel's silences and one particular 'violent hierarchy'. Numerous other oppositions will be found throughout the text: indeed, a close, analytical reading should not neglect to explore such oppositions, for they make up the very stuff of the novel. Here, for example, is Gwendolen thinking of Grandcourt as a possible husband:

> True, he was not to have the slightest power over her (for Gwendolen had not considered that the desire to conquer is itself a sort of subjection) . . . (p. 106)

And here is Grandcourt thinking about his mistress:

> It was too irritating that his indulgence of Lydia had given her a sort of mastery over him in spite of her dependent condition. (p. 349)

Moments like these are reasonably describable as 'deconstructive' in the sense that they clearly challenge conventional ways of thinking. Grandcourt's mistress is temporarily his master; and power is shown to be a kind of subjection. Such passages anticipate readerly attempts at deconstruction. But the reader will often have to work harder than this. Take Deronda's impression of Gwendolen some time after her marriage: 'the glimpses he had of Gwendolen's manner deepened the impression that it had something newly artificial' (p. 410). Since Deronda's view is that this change is a change for the worse, the implication is that what is 'natural' is to be preferred to anything 'artificial'. The nature/artifice hierarchy is no more common in this text, no doubt, than in many others: in Jane Austen's *Emma*, for example, the reader is treated to a witty conversation between Mr Knightley and Mrs Elton on the subject of what *really* constitutes 'the natural'.[22] But in *Daniel Deronda* the hierarchy nature/artifice can be read as deconstructing. Compare Deronda's impression of Gwendolen in the above passage with the account of Deronda's behaviour on being surprised with Gwendolen by her husband rather later in the novel:

> It was not a moment in which [Gwendolen] could feign anything . . . What she felt besides was a dull despairing sense that her interview with Deronda was at an end: a curtain had fallen. But he, naturally, was urged into self-possession and effort by susceptibility to what might follow for her from being seen by her husband in this betrayal of agitation; and feeling that any pretence of ease in prolonging his visit would only exaggerate Grandcourt's possible conjectures of duplicity, he merely said -
> 'I will not stay longer now. Good-bye.' (pp. 610–11)

Deronda's behaviour in this instance is *not* 'naturally' motivated, whatever his feelings for Gwendolen. He acts a part (as Gwendolen is unable to) with unimpeachable good manners, the very model of consummate artifice and socialized decorum. Deronda does not 'feel' it would be unwise to pretend; he *knows* it would, as an intelligent man of the world.[23] Deronda's 'natural' impulse – had it been unfettered by his adroit sense of what passes for proper behaviour in society – would presumably have led him to act rather differently. Deronda, in fact, behaves in this instance much as Gwendolen was behaving in the earlier instance: each behaves with 'artifice' – though the artifice in the later example is passed off by the narrator as 'natural'. Clearly the privileging of the natural over the artificial (over the constructed) will not do – if only because as a way of commenting on human behaviour it is crude in the extreme, as a deconstructive reading of passages such as this brings out.

To read *Daniel Deronda* deconstructively, then, is to read with a sharp sense of how at every turn the novel marginalizes, represses, omits, disguises and assumes, in ways which are open to question. Analysis will often be of specific textual cruxes – in particular of those instances where the linguistic texture seems to show signs of cracking under pressure. Thus, some of the novel's chapter epigraphs (especially those unattributed by Eliot) will be found to offer in a condensed form metaphors of wider applicability, to which readers would do well to direct their attention. (A comparative analysis of the epigraphs to Chapters 22 and 27 might be found to be especially interesting.)

But while a deconstructive reading – like any other good reading – is always more than the sum of the readings of the various parts of the novel, it would be self-contradictory and absurd to attempt to offer here anything like an exhaustive reading of the 'whole' of such a complex novel (or of any novel, for that matter). None the less, a few points are worth making to supplement and round off our discussion. Most commentators on the novel seem to agree that what is presented throughout the text is a philosophical, moral and social argument. The argument runs (roughly) as follows. In so far as individuals are free to live their lives as they choose – and this is, as the novel recognizes, a big 'if', given the various determinants of human behaviour – they will best find the happiness they seek by eschewing the state of egoism or 'moral stupidity' (pp. 175, 509, 596), in which individuals 'do as they like' (pp. 137, 445), and by opting instead for a life which recognizes the claims of other people – even if others regard such an attitude as 'moral eccentricity' (p. 178). Ideally, individuals find fulfilment through altruistically dedicating themselves to a larger cause (p. 803) and/or taking up the duties and responsibilities which attach to specific roles within society. If this inevitably over-simple summary makes the novel sound as if it is peddling a philosophy akin to John Stuart Mill's version of Utilitarianism (with its concept of enlightened self-interest), together with a dash of Arnoldian socio-cultural analysis, it should be emphasized that the model of society being held up for approval is predominantly Romantic and organicist. Here is Gwendolen's culminating, key recognition, as Deronda explains where his destiny lies:

> That was the sort of crisis which was at this moment beginning in Gwendolen's small life: she was for the first time feeling the pressure of a vast mysterious movement, for the first time being dislodged from her supremacy in her own world, and getting a sense that her horizon was but a dipping onward of an existence with which her own was revolving. (p. 804)

Gwendolen's world-view is, in other words, deconstructing in front of her. To read *Daniel Deronda* deconstructively involves, first and foremost, an abandonment of any sense of the 'wholeness' of the novel, and an analysis of the relationships of its constituent parts. In the paragraph just quoted, the novel's idealistic, visionary aspect is most in evidence: it would be worth contrasting that with the aspect of the

novel which presents a thoroughly damning critique of the society of
Eliot's own day. What is the relationship between these two aspects?
And to what extent is the novel's idealistic superstructure adequately
sustained by its (realist?) substructure? What are the values which
seem to be taken for granted in this novel? (What is the force of 'small'
and 'vast' in the above quotation?) How far *is* it tenable to view the
novel as self-deconstructing? To return to Hillis Miller's claim,
referred to at the beginning of this chapter: this novel certainly explicitly anticipates the terminology of today's deconstructive readers: *vide*
the reference to 'the play of various, nay, contrary tendencies' (p. 42),
and Gwendolen's thought of the writing of her letter to Grandcourt
being 'endlessly deferred' (p. 294) – and perhaps such features *are*
indications of the extent to which *Daniel Deronda* contains 'warring
forces of signification', and so is critically different from itself?

This brings us back – appropriately enough – to the beginning of
this chapter. The chapter has explored the relationship between
reading and deconstruction in relation to *Daniel Deronda*, largely by
attempting to focus on what is involved in reading Eliot's novel
deconstructively. Deconstruction is not, of course, the same as *re*construction. As Christopher Norris writes:

> The most rigorous reading . . . is one that holds itself provisionally
> open to further deconstruction of its own operative concepts.[24]

All readings are, to varying extents, misreadings, and the provisionality of the readings offered in this chapter should be taken 'as read' and
'as misread'. To read deconstructively is to read with a particular
(though not peculiar) critical stringency. Yet perhaps we should not
lose sight here of the fact that this is but one mode of reading among
the infinite variety of possible ways of reading (and misreading) which
exist in theory and in practice. And as a result of the recent, painstak-
ing work of scholars such as Alberto Manguel, our sense of the realities of the activity of reading throughout history is sharper and fuller
than previously.[25]

It should seem neither perverse nor obvious to claim that reading
deconstructively need be no less pleasurable and fulfilling than in
engaging in other kinds of reading. But if taking pleasure in acts of
reading should not be the only yardstick against which the value of
such acts is to be measured, its absence (apparent or real) is surely
revealing. Critics as diverse as Robert Alter, Roland Barthes, John

Carey, Philip Davis, Hermione Lee, David Lodge, Hillis Miller and Tony Tanner all clearly share at least one characteristic: readerly delight in their interpretations of the novels about which they so patently care. One might proceed further and argue that reading, for such deft practitioners of the science-in-art that is literary criticism, offers its own rewards, and requires no other justification.[26] The proto-deconstructor and morally circumspect author of *Daniel Deronda*, at least, would – no doubt – have approved.

6 Reading as Revelation: A Portrait of the Artist as a Young Man

According to Derek Attridge in his illuminating discussion, 'Reading Joyce', '[f]ar more people read Joyce than are aware of it'. In advancing this claim, Attridge is not being perverse: he is simply acknowledging the scale of Joyce's impact on so many aspects of twentieth-century culture. Given 'the ubiquity of [Joyce's] influence', Attridge goes on to argue, '[t]here is a sense, therefore, in which we can *never* read Joyce "for the first time"'. Attridge continues:

> If we can never read Joyce's works for the first time (though our pleasure may be enhanced if we always do our best to approach them with open minds), we can also never come to the end of our reading of them.

This is because 'Joyce's work in particular seems to have a built-in principle of openness to further investigation, further interpretation, further enjoyment'. Attridge 'emphasize[s] the pleasures of reading Joyce, because . . . an account that loses sight of this fundamental point is in danger of forgetting why we read, or write about, Joyce at all'.[1] Attridge's point about the openness of Joyce's writings 'in particular' to readerly pleasure and interpretation is one which we have been concerned to make more generally throughout this study, in relation to each of the novels explored. However, open texts demand open readers: readers who approach novels with their minds' eyes 'wide shut' will not experience fully the pleasures of interpretation. For such readers, reading becomes more a matter of restriction rather than of revelation.

But Attridge's phrase 'in particular' could be interpreted as meaning not simply 'in this particular case' but 'unlike in other cases'.

In other words, the claim would be that Joyce's writings are *more* open than those of other writers – that they are, in some sense or senses, uniquely open. (Presumably, the point does not advert merely to the issue of closure, since it is a critical commonplace that the endings of modernist novels tend, on the whole, to be more open than those of their nineteenth-century realist forerunners.) How 'open' a novel *A Portrait of the Artist as a Young Man* really is, and the consequences of this for the reading process in practice will be discussed in the pages that follow.

Compare this 'particular' novel first, though, with the novels thus far considered. The similarities of *A Portrait* with Sterne's *Tristram Shandy* are plain enough, and numerous critics have commented upon them. There is a self-consciousness about both novels, as John Paul Riquelme notes, comparing 'Joyce's autobiographical fiction' with Sterne's 'fictional autobiography'.[2] Both novels, in their different ways, explore quite brilliantly the individual human being's 'streams of consciousness'. Both novels in their time were ground-breaking, technically innovative, experimental, and readers and reviewers found them puzzling and difficult; but whereas much of Sterne's experimentation is plainly playful (which is not to deny the philosophical profundity of *Tristram Shandy*), Joyce's modernist project has a seriousness befitting its titular hero, Stephen Dedalus. Yet this seriousness is double-edged: like *Pride and Prejudice*, *A Portrait* is a highly ironic text, forcing the reader to make conscious interpretative choices throughout. Stephen Dedalus, like Elizabeth Bennet, is portrayed both sympathetically and ironically, but while in Austen's novel it is almost always quite clear what we are supposed to be thinking of her heroine, Joyce's presentation of his 'hero' is far more complex and ambiguous, so that the reader is left wondering on many occasions whether this 'young man' is to be taken wholly seriously or not. Joyce's narrator (and ultimately Joyce himself as the artistic creator of the novel), in Stephen's 'own' words, 'impersonalises itself, so to speak'. Then we read a famous sentence:

> The artist, like the God of the creation, remains within or behind or beyond or above his handiwork, invisible, refined out of existence, indifferent, paring his fingernails. (p. 233)

Hardly words which could be applied to Austen or her narrator. Indeed, it is only at the end of *A Portrait*, when Stephen briefly becomes his own narrator, as we are given extracts from his journal, that the narrative – in terms of its form – is faintly reminiscent of a type of nineteenth-century romantic-realist fiction, the first-person *Bildungsroman*. Yet somehow *A Portrait* seems much further removed in time from *Great Expectations* than the half-century which separates their publication dates. The wonderful account of Stephen's first Christmas dinner undoubtedly echoes Dickens's typically flamboyant description of Pip's festive ordeal of passage. However, the developing consciousness under inspection in the later novel is that of an artist in embryo, and the emphases fall accordingly: this is not only a *Bildungsroman*, we have to remind ourselves, but also a *Künstlerroman* (a novel with an artist for its protagonist). Actually, in some respects Stephen's discovery of his artistic vocation finds a closer analogue in Daniel Deronda's uncovering of his religio-political destiny in Eliot's novel. Both protagonists have to contend with familial, racial, cultural and social forces which delimit the choices available to them. Deronda espouses a cause; Stephen rejects all causes other than that of his artistic calling: both novels radically call into question the role of religion, the politics of statehood, and the nature of artistic vocation. Indeed, as we shall see, the self-deconstructive tendencies of *Daniel Deronda* are more than replicated in the warring schematic complexities of *A Portrait*.

Some of the above points could be summarized baldly by stating an obvious distinction: *A Portrait of the Artist as a Young Man* (1916) is a *modernist* novel. Modernist novels differ from realist (or semi-realist) novels not merely in degree but in kind. Mark Schorer puts the point well:

> *A Portrait of the Artist as a Young Man*, like *Tono Bungay* and *Sons and Lovers*, is autobiographical, but unlike these it analyses its material rigorously, and it defines the value and the quality of its experience not by appended comment or moral epithet, but by the texture of the style.[3]

The *locus classicus* where the implications of the modernist emphasis upon interiority (or 'stream of consciousness' in William James's phrase) for fictional technique are explicitly stated is, of course, Virginia Woolf's essay, 'Modern Fiction' of 1919 (reprinted in *The Common Reader*, 1925). The crucial passage reads thus:

Examine for a moment an ordinary mind on an ordinary day. The mind receives a myriad impressions – trivial, fantastic, evanescent, or engraved with the sharpness of steel. From all sides they come, an incessant shower of innumerable atoms; and as they fall, as they shape themselves into the life of Monday or Tuesday, the accent falls differently from of old; the moment of importance came not here but there; so that, if a writer were a free man and not a slave, if he could write what he chose, not what he must, if he could base his work upon his own feeling and not upon convention, there would be no plot, no comedy, no tragedy, no love interest or catastrophe in the accepted style . . . Life is not a series of gig lamps symmetrically arranged; life is a luminous halo, a semi-transparent envelope surrounding us from the beginning of consciousness to the end. Is it not the task of the novelist to convey this varying, this unknown and uncircumscribed spirit, whatever aberration or complexity it may display, with as little mixture of the alien and external as possible? We are not pleading merely for courage and sincerity; we are suggesting that the proper stuff of fiction is a little other than custom would have us believe it.[4]

In retrospect, this seems a peculiarly astute analysis of the situation of the novel at that time. When it was first published, the essay's iconoclasm must have seemed breathtaking: with complete self-assurance and audacious polemical verve, Woolf dismisses the dominant tradition of the English novel, in favour of something new, different, experimental. Later in the same essay Woolf specifically singles out Joyce as writing the kind of fiction she so evidently prefers. The modernist novel is, in these terms, 'the novel of fine consciousness', aiming at 'a higher realism' than realism proper by being 'truer to the feel of life'.[5]

Indeed, some of the early reviewers of *A Portrait* thought the novel *too* realistic.[6] Thus J. C. Squire, reviewing the novel for the *New Statesman*, commented that 'one is left with the impression that almost all the way one has been listening to sheer undecorated, unintensified truth', while John Macy succinctly observed of *A Portrait* in the *Dial*, that 'Life is so'. Of the 27 reactions to the novel collected in *James Joyce: The Critical Heritage* (Volume I: 1902–27), no fewer than 17 use words and phrases such as the following: 'complete realism', 'genuine realist', 'quintessential and unfailing reality', 'perfect fidelity', 'absolutely true to life', 'veracity', 'rich concreteness', 'convincing' and 'pitiless accuracy'. Some refer to Joyce's 'extraordinary naturalism', while others write of his 'naturalness', or describe the novelist's method in terms of its 'impressionism'. (Joyce's 'symbolism' is largely ignored.) A few find Joyce's explicitness concerning bodily functions repulsive, complaining that his novel reeks of 'drains', 'sewers', and 'the dunghill'. The novelist with whom he is most frequently compared is Sterne.[7]

The responses of these early readers (and these are *real* readers) are themselves revealing about the practice of interpreting *A Portrait*. A number of points suggest themselves. First, they remind us of the inescapably comparative, contrastive and evaluative nature of the critical act: in order to make sense of *A Portrait* the reader has to have other appropriate textual reference points. As a novel it can only be properly understood in relation to other novels (especially those which have gone before) and in relation to other modernist literary texts. In other words, interpretation is always intertextual – a point to which we shall have occasion to return in the course of our discussion of *Possession* in Chapter 8. All novels exist within particular traditions of novel-writing and novel-reading, which traditions they at once constitute and modify. Secondly, taken as a whole these contemporary reviews offer powerful evidence in support of two later critical concepts: Jauss's notion of the 'horizon of expectations', and Fish's theory of 'interpretive communities'. For although contemporary interpretations of *A Portrait* differ considerably in matters of detail, they tend to share the same broad assumptions about Joyce's novel *as a novel* – assumptions which reflect a common understanding of the conventions of writing novels in the late nineteenth and early twentieth centuries. Even the cries of moral outrage reveal something about an emerging aesthetic perception: the tried-and-tested realist mode, carried to one extreme, appears to lead to the brand of modernism so graphically illustrated by the author of *A Portrait*. Such a perception is necessarily limited, of its time. Six years later, with the publication of *Ulysses* (1922), the earlier novel seemed neither so extreme in terms of its subject-matter nor so radical an experiment in terms of its method and style. Horizons change, paradigms shift, and communities adapt their interpretations accordingly.

The realist/modernist split reveals something else about ways of reading in more general terms. To read critically is to attempt to understand, to try to make sense of, to interpret a literary text. But the very act of thinking about a text in relation to other texts seems to involve the kind of analysis which leads, ineluctably, towards the creation of a generic or modal taxonomy. The simplest way of distinguishing one text from another is to classify each on either side of a binary divide. Yet this 'either/or' way of thinking can lead to serious misconceptions, as we saw in the previous chapter. To think in dualistic, polar opposite terms is certainly convenient, and the neatness and clarity of such a binary logic are perhaps tempting – all the more so when faced with a complex mass of different, though related, materials. However, as we saw in the case of *Daniel Deronda*, the product of George Eliot's 'both/and' imagination, it can be naïve to classify a novel as simply and purely 'realist'. Eliot's final novel contains elements which are distinctly 'non-realist', and therefore it makes more sense to conceive of *Daniel Deronda* in terms of its position somewhere along a continuum between romance and realism. Or, to look at the novel from another angle, somewhere on a spectrum between classic realism and high modernism. This is not to fudge a critical issue, but to give the complexity of a literary text its due.[8]

A similar point might be made in discussing the temporal process of reading novels such as *Daniel Deronda* and *A Portrait*. To read, to interpret, is – in practice – to take part in a cyclical (if not circular) process. And there are different kinds of 'hermeneutic circles', a point we touched on in Chapter 4. There is the part/whole circle: we can only properly understand one part of a novel if we have some sense of the whole novel, and yet our sense of the whole novel depends upon our understanding of its constituent parts. There is the past/present circle: our present sense of the past is past-dependent, yet we can only make sense of the past from our position in a (disappearing) present. And there is the subject/object circle: but in the case of the reader and the text which is the subject and which is the object – in practice, not just in theory? As we saw in Chapter 1, it is not enough to pay lip-service to the notion that the text and the reader are mutually reinforcing in the production of meaning. Which is which? (We shall return to this apparent 'Catch-22' when we consider the title of Joyce's novel.)

Readings of *A Portrait* which are built around basic dichotomies or oppositions may appear to solve some problems but will often be found to throw up further problems. One attractive feature of a deconstructive reading of a novel, as we observed in the previous chapter, is that because it refuses to over-simplify – and thus falsify – by automatically privileging a thesis over its antithesis, it can result in a reading (a new synthesis) which does justice to a novel by taking account of apparently (or really) discordant elements: in other words, it *re*solves problems by *dis*solving them. It replaces rigid readings by flexible readings. Consider those readings of *A Portrait* which insist upon the rightness of a particular attitude towards the novel's protagonist, Stephen Dedalus. Does the novel encourage the reader to sympathize with Stephen (if not to identify or empathize with him)? Or does the novel present Stephen in an ironic light, fostering in the reader a more detached attitude? Hugh Kenner regards Stephen ironically, while William Empson takes issue with Kenner, considering Stephen to be an essentially sympathetic figure. Does it have to be *either* sympathy *or* irony? Empson *versus* Kenner? Or is there room for both Empson's and Kenner's readings?[9] Could it be that the distance between Stephen and the reader varies – here close, there far apart? Or, to switch from a spatial to a temporal metaphor, is it possible that at times we sympathize with Stephen while at other times we regard him with indifference (or even distaste)? Do we perhaps sometimes find ourselves in the position of Tertius Lydgate in George Eliot's *Middlemarch* (1871–2) as he looks at Edward Casaubon, with 'contempt' for the latter's 'futile scholarship' but also feeling 'a little amusement mingling with his pity' for him?[10] Or is it the case that to generalize about readers' responses and reactions in this way is to underplay the practical significance of the fact that individual readings do, inevitably, differ? Just how much are we taking for granted, here and now, about what it is to 'read' *A Portrait*?

One way of beginning to answer this question is to adopt a similar procedure to that in Chapter 5, when we paused over the title-page of *Daniel Deronda*. For what aspect of a novel is less arbitrary or more important than its title? A title is more than a bill of fare, and much more than an identificatory label. It is the novelist's preferred and most succinct indication of what the novel *is*, and of what he or she is *doing* in, with, and through it. So what happens when we read – closely, thoughtfully – the title of Joyce's novel? The full title is: *A Portrait of the Artist as a Young Man*. A title which, through the initial indefinite article, proclaims a certain indeterminacy: not *The* Portrait – as in Henry James's novel, *The Portrait of a Lady* (1881)[11] – but *A* Portrait, suggesting that other, different portraits might have been painted – and that this is but one portrait. The note struck is relativist, sceptical, ironic, as if announcing an unauthorized (albeit authored) autobiography.[12] But it is A Portrait *of the Artist* which we are to be given. The analogy is with painters' self-portraits. The metaphor suggests a view of art consonant with the concept *ut pictura poesis* (a poem is like a picture); yet the Paterian notion that '[a]ll art constantly aspires towards the condition of music' is absent here, despite the young Joyce's dabblings in a Paterian-Wildean aestheticism.[13] The title is both reflective and reflexive: Johnson's Shakespearean mirror is not only held up to nature but to art, and the art in question is not so much 'natural', therefore, as peculiarly, self-consciously 'artificial' – it is the art 'of' the artist (the portrait not only *depicts* him, it is *by* him).[14] The title may be said to self-deconstruct in the same way that any sentence containing the (unique) pronoun 'I' self-deconstructs because of the splitting of the subject between subject and object, nominative and accusative. Joyce announces, in effect, both his presence and his self-(re)presentation. The 'I' is both 'I' and 'me' (or 'myself'): it (he) is painting and being painted. This presents the reader with an interpretative crux: where is the emphasis here? On the portrait (the object)? Or on the artist (the subject)? Is it even possible to distinguish between the two? Each includes, or is defined by, the other: the subject is represented in the object; the object is the project of the subject. The title continues: *as a Young Man*. This would appear to privilege subject over object, artist over portrait, as if Joyce is requiring his readers to make due allowance for the fact that it is a version of his younger self which he is (re)presenting. Yet it is difficult to avoid the impression that Joyce is here being ironic about being ironic. After all, much of *A Portrait* does not describe the artist 'as a young man', but as a boy and (later) as an adolescent. Moreover, the last four words of the title open up other interpretative possibilities. Is the stress on the artist's (developing) personality as a human being? Or on the human being's (developing) artistry? Can the human subject and the creative artist be separated out in this way any more easily than 'I' and 'me'? Is Joyce implying, after Wordsworth, and with Freud, a deterministic view of human and artistic development – that, in George Eliot's words, 'what we have been makes us what we are'?[15] In which case, is the cause or the effect the worthier of our attention? Why 'as a young *man*'? Is the artist's gender of special significance? How representative is this portrait of '*the* artist'? The word 'the' has a denotative particularity (specifically, Stephen Dedalus – or, more tendentiously, James Joyce) but also possesses a connotative generality (the universal artist). Really, reading this title, one wonders where to stop.

Or whether to stop. The front cover of the Penguin Twentieth-Century Classics edition of 1992 reproduces a photographic portrait

of Joyce as a young man of twenty-two, and it shows him staring –
resolutely, appraisingly, perhaps ironically – at the camera. The relevant caption to the same photograph in Ellmann's biography gives
the older Joyce's interpretation of his younger self's teasing facial
expression: 'I was wondering would he [C. P. Curran, the photogra-
pher] lend me five shillings.'[16] The steady gaze (Joyce's eyesight had
not by then markedly deteriorated) fixes us as we 'read' this portrait.
The ironies multiply. Interpretation, seemingly, is never-ending. The
reader reads and is likewise read. The text is interrogated and interrogates in turn. *All* texts are 'portraits': not merely 'representations',
'likenesses', but, in keeping with the etymology of the word – it can be
traced back through Old French and Romanic to the Latin *pro trahere*,
'drawings from' life which 'draw from' readers endlessly 'protracted'
responses to the life-like representations verbalized therein.

The text as subject and object, then – and one can imagine a playful
James Joyce coining the portmanteau word 'soubject' for it in
Finnegans Wake (1939) – is what we are presented with in *A Portrait*.
Like *Tristram Shandy, Great Expectations* and *Daniel Deronda*, it
appears to present its readers with a unified subject in the shape of
the unfolding life of its protagonist. Like these earlier novels, but to an
even greater degree than any of them, its unity is fissiparous (appropriately enough for a product of a nuclear century). The splits veining
the title run all the way through the novel to its final two journal
entries, as Stephen (at last an 'I'-narrator) makes his exit, followed by
his creator:

> *26 April:* Mother is putting my new secondhand clothes in order.
> She prays now, she says, that I may learn in my own life and away
> from home and friends what the heart is and what it feels. Amen. So
> be it. Welcome, O life! I go to encounter for the millionth time the
> reality of experience and to forge in the smithy of my soul the uncre-
> ated conscience of my race.
>
> *27 April:* Old father, old artificer, stand me now and ever in good
> stead.
>
> Dublin 1904
>
> Trieste 1914   (pp. 275–6)

This pseudo-doxological ending contains verbal echoes from the
endings of the Bible (specifically from the final book of the New

Testament, Revelation, sometimes known as Apocalypse), *Jane Eyre*, and (inevitably) *Great Expectations*. The dichotomies which pervade these paragraphs culminate for Stephen in the Daedalus/Icarus reference in the final sentence, and for Joyce in the appended dates. Stephen's expectations, with which the novel ends, may be a far cry from Pip's on leaving Joe's forge in the earlier *Bildungsroman*. But what of the twelve years which separate the inception of *A Portrait* and its publication in 1916, the year of the 'Easter Rising', and two years into the First World War? It is as if *A Portrait* was conceived in one world only to be born into another. While Stephen discourses learnedly upon the *Summa* of Aquinas, the Battle of the Somme was being fought. Such a disjunction replicates in a major key the many minor bifurcations which make up the labyrinthine structure of *A Portrait*.

Not that the structure of *A Portrait* seems especially labyrinthine when the novel's ostensible subject-matter is summarized. At the 'centre' of the novel is Stephen Dedalus, the artist-in-the-making, the growth and development of whose personality this fictional autobiography and *Künstlerroman* gradually presents to the reader. The novel has a clear, linear, chronological shape, divided into five chapters, each of which ends with a significant moment of realization or illumination. In *Stephen Hero* these revelatory, quasi-spiritual moments are referred to as 'epiphanies';[17] in narrative terms they symbolize successive phases in Stephen's increasingly complex awareness of himself and external reality. Stephen's growing self-consciousness is also conveyed by the emergent linguistic sophistication of the novel's discourse. The novel strongly implies that it is through a combination of the language of the senses and language itself that Stephen is enabled to make sense of his experience of the world around him. Reinforcing and elaborating the novel's narrative structure are various patterns: certain words and phrases, images and motifs, ideas and themes recur throughout. On a conceptual level, for example, the novel foregrounds the rebellion of the artist-sinner-son-nationalist against the authority figures of the English literary tradition, the Roman Catholic religion, his father Simon Dedalus, and (last but hardly least) Ireland. The movement is away from conformity, obedience, dependence and oppression, towards self-expression, freedom, independence and exile. It is a novel of becoming rather than of being. The portrait of the artist, rather like the portrait in Wilde's *The Picture of Dorian Gray* (1891), is protean, mobile, unstable.

The same is true of the novel's many hierarchical oppositions. A list of some of the key opposed terms might include the following pairings:

art/life	art/religion	artist/priest
soul/body	word/world	right/wrong
church/country	heaven/hell	god/devil
man/woman	virgin/prostitute	white/red
warm/cold	nice/nasty	stasis/kinesis.

Such rigid 'either/or' ways of dividing up reality strike even the young Stephen as problematical:

> White roses and red roses: those were beautiful colours to think of . . . and he remembered the song about the wild rose blossoms on the little green place. But you could not have a green rose. But perhaps somewhere in the world you could. (p. 9)

The creative ur-artist, freely exercising his imagination, is beginning to grasp how words can provide what the world cannot – hence art's superiority over life. Art is presented not as mere product, but as processing life (art's raw material), moulding and controlling it, above it and beyond it, the ultimate 'transcendental signifier'. And certainly there is the suggestion that art has more to offer than a religion involving a (Jansenistic) denial of sensory and sensuous experience. Where religion offers only repression (so the thesis runs), art appears to offer freedom and power.

The crucial passage in which the art/religion opposition is so impressively explored is the 'wading girl' epiphany at the end of Chapter 4. Just before this particular episode, Stephen is deliberating over whether he has a religious vocation or not:

> From the door of Byron's publichouse to the gate of Clontarf Chapel, from the gate of Clontarf Chapel to the door of Byron's publichouse and then back again to the chapel and then back again to the publichouse . . . (p. 178)

He rejects the priestly vocation of a Jesuit: 'the oils of ordination would never anoint his body. He had refused. Why?' (p. 179). The answer emerges only slowly. It has something to do with 'the rhythmic rise and fall of words': Stephen is drawn to 'the glowing sensible world through the prism of a language manycoloured and richly storied . . .' (pp. 180–1). But there is more to it than this, we are told, as Stephen begins to feel 'the call of life to his soul' (p. 184). Stephen realizes that a higher calling awaits him:

> He would create proudly out of the freedom and power of his soul, as the great artificer whose name he bore, a living thing, new and soaring and beautiful, impalpable, imperishable. (p. 184)

Almost immediately, Stephen has a wonderful vision of a beautiful, bird-like wading girl:

> —Heavenly God! cried Stephen's soul, in an outburst of profane joy . . .
> Her image had passed into his soul for ever and no word had broken the holy silence of his ecstasy. Her eyes had called him and his soul had leaped at the call. To live, to err, to fall, to triumph, to recreate life out of life! (p. 186)

It is a moment of revelation, a moment of awakening. It is a deeply sensual moment. It is also a sublimely religious moment, as the language of the passage amply demonstrates. Yet if this is art's supreme triumph over religion, as Stephen responds positively to the call of beauty, it is an odd kind of triumph. For the concept of art revealed here is itself essentially religious, or – more specifically – sacramental. One kind of cultural order or tradition replaces another, and both involve the making of meanings, reverently, feelingly interpreting reality. Dorothy van Ghent's definition of the Joycean epiphany is apposite here: 'an image, sensuously apprehended and emotionally vibrant, which communicates instantaneously the meaning of experience'.[18] Stephen's dedication to art, for the moment at any rate (it will be revised in the following chapter), is as much a matter of the soul as of the body. The kind of art envisaged presupposes a fundamentally metaphysical understanding of the circumambient universe. The hierarchy art/religion thus collapses at this point: there is no essential difference between the two. Stephen remains Stephen, and his view of reality is still shaped by his very literate Irish

Catholicism. Art, for him, will henceforth take on the role of religion. Indeed, the persistence of the spiritual in the aesthetic becomes a key emphasis of the fifth (and final) chapter. Even when Stephen pronounces his *non serviam*, refusing to make his Easter duty to please his mother, the born-again artist betrays his anxiety of (Catholic) influence.[19] As Cranly tells Stephen (and Cranly is Stephen's most astute and sensible critic): 'your mind is supersaturated with the religion in which you say you disbelieve' (p. 261). Wilde defined art thus: 'Art is our spirited protest, our gallant attempt to teach Nature her proper place.'[20] Art is Stephen's *spiritual* protest.

So, as we saw in the case of *Daniel Deronda*, 'either/or' modes of ratiocination simply will not do. The greatest of novels render the multitudinous complexity of reality complexly. We are obliged to recognize, like Stephen over his Oedipal dilemma as to whether it is right or wrong to kiss his mother, that to some questions there are no right answers (pp. 10–11). However, even the 'rightness' of that assertion must be balanced against Stephen's pre-structuralist meditation upon language a couple of pages later! Stephen reflects:

> God was God's name just as his name was Stephen. *Dieu* was the French for God and that was God's name too; and when anyone prayed to God and said *Dieu* then God knew at once that it was a French person that was praying. But though there were different names for God in all the different languages in the world and God understood what all the people who prayed said in their different languages still God remained always the same God and God's real name was God. (p. 13)

This passage ushers in an evocative interior monologue in which Stephen is made to ponder on the passing of time in a Proustian vein. Here too Stephen's felt thinking is binary in nature, as if the young schoolboy can only work things out to his satisfaction in terms of 'sides'. Self/other, big/small, term/vacation, light/dark, warm/cold . . . 'like a train going in and out of tunnels' (p. 14). It is a remarkable piece of writing, and Stephen's growing self-consciousness – the self splitting, one part aware of and examining the other – is replicated in the duplex interpretative activity of the reader who is called upon both to feel with Stephen and to think about this stunning instance of 'action in character'. 'By thinking of things', it occurs to Stephen much later, 'you could understand them' (p. 43).

Revelations in *A Portrait* vary in magnitude and intensity. Each major epiphany at the end of the first four chapters is succeeded by a minor epiphany in a lower key at (or near) the beginning of the subsequent chapter. Thus the breathtakingly beautiful conclusion to Chapter 1, which sees the quiet evening transformed for Stephen, fresh from his triumphant visit to the rector, is followed by a couple of gritty characterizations in the sketches of Uncle Charles and Mike Flynn at the beginning of Chapter 2. The 'soft grey silence' and 'smell of evening' (p. 61) give way to 'the grey and blue coils of smoke' from Uncle Charles's 'black twist' tobacco (p. 62), and Mike Flynn's 'flabby stubblecovered face, as it bent over the long stained fingers through which he rolled his cigarette' (p. 63). If, as Anthony Burgess remarks, *A Portrait* has for its fundamental symbol 'a creature trying to escape from the bondage of the grosser elements, earth and water, and learning painfully how to fly',[21] there are certainly several occasions when Stephen – and the reader – is brought down to earth with a shuddering bump. In Joyce's own words, these are the incursions of 'that sudden reality which smashes romanticism into a pulp'.[22] (Flaubert and Ibsen were two major influences on Joyce at this time. Similar notes are to be found in Hardy and Larkin, and in Joyce's greatest successor, Beckett.) Such ironic contrasts, powerfully eidetic as they are (and their vividness really is extraordinary), pose few interpretative problems for the reader.

Rather subtler are those revelations of Stephen's character which are conveyed through a finely modulated, nuanced prose which Joyce uses to render Stephen's evolving consciousness. Stephen's adolescent fantasy about Mercedes – a character in Alexandre Dumas's *The Count of Monte Cristo* (1844–6) – is not difficult to read:

> They would be alone, surrounded by darkness and silence: and in that moment of supreme tenderness he would be transfigured. He would fade into something impalpable under her eyes and then in a moment, he would be transfigured. Weakness and timidity and inexperience would fall from him in that magic moment. (p. 67)

But what is the reader supposed to do? Laugh? The repetition of 'transfigured' (another word of religious – and indeed revelatory – significance), and the final, clinching 'that magic moment' give the cognitive game away. It must be conceded that it is not easy to place the reader emotionally in such passages.

Such interpretative quandaries are in part a consequence of Joyce's use of free indirect style, when the dividing line between Stephen and the narrator is not always clear. Thus we read:

> The hour when he too would take part in the life of that world seemed drawing near and in secret he began to make ready for the great part which he felt awaited him, the nature of which he only dimly apprehended. (p. 64)

How much of this is Stephen? How much of this is Joyce's narrator? (Does Stephen reflect that 'he too' is about to enter a new phase in his life, or is this a narrative intervention, 'placing' Stephen, as it were? What is the application of 'seemed' in the sentence? How self-conscious, if at all, is Stephen about making ready 'in secret' for his future role? And so on . . .) Riquelme cites such passages as examples of an 'oscillating perspective' in the narrative, and sees the device as preparing the way for the more obviously polyphonic *Ulysses* or (even more radically) *Finnegans Wake*.[23] Riquelme observes:

> This device involves the rendering of the character's consciousness in the third person and the past tense. Although there may be no explicit announcement of the mental process in the narrator's language, we understand the passages as thoughts occurring to the character in the first person and in the present tense . . . The reader translates the third person into 'I' during the reading process . . . The ambiguous merger of voices makes it difficult, even impossible, for the reader to distinguish between the cunningly combined voices of character and narrator . . . [and] necessitates the reader's active recreative rendering of the narration. The reader *performs* the text of narrated monologue with a special kind of involvement because of the device's unusual nature.[24]

(The italics are Riquelme's.) The device is hardly 'unusual' – Austen, Flaubert and Eliot, for example, all make copious use of it – but, none the less, Riquelme's lucid narrative analysis is accurate in essentials. He proceeds to develop and illustrate his thesis persuasively, in a reading which cites Booth and Genette, but which would also appear to owe something to a range of theorists and critics including Bakhtin, Jauss, Iser, Fish and Lodge. Rightly, Riquelme stresses the reader's self-conscious, active involvement in attempting to differentiate between the two voices of the Möbius strip that is *A Portrait*, and highlights the provisional/revisional and prospective/retrospective nature of all of the reader's interpretations and judgements.[25] His emphasis on reading as performance seems especially apt: shades of Pip reading Wemmick's note in the light of the watchman's lantern . . .

The nature and extent of the involvement required of the reader is different again in the famous hell-fire sermon of Chapter 3. In the nineteenth century more sermons than novels were published (if not read). At the end of the twentieth century, sermon-readers – even more than sermon-listeners – are probably an endangered species. Inevitably, this raises fundamental questions about how we read Joyce's powerful, chilling pastiche of a sermon. The didactic intrusions of Eliot's narrator in *Daniel Deronda* provide one kind of paradigm, but given (and it is not a large 'given') that we are not supposed to be agreeing with Father Arnall's elaboration of Catholic eschatology, the parallel is not, perhaps, a helpful one. A more promising analogy is suggested by the fact that one of Joyce's sources for the sermon, Giovani Pietro Pinamonti's *Hell Opened to Christians, to Caution Them from Entering into It* (1688; translated 1868), uses as its approach the methods recommended by the founder of the Society of Jesus, St Ignatius Loyola, in *The Spiritual Exercises* (1548). These exercises, a translator remarks, are 'not a subject for mere reading but a handbook for those engaged in the energetic activity of "making a retreat"'; as such they 'are not to be *read* so much as *prayed*' (translator's italics).[26] The relevant section of *The Spiritual Exercises* is 'First Week, Fifth Exercise: A Meditation on Hell'. The retreatant is enjoined to recreate mentally as vivid a picture of hell as possible, in its 'length, breadth and depth', so that 'in imagination' all five senses may actively contemplate the sufferings of the damned.[27] This is the characteristic Ignatian method of meditation, entailing the vivid re-presentation to oneself of a particular scene or situation. It offers a model of reading which is at once personal and felt, and precisely orientated to the object of attention in question – a kind of seventeenth-century anticipation of Keats's practice of 'negative capability'. As such, it provides us with one way into Joyce's homiletic *tour de force* in *A Portrait*. For the retreatants are called upon to do many readerly things: to 'remember', to 'examine', to 'reflect', to 'try to understand', to 'give all their attention', with their 'whole heart' and 'whole mind', in a spirit of 'quiet' and 'devotion' (pp. 116–19). Then comes the moment when the preacher gives an intensely vivid, terrifying representation of hell's physical and mental qualities for his auditors' spiritual edification. It is an attempt 'for a moment to realize, as far as we can, the nature of that abode of the damned' (p. 128). In other words, it is a matter of 'bod[ying] forth/The forms of things unknown',[28] making real what is unreal, making present what is absent.

Stephen, in this context, is the ideal listener/reader, as certain crucial realizations follow the 'realization' of hell in the sermon he has just heard. Through the words of the sermon, he has connected with the world and the world-view therein represented: he has made it totally real to himself, personally, in both thought and feeling. And the experience makes a difference to his life: Stephen confesses his sins, and reality is transformed for him as a result:

> He sat by the fire in the kitchen, not daring to speak for happiness. Till that moment he had not known how beautiful and peaceful life could be . . . On the dresser was a plate of sausages and white puddings and on the shelf there were eggs . . . White pudding and eggs and sausages and cups of tea. How simple and beautiful was life after all! And life lay all before him. (pp. 157–8)

The apocalyptic echo from the end of Milton's *Paradise Lost* acts as a coda to this particular epiphany, this revelation of reality. (The word 'epiphany' can be translated as 'showing forth' or 'manifestation'; the word 'apocalypse', likewise, can be rendered as 'revelation' or 'uncovering'.) Some readers – Roman Catholic readers especially (whether practising or lapsed)[29] – will sympathize with Stephen, and perhaps even empathize with him. But most readers will marvel at Joyce's extraordinary psychological, moral and social realism. To compare the last page of Chapter 3 with the opening paragraphs of Chapter 5 (a 'kitchen sink' scene) is to appreciate the centrality of Joyce's exploration of the reciprocal relationship between inner and outer reality, between subjective perception and objective 'brute facts', to the concerns of this novel.

Less impressive is the section dealing with Stephen's aesthetic theories in Chapter 5. The mass of abstract detail suggests that Joyce probably (but not unarguably) meant his readers to take Stephen's theories seriously, even though Stephen's priggish and pretentious young adult self is treated with suitable irony. In particular, the privileging of 'stasis' over 'kinesis' in Stephen's model of aesthetic response was to find its parallel some twenty years later in American

New Criticism with its attention to literary (and especially poetic) works of art 'as self-sufficient objects without attention to their origins or effects'.[30] Or affects: both approaches involve arguing against a dynamic model of aesthetic response.

And yet, as we have seen, the active involvement of the reader is a crucial condition for a successful critical reading of *A Portrait* itself. Even with such an engagement, interpreting parts of *A Portrait* (Stephen's villanelle, say) is difficult enough; without it, a satisfactory interpretation of the novel becomes utterly impossible. Stephen himself misreads reality throughout: during the pandybat triumph, after the Easter retreat, in the wading girl episode . . . But in each of these instances he is at least personally engaged in *reading* reality, responding actively to it with his 'whole heart' and 'whole mind'. The artistically detached Stephen, with his newly discovered aesthetic theories, is, on the contrary, an indifferent reader and interpreter of reality. Here, for example, is Stephen's rapturous reading of reality at the end of Chapter 4, where he sees the girl

> before him in midstream, alone and still, gazing out to sea. She seemed like one whom magic had changed into the likeness of a strange and beautiful seabird. Her long slender bare legs were delicate as a crane's and pure save where an emerald trail of seaweed had fashioned itself as a sign upon the flesh. Her thighs, fuller and soft-hued as ivory, were bared almost to the hips where the white fringes of her drawers were like featherings of soft white down. Her slateblue skirts were kilted boldly about her waist and dovetailed behind her. Her bosom was as a bird's soft and slight, slight and soft as the breast of some darkplumaged dove . . .
> —Heavenly God! cried Stephen's soul, in an outburst of profane joy. (pp. 185–6)

Compare the above passage with a much later specimen of 'bird-watching':

> What birds were they? He stood on the steps of the library to look at them, leaning wearily on his ashplant . . .
> He watched their flight; bird after bird: a dark flash, a swerve, a flash again, a dart aside, a curve, a flutter of wings. He tried to count them before all their darting quivering bodies passed: six, ten, eleven: and wondered were they odd or even in number. Twelve, thirteen: for two came wheeling down from the upper sky . . . (p. 243)

In the first passage Stephen's sensuous, lively engagement with reality is as close to spontaneity as it is possible to get: he is clearly, visibly, audibly moved (a good example of 'kinesis'). The second passage is too long to quote in full here. It is an extended, self-conscious, highly literary meditation. (There follow allusions to the Bible, Cornelius Agrippa von Nettesheim, Swedenborg, Tennyson and Yeats.) Stephen, as befits a D[a]edalus, is treating the spectacle as a possible oracle for divination, with thoughts of flying to freedom already in his mind. But although he comes away from the scene soothed, experiencing a 'soft liquid joy' (p. 245), his reading of that quiet (if not 'static') scene will probably strike the reader as rather more clinical in its detachment than the earlier passage. When, at the end of the episode (hardly an 'epiphany'), movement occurs, it is movement of an orderly, mechanical kind:

> A sudden swift hiss fell from the windows above him and he knew that the electric lamps had been switched on in the readers' room. He turned into the pillared hall, now calmly lit, went up the staircase and passed in through the clicking turnstile. (p. 246)

Joyce's journeyman prose is deft and precise. To learn how to read reality and render it artistically Stephen will have to move further afield: he will have to journey into exile.

Derek Attridge has this to say about the experience of reading Joyce:

> Reading Joyce is only one of many ways to pursue an interest in the unceasing traffic – in both directions – between words and the world . . . his texts themselves teach us how to read them . . . If there *is* a way of reading Joyce that could be thought of as less than fully worthwhile, as something of a waste of human energy, it would be one that fails to bring together an active and curious attention to the words on the page with whatever store of knowledge and experience the individual reader has accumulated.[31]

He goes on to emphasize the 'teeming generosity' with which the Joycean *œuvre* 'entices us into repeated acts of interpretation'.[32] Attridge's words are themselves both generous and just. To read *A Portrait* critically is necessarily to become engaged actively in the inspirational, interpretative quest for meaning and meanings. Reality, in this meaning-full modernist novel, reveals itself as multifaceted and (ultimately) as mysterious. As we read *A Portrait*, the winding, tantalizing ways of the reading process itself are sketched out for us in a dazzlingly original series of profound revelations. And as we read the novel, as we are (in Attridge's words) 'entice[d] . . . into repeated acts of interpretation', the novel's revelatory power becomes more and more apparent.

Paul Ricoeur discusses the reading process in the following terms:

> Reading is an appropriation-divestiture. How can this letting-go, this relinquishment, be incorporated into appropriation? Essentially by linking appropriation to the revelatory power of the text . . .

In the process, Ricoeur continues, 'the *ego* divests itself of itself' so that the 'process' becomes one 'of dispossession'. However, this only happens in those instances where the reader 'lets go' and opens herself or himself to the text's possibilities. The condition of openness is crucial, as the quotation from Attridge quoted at the beginning of this chapter makes plain. Paradoxically, this 'dispossession of the narcissistic *ego*', according to Ricoeur, leads to a truer, deeper, fuller '*self*-understanding', but

> Only the interpretation which satisfies the injunction of the text, which follows the 'arrow' of meaning and endeavours to 'think in accordance with' it, engenders a new *self*-understanding.[33]

A Portrait richly rewards those readers who (feel and) 'think in accordance with it', by giving them a *new* understanding of themselves and the reality in which they live. According to Georges Poulet, '[r]eading is just that: a way of giving way . . .'. He elaborates:

> The phenomenon is indeed hard to explain, even to conceive, and yet, once admitted, it explains to me what might otherwise seem even more inexplicable. For how could I explain, without such take-over of my innermost subjective being, the astonishing facility with which I not only understand but even *feel* what I read. When I read as I ought – that is without mental reservation, without any desire to preserve my independence of judgement, and with the total commitment required of any reader – my comprehension becomes intuitive . . . In other words, the kind of comprehension in question here is not a movement from the unknown to the known, from the strange to the familiar, from outside to inside. It might rather be called a phenome-

non by which mental objects rise up from the depths of consciousness into the light of recognition . . . Reading, then, is the act in which
the subjective principle which I call *I*, is modified in such a way that I
no longer have the right, strictly speaking, to consider it as my *I*. I am
on loan to another, and this other thinks, feels, suffers, and acts
within me . . . When I am absorbed in reading, a second self takes
over, a self which thinks and feels for me.[34]

This phenomenological understanding of the reading process brings
us back to Derrida's notion of reading as 'transformational', encountered earlier in this study. If, as readers, we genuinely open ourselves
to the transformational possibilities of Joyce's text, the experience of
reading it becomes truly revelatory. In short, reading *becomes* revelation in *A Portrait*, whilst revelation is shown to be . . . reading.

7   Reading the Self: Beckett's *Trilogy* – *Molloy; Malone Dies; The Unnamable*

> The fact would seem to be, if in my situation one may speak of facts, not only that I shall have to speak of things of which I cannot speak, but also, which is even more interesting, but also that I, which is if possible even more interesting, that I shall have to, I forget, no matter. (p. 294)

Reading Beckett's novels is not easy. In part, this is because syntax, in Beckett, collapses under the pressure of the unsayable. For the 'Unnamable' narrator of the third part of Beckett's *Trilogy* (1959), most obviously unsayable is the nature of the self that cannot be named. We have seen Tristram Shandy, too, lose track of his ostensible subject – himself, his life and opinions – apparently the victim of association and contingency. We have also seen him lose his way with a sentence, forget where it was leading, and have to begin it again. But in Sterne's novel, digression from self and the syntactic convolutions that go with it have an essentially narrative reference. Tristram's loss of way is not seen to present a crisis of identity: the questioning of self is itself only part of the narrative humour which makes it impossible for Tristram to get on with his account:

> —— My good friend, quoth I —— as sure as I am I —— and you are you ——
> —— And who are you? said he. —— Don't puzzle me; said I.
> (*Tristram Shandy*, p. 434)

So whilst the reader might have similar superficial problems in following the thread of Sterne's and Beckett's sentences, the experience of these problems is different, and creates different expectations. Our response to Tristram's difficulties confirms the comic nature of the digressive, associative tendency. In Byatt's terms, the pleasure of long sentences is the revelation of 'the way the mind puts the world together' (see Chapter 8). Tristram, 'notwithstanding all that has been said upon *straight lines*', defies us to move straight forward to complete one idea when there are always other worthwhile ideas starting up to distract us (so cabbage-planters, in his analogy, cannot plant their cabbages in straight rows when local beauties have their 'slits in petticoats' unmended – *Tristram Shandy*, p. 449). The reader of Beckett's convoluted, unfinished sentences encounters not a positive celebration of chance, opportunism and connection, but a sense of desperate futility. Tristram finds he has nowhere particular to go; Beckett's narrators – Molloy and Moran in the first part of the trilogy, Malone in the second, and the Unnamable in the third – all positively *have* to get somewhere, but cannot. Our response, then, to the local difficulties of getting from the beginning of a sentence to the end is transformed by a very different sense we have of the significance of *ends*. That the Unnamable should lose 'his' way in the opening quotation refers us not primarily to the problem of telling stories but to the connection between questions of artistic representation and philosophical questions about the nature of reality itself. On the representational level, the Unnamable's qualification – 'if in my situation one may speak of facts' – is important. One may *not*, on one level, speak of facts in fiction. The declarative opening of Moran's narrative – 'It is midnight. The rain is beating on the windows.' – has a provisional status confirmed by its cancellation at the end of Moran's account:

> Then I went back into the house and wrote, It is midnight. The rain is beating on the windows. It was not midnight. It was not raining. (p. 176)

In fiction such statements of 'fact' have the same 'truth'. 'It is midnight' *is* as true or as false as 'it was not midnight'. The revision also makes it impossible to distinguish, as Calinescu puts it,

> what is fictionally true (what a protagonist does or says, 'what really happens' in the story) from what is fictionally fictitious (what a protagonist dreams, dreams up, fantasizes, vividly anticipates, imagines, hypothesizes, falsely remembers, projects, and so on).[1]

This distinction is one which readers do not wish to sacrifice, because without it we cannot believe in the integrity of the fictional world as a representation of the real world. No sooner are we told it was *not* raining than we would like to class this as the new 'fictional truth' making the idea that it *was* raining 'fictionally fictitious'. But the new statement has also now acquired the same uncertainty. We realize that the next paragraph could just as easily retract it. The perversity of the 'correction' has made us aware, as readers, that we, like Calinescu, must put inverted commas around the fictionally true 'what really happens' (these inverted commas will return to haunt this chapter later). The effect, inversely, is to remind us 'how dramatically important the concept of fictional truth is in the reception of narrative works'.[2] The reader of Beckett will forever be trying to establish the level of fictional truth to make sense of what 'really' happens to the characters. So strong is this impulse that its denial is never completely successful. We know that it is not raining, we know that it is not *not* raining, but we would still like to think that it was either one or the other. To read Beckett, then, is to encounter the urgency of our own narrative need for a kind of truth.

But Beckett is not simply concerned with the unrepresentability of a world of facts in fiction (a world where it actually rains or does not), but, more importantly, with the unspeakability of the world itself. The facile point that 'fiction' cannot be 'truth' opens onto the profound question of the 'true' nature of the world and the self that perceives it and tries to express it. Tristram Shandy wants to tell his story, and embraces the comic discovery that his story is embedded in the stories of others, that to describe himself he must digress from himself, but it is his 'story' not his sense of self-identity which is at stake. 'Story', in Beckett, is persecution; digression is tragic, as the 'I' tries to shed all *stories* of itself to tell who it *really* is. Who you are, in Beckett's fiction, is not a playful question of narrative representation but an urgent question of being. To 'have to speak of things of which you cannot speak' is to be forced to face an unspeakable and unknowable self.

Hillis Miller's description of reading is relevant here. Drawing out the implications of Paul de Man's arguments, Hillis Miller gives 'reading' the broadest possible application. In a sense every response we have is a kind of 'reading'. Our version of reality, our perceptions and sensations, are 'permeated by language through and through'.[3] But this means we are somehow trapped inside language. We cannot 'get outside the limits of language by means of language',[4] and therefore cannot know if our reading *actually* refers to anything beyond itself:

> Everything we reach that seems outside language, for example sensation and perception, turns out to be more language. To live is to read, or rather to commit again and again the failure to read which is the human lot. We are hard at work trying to fulfill the impossible task of reading from the moment we are born until the moment we die. We struggle to read from the moment we wake in the morning until the moment we fall asleep at night, and what are our dreams but more lessons in the pain of the impossibility of reading, or rather in the pain of having no way whatsoever of knowing whether or not we may have ... stumbled by accident on the right reading?[5]

Such ideas might seem both provocative and difficult, but they can be applied quite straightforwardly both to the stories Beckett's narrators are trying to tell and to the experience of reading them. Beckett's narrators explicitly confess that they have to go on telling, without ever knowing if they have at some point, accidentally, stumbled on the right formula of telling – the story to end all stories, the tale of 'How It Is'. They assume they have not found this formula because they find they are still telling *stories* about who they 'are' and about the 'world' rather than telling the *truth*. If they could tell the truth then they could be silent. Likewise we read knowing we can get no closer to the 'reality' than they can – we cannot complete or close our reading; there is no final say about the readings we can give, no reading *truth* beyond which the rest is silence. Our reading of Beckett's *Trilogy*, then, repeats the lesson its narrators are forced to learn. We encounter the same crisis of identity. Who is it who is reading? Beckett's fiction makes this understanding explicitly a part of our experience. But we ought to note that Hillis Miller, here, admits that the condition of reading the unreadable is not without its 'pain'. Beckett's Unnamable does not 'forget' what he was trying to say because of an elaborate narrative game whose humour would enlighten the reader about the limitations of narrative. He 'forgets' because what is to be said cannot be said. And our interest ('which is even more interesting') is an urgent interest, because our own sense of self is at stake.

The problem affecting all theories of reading – the identification of the 'reader' discussed – is usually a rhetorical problem: when we are discussing the reader what are the reading characteristics to be attributed to him or her? The question of the reader in Beckett's world is shared by the narrators: not a matter of who do we mean when we say 'the reader', but rather who *is* the one who reads? In a sense Beckett's novels thus transcend the problem of definition that theories of response have not been able to solve. Whatever the term used for the reader (the implied reader, the intended reader, the superreader . . .) the analysis of the reading role has always left the real readers – *us* – strangely dislocated. To adapt the words that end Gérard Genette's *Narrative Discourse*, we become those 'people' who are 'always off to the side'.[6] Not so in Beckett's *Trilogy*, where our real status is the issue. 'I'm listening', says the Unnamable, 'Well I prefer that, I must say I prefer that, that what, oh you know, who you, oh I suppose the audience, well well, so there's an audience' (p. 385). The reader of Beckett is simultaneously the 'who you' within the narrative, addressed by the narrative, and the 'who you' who actually reads, because the problem of identity is both within and without the text. Winnie's 'story', in Beckett's play *Happy Days*, is instructive here. She recounts how a man, possibly named Shower or Cooker, complains to his wife about the meaning of Winnie, buried in the sand. The wife's response becomes Winnie's question to the 'real' audience as the stage direction has her stare at the auditorium: 'And you, she says, what's the idea of you, she says, what are you meant to mean?'[7]

It is hardly surprising, since the central issue is the nature of identity, that we should have such provisional 'naming' in Beckett's world. Moran, who has the mysterious mission of tracking down the missing Molloy, immediately recognizes that what 'Molloy' means is always provisional. 'Is it possible', writes Jean-François Lyotard,

> that the number of senses attached to a named referent . . . increases without limit? . . . [I]t cannot be proven that everything has been signified about a name (that 'everything has been said about *x*') not only because no such totality can be proven, but because the name not being by itself a designator of reality . . . the inflation of senses that can be attached to it is not bounded by the 'real' properties of its referent.[8]

What we 'are' continually changes as we change and as others perceive us differently – we continually acquire new, different and potentially limitless attributes (we are 'changed' by everything we experience). Never will there be a point where we simply are what we are – when nothing else could conceivably be added to the description of what it means to be us. And our names never pretend to tell what we 'are'. We cannot test our possible properties by referring to our names. When accounting for ourselves, when saying who we 'are', we tell stories, and others tell other stories about us. We are the subject of potentially infinite readings.

We have already encountered 'dubious concepts of the self' in Chapter 5. In Beckett the problem becomes a crisis. 'The fact was', writes Moran, 'there were three, no, four Molloys.' He continues:

> He that inhabited me, my caricature of same, Gaber's and the man of flesh and blood somewhere awaiting me . . . I will . . . add a fifth Molloy, that of Youdi. But would not this fifth Molloy necessarily coincide with the fourth, the real one as the saying is, him dogged by his shadow? I would have given a lot to know. There were others too, of course. But let us leave it at that, if you don't mind, the party is big enough. (pp. 115–16)

Once again a Beckett narrator gives the declarative 'the fact was' only to make absurd the notion of such a fact. He wonders if one 'version' of Molloy is not the right one, that Youdi possibly knows Molloy in essence, in reality (as the saying is). It is not surprising that he would 'have given a lot to know' this. The 'real' reality of Molloy is the concern. But Lyotard's idea of 'inflation' is borne out by trying to number the Molloys – not four, but five . . . and then, 'there were others too, of course'. The idea that the reader might protest that these 'others' are not properly introduced is laughable, as if we were not struggling sufficiently with five Molloys. Some party! Soon, under such pressure, the name itself begins to slip and slide. It might not be Molloy, but rather Mellose, or Mollose:

> Of these two names, Molloy and Mollose, the second seemed to me perhaps the more correct. But barely. (p. 113)

A fortuitous accident relates the point beyond the text. Christopher Ricks notes as an 'inspiration' the biographical slip of Alice and Kenneth Hamilton (or one of their sources) in recording the entry on Samuel Barclay Beckett's birth certificate as 'Samuel Barely Beckett'.[9]

Molloy is 'barely' Molloy (or Mollose); Beckett is 'Barely Beckett'. Our names, accurate or not, do not designate our reality. So Lyotard makes a crucial distinction between the 'nominative' function and what he calls the 'ostensive' (in the sense of 'manifestly or directly demonstrative'):

> 'This is Caesar' is not an ostensive phrase, it is a nominative phrase. Now it 'takes place' just as well in front of a portrait of Caesar as in front of Caesar . . . this is because to name the referent is not the same as to show its 'presence'.[10]

Whatever name we use, if its aim is to *constitute* that which it names, it will never be the 'right' one. In this sense Beckett's narrators are one and the same doomed narrator trying to find the 'right' name for whatever 'they' are:

> All these Murphys, Molloys and Malones do not fool me. They have made me waste my time . . . when, in order to stop speaking, I should have spoken of me and of me alone. (p. 305)

So Moran is another version of Molloy, not just someone trying to find Molloy, but someone trying to find 'himself'. And we can reject every unsatisfactory name – 'it' is not Molloy, nor Malone, nor Moran, nor Mahood, nor even the Worm of the third part of the *Trilogy* – and call it 'unnamable', only to find that the 'Unnamable' is a name too, that it too is subject to absence not presence. The 'I should have spoken of me and of me alone' simply transfers the problem from the proper nouns to the pronouns:

> . . . it's the fault of the pronouns, there is no name, for me, no pronoun for me, all the trouble comes from that, that, it's a kind of pronoun too, it isn't that either. (p. 408)

In this way all of Beckett's narrators are uttering versions of the 'not I', the 'I' being the minimalist version of the problem. It is not simply that 'I' am '*not* I', but also that the '*not* I' is essential to the (impossible) definition of what I am.

We ought to admit, of course, that these kinds of issue do not make for comfortable reading experiences. Lennard Davis puts this colourfully, when he notes:

While reading we do not want the centrality of the character's existence to be tampered with any more than we want to be reminded
about harmful additives and chemicals while enjoying our favorite
ice cream.[11]

Ben Knights is more sincere about his concerns for the reader, and
suggests that the reader's wish to see character as stable fulfils a
psychological need:

> Literary character must in some sense be a projection of what people
> want to be able to think about themselves . . . That is to talk of such
> properties as stability and coherence through time, and of people as
> possessing a recognisable identity even in different circumstances, as
> having attributes (strengths and weaknesses) which they would wish
> others to judge charitably, to be possessed of a core of being which is
> invulnerable to damage from the outside world, and so on.[12]

By these criteria reading Beckett is radically destabilizing, as the
problem of names merges with the problem of reality. But we ought
also to note that this is a problem with a long history, not just the
preoccupation of twentieth-century sceptical and relativist philosophy. The empiricists had shown that our ideas of real substances were
always, inevitably, incomplete and that the names of our ideas of
things in the world did not constitute the things themselves. So, for
John Locke, the word 'gold' can never indicate the essence of the
substance, and the question of what 'gold' really *is* must remain a
question. To say that 'gold' is a substance defined by its properties –
that it is 'yellow, fusible, ductile, weighty, and fixed' – is to define it in
terms of its relationship with other substances: 'Put a piece of *Gold*
any where by it self, separate from the reach and influence of all other
bodies, it will immediately lose all its Colour and Weight, and perhaps
Malleableness too; which, for ought I know, would be changed into a
perfect Friability.'[13] Furthermore, 'gold' will always have properties
unknown to us:

> If we make our complex *Idea* of *Gold*, a *Body yellow, fusible, ductile,
> weighty*, and *fixed*, we shall be at the same uncertainty concerning
> *Solubility* in *Aqua regia*; and for the same reason. Since we can never,
> from consideration of the *Ideas* themselves, with certainty affirm or
> deny, of a Body, whose complex *Idea* is made up of yellow, very
> weighty, ductile, fusible and fixed, that it is soluble in *Aqua regia*: And

so on of the rest of its Qualities. I would gladly meet with one general Affirmation, concerning any Quality of *Gold*, that any one can certainly know is true.[14]

In this sense assertions about identity ('this is what I am') and assertions about external reality ('this is what the world is') suffer the same indeterminacy, unrelieved by the assumption that the name indicates properties (that Molloy is 'like' this, that Gold is 'like' that). So Lyotard notes that ostensive and nominative referents have this in common:

> Phrases which are not the current phrase and which are currently unknown refer to them by assigning them senses other than the current sense . . . Just as *This page is white* (seen from here) *and is not white* (seen from there, it is grey), so *Napoleon is a strategist* (in one network of names) *and is not a strategist* (in another, he is an emperor).[15]

The emphasis falls aptly on perspective and point of view, and hence is another expression of the conditions of response. The position of the viewer or interpreter is the 'determining' factor, and since there is a multiplicity of views nothing is actually 'determined'. If we see Molloy from one perspective he is one thing; from another he is something completely different. Furthermore, any definition of properties depends on the proof of non-properties: 'Reality is not expressed therefore by a phrase like: *x is such*, but by one like: *x is such and not such*'.[16] Consequently, Lyotard argues that 'negation is at the heart of testimony'.[17]

Beckett's 'not I', then, is a paradigm for all forms of scepticism. The passion for truth that his narrators express results in an impossible process of negation and cancellation that proves the self and the world to be unknowable and unsayable: 'What I liked in anthropology', writes Molloy, 'was its inexhaustible faculty of negation, its relentless definition of man, as though he were no better than God, in terms of what he is not' (p. 39). Wolfgang Iser, in a chapter on Beckett in his book *Prospecting*, shows that the 'pattern of negativity in Beckett's prose' forces the reader to reassess her/his sense of reality:

> In our everyday lives we are always guided by the conviction that our conceptions can grasp realities; we are not aware that they may represent mere fictions formulated because we find ourselves

confronted by realities of whose existence we are conscious but which we can never actually know.[18]

Despite Iser's consequently misplaced confidence in the 'indisputable' nature of this reality that cannot be known, do not such observations necessarily lead us to place 'reality' itself in those inverted commas which indicate its uncertain, unknowable, and unsayable status? Surely our reference to the 'real' comes to deserve Beckett's 'as the saying is'. But then we will be using a formula despised by as astute a critic of Beckett as Christopher Ricks. Ricks quotes a number of what he considers to be inept criticisms which confirm for him the 'professionalised orthodoxy' of a feeble 'postmodernist' reading of Beckett. One of his pilloried passages, worth requoting, comes from Frederik N. Smith:

> 'By everywhere undermining the connection between language and reality, Beckett has deliberately run words aground, leaving them no longer usable as signs for meanings beyond themselves, but oddly free to express meaning by reference to other words . . . Once the referential function of language has been exposed as a sham, the lyrical is put on an equal footing with the less than lyrical . . . The language of Beckett's minimalist fiction can, by definition, cut away everything but language. And once language is accepted as relying not on external 'reality' for its significance but is understood rather as the source of its own meaning, the more poetic, more conventional use of it lends at least a linguistic significance to what is said.'[19]

In attacking this passage Ricks is, in a sense, shadow-boxing. The passage manifestly reduces postmodern ideas of indeterminacy to the vaguest, most meaningless gestures. Beckett does not seek to 'undermine' the connection between language and reality: he rigorously exposes the problem of their relationship, a problem which *depends*, however hopelessly, on the notion of such a connection. The idea that words are 'no longer usable as signs for meanings beyond themselves' is a facile reduction of the struggle to signify which has such urgency in Beckett's prose. If the 'language' of Beckett's vaguely 'minimalist' fiction did 'cut away everything but language', then any debate about it would be both easy and pointless (it would *be* what it so self-referentially *is*). For the idea that language is 'the source of its own meaning' Ricks's own dismissal of this as 'wisely unfathomable' cannot be bettered. But Ricks's comment on the use of 'reality' in the passage raises a more important objection:

> Meanwhile, reality – which is haled in as just another of those shams – is given the usual treatment, the infected hygiene, iatrogenic, of inverted commas: *external 'reality'*.[20]

Ricks's point is that Beckett's art is never 'so complacent as to deny the existence of "the without", "impregnable" as it yet fertilely is'. But the real motive for his attack on those 'iatrogenic' inverted commas implies that the critical physician does ill to Beckett's art by pretending to cure the ills that Beckett's characters so 'really' suffer (an 'iatrogenic' disease is one caused by medical treatment). Ricks quotes a number of passages, the last from *Ill Seen Ill Said*: ' "She sits on erect and rigid in the deepening gloom. Such helplessness to move she cannot help" ':

> In all of these, supremely in the last . . . it is not simply the 'syntax of weakness' but the incarnation of the human reality of it all, of piteous bodily weakness, and of the strength to contemplate it, and to realize it, which is so moving.[21]

This is marvellous criticism, but we might feel that the syntax of suffering shows even the incarnation of pain to be inexpressible. The 'human reality of it all' may be accurately *vague*. Here is Molloy trying to explain his leg problem:

> Follow me carefully. The stiff leg hurt me, admittedly, I mean the old stiff leg, and it was the other which I normally used as a pivot, or prop. But now this latter, as a result of its stiffening I suppose, and the ensuing commotion among nerves and sinews, was beginning to hurt me even more than the other. What a story, God send I don't make a balls of it. For the old pain, do you follow me, I had got used to it, in a way, yes, in a kind of way. Whereas to the new pain, though of the same family exactly, I had not yet had time to adjust myself. Nor should it be forgotten that having one bad leg plus another more or less good, I was able to nurse the former, and reduce its sufferings to the minimum, to the maximum, by using the former exclusively, with the help of my crutches. But I no longer had this resource! For I no longer had one bad leg plus another more or less good, but now both were equally bad. And the worse, to my mind, was that which till now

had been good, at least comparatively good, and whose change for the worse I had not yet got used to. So in a way, if you like, I still had one bad leg and one good, or rather less bad, with this difference however, that the less bad now was the less good of heretofore. (pp. 76–7)

The reader can, just about, follow this, but its 'intents and purposes' are rather hopeless. Molloy has two extremely painful legs and he is trying to make nice distinctions about the different perception of the pain in each leg. Molloy is still speaking of things of which he cannot speak (the fuller account of his problems ends with the usual formula: 'I'm lost, no matter'). Typically, the reader's struggle to follow the sense through this passage is directly acknowledged by the narrator. When Molloy moves on to the 'dastardly desertion' of his toes, he considers the problem of the reader's possible, reasonable, uncertainty: 'do you as much as know what foot we're talking about? No. Nor I' (p. 80). That our pain is inexplicable and incommunicable makes our predicament all the more painful. But how much more inexpressible than this physical suffering is the 'not I' of metaphysical suffering. Ironically the removal of those inverted commas from our sense of 'reality' may be more iatrogenic than their retention. To suffer without knowing what it is to *be*, without knowing what it is that suffers, is indeed to perpetuate suffering. The 'not I' is forced to continue its lesson of pain until it is allowed to cease to be. How can it cease to be until it has defined its own existence, its own 'reality'? Here Iser's suggestion that negativity in Beckett offers an 'infinite potentiality' in effect misses the point as much as the bland offerings of the vague advocates for the 'free play' of words. But perhaps even Ricks underestimates the crisis of suffering that those inverted commas of 'reality', when used with a full sense of the philosophical concerns of Beckett's prose, may betray.

Ricks's critique of the looseness of 'postmodern' readings has an interesting affinity with arguments from very different critical quarters. Christopher Norris, with his impeccable Derridean credentials, is similarly forceful in his attacks against the idea that 'reality' (still with its 'perverted commas') is 'just a matter of "phrases" – a construct out of various descriptions, vocabularies, language-games, tropes, narratives etc.'.[22] The 'ultra-relativist orthodoxy', according to Norris (in strikingly Ricksian terms)

　　erects its own lack of critical and ethical resources into a quasi-

universal 'postmodern condition', a terminal indifference with regard
to issues of truth and falsehood, or – to paraphrase Jonathan Swift –
that state of perfect self-assurance which comes of being blissfully
well deceived.[23]

But there is a middle ground in this debate about relativism. We do
not need to dispense with a notion of reality simply because it needs
the inverted commas to show that we cannot determine it. Barbara
Johnson's advocacy of an analysis that tests 'the specificity of a text's
critical difference from itself' (see Chapter 5) hardly promises an ultimate confidence in the discovery of 'truth', but accepts that we must,
rigorously, continue to seek it. Norris's own reference to Swift could
be seen as instructive here. The allusion is to a famous passage in *A
Tale of a Tub* (1704), where Swift's mock-author describes an anatomy
lesson: the more deeply the corpse is investigated to discover the
source of its ills, the more abundant and unfathomable become its
discovered flaws. Swift's ironic persona cannot tolerate this state of
affairs, so he recommends a general patching-up to return us to that
state of 'blissful' self-deception. An analysis of response does suggest
that all claims to truth are subject to a radical scepticism, but this does
not mean that we should throw away the instruments of analysis.

The reader of Beckett, certainly, is not allowed the comfort of terminal indifference. Issues of truth and falsehood are crucial to Beckett's
narrators and central to the reader's experience. Molloy's 'truly it little
matters what I say' (p. 32) is not a feeble abnegation of narrative
responsibility, but a desperate acknowledgement of the problems of
'truly' saying anything that *does* matter. The idea that 'reality' might
be 'a matter of phrases' is not, in Beckett, a conveniently liberating
impulse, but an intolerable fear. 'I always say either too much or too
little', comments Molloy, 'which is a terrible thing for a man with a
passion for truth like mine' (p. 34). Neither the 'passion' nor the
'terror' here should be underestimated. That usually harmless gesture
of integrity implied in the commonplace 'to tell the truth' becomes, in
the *Trilogy*, an expression of crisis. It *deserves* its exclamation mark:
'But to tell the truth (to tell the truth!) . . .' (p. 32). And when a truth
can be told in more than a mere figure of speech it tends to produce a
typically self-defeating logic:

> To tell the truth, let us be honest at least, it is some considerable time
> now since I last knew what I was talking about. (p. 325)

If this is comedy then it conforms only to Beckett's 'laugh of laughs' ('the laugh that laughs – silence please – at that which is unhappy')[24] which confirms our helpless impotence. Malone's 'what truth is there in all this babble?' has an aptly embittered edge (p. 236).

The same sense of desperation affects the presentation of self. And again, while Beckett may provide textual evidence for a relativist view, he allows no saving sense of indifference. Norris, labelling Richard Rorty as a neo-pragmatist, accuses him of believing that

> we can happily get along with a minimalist notion of the 'subject' which dispenses with any principle of integrity, selfhood or continuous identity over time, and which rejoices in the range of optional subject-positions.[25]

The disunity of self in Beckett brings the reader no such sense of 'happiness' and 'rejoicing', and though the *Trilogy* challenges the principles of integrity, selfhood *and* continuous identity, it does not readily dispense with them. Rather, it incessantly worries at them. The narrators of the *Trilogy* teach us that 'playing' with versions of self is a form of torture ('playing with yourself', after all, is a form of self-abuse – the joke is Beckett's own):

> What tedium. And I call that playing. I wonder if I am not talking yet again about myself. Shall I be incapable, to the end, of lying on any other subject? (p. 189)

Lyotard may be the archetypal relativist villain of Norris's critique,[26] but his description of the 'differend' aptly, without indifference, captures the sense of Beckett's commitment to an impossible truth:

> The differend is the unstable state and instant of language wherein something which must be able to be put into phrases cannot yet be. This state includes silence, which is a negative phrase, but it also calls upon phrases which are in principle possible. This state is signaled by what one ordinarily calls a feeling: 'One cannot find the words'.[27]

The relevant silence, the phrases in principle possible, and the explicit 'one cannot find the words' are recurrent features of Beckett's exploration of self and world. But most significant is the sense that something '*must* be able to be put in phrases' but '*cannot* yet be' (even the 'yet' is apt; there is always the sense shared by Beckett's narrators that there might 'yet' be a right formula of words to say 'it'): 'I shall *have to* speak of things of which I cannot speak' (p. 294; our italics). Lyotard's 'differend', according to Bill Readings, is 'the incommensurable presence of the absolutely unspeakable in and against speech'.[28] Further, the *feeling* that remains (that one 'cannot find the words') is a feeling of injustice. We are 'wronged' by the inexpressible; it makes us suffer. Beckett reveals 'the ontological gulf that opens up between word and world, subject and object'.[29] But he does not wish us to *enjoy* the 'disarticulation of sense and reference' that has been termed 'the textual aporia'.[30] To label the gulf, however *de rigueur*, is not to close it, as the Unnamable reminds us: 'I should mention before going any further, any further on, that I say aporia without knowing what it means' (p. 293). How apt, here, is the definition of an 'aporia' as a 'pathless path' (see Chapter 8).

Readers of the *Trilogy* are placed in an impossible position. They are forced to see the urgent importance of all claims to truth, but face every form of textual scepticism. They find the establishment of the self to be absurdly frustrated by every narrative development and every new naming, but learn to yearn for the kind of identity denied them. They read a language which continually cancels and corrects itself in a rigorous attempt to speak 'truly', but which sounds its own doom in the process. They encounter a suffering vision which makes all talk of textual 'freedom', 'play' and 'rejoicing' deserve the kind of critique offered by Ricks and Norris, but also find the fullest confirmation of the unsayable self and unspeakable world so characterized by the deplored postmodern relativism of Rorty or Lyotard.

Iser's idea that Beckett's negativity 'constitutes the point at which [his] texts sink their roots into life itself' and that it 'stimulates communicative and constitutive activities within us'[31] offers an odd triumph of hope over the rootless experience of reading the *Trilogy*. Nothing, in Beckett's text, will stay still. The crisis of naming we have been discussing spreads as the *Trilogy* proceeds, and is worth following a little further.

Molloy is not the only 'chameleon in spite of himself' (p. 30). He soon meets with a 'Mrs Loy' or 'Lousse', provisionally called 'Sophie' until a typical disclaimer: 'no, I can't call her that any more, I'll try calling her Lousse, without the Mrs' (p. 35). Here we can imagine one of Beckett's favoured exhaustions of the subject: she is either Mrs Loy or Mrs Lousse or Loy or Lousse or Sophie or Sophie Loy or Mrs Sophie

Loy or Sophie Lousse . . . but then a new possibility would arise threatening the combination of possibilities with geometric progression. When Malone tells the story of 'Sapo' he drops the name with more of a sense of outraged disgust: 'no, I can't call him that any more, and I even wonder how I was able to stomach such a name till now' (p. 229). It is to be wondered how that much-needed aid, a dictionary of Beckett's characters, could ever be compiled to help the floundering reader. There is not even a guarantee as to the biological sex of some characters. Molloy describes his grotesque sexual experience with a 'Ruth' or 'Edith' ('is it true love, in the rectum?'), only to add: 'Perhaps she too was a man, yet another of them' (p. 57). Beckett's characters, as expressions of the 'not I', are inevitably protean. To name is to invent a version of the 'I' which is bound not to be the 'real' I, and which has therefore to be dropped in favour of an equally hopeless alternative. The Unnamable, with cruel irony, is the greatest shape-changer of all, becoming the anti-hero of each of his stories of who he is not:

> But let me complete my views, before I shit on them. For if I am Mahood, I am Worm too, plop. Or if I am not yet Worm, I shall be when I cease to be Mahood, plop. On now to serious matters. No, not yet. (p. 340)

There is, of course, no more serious a matter than who the Unnamable is: the 'on now to serious matters' is forgivably disingenuous. It is Iser's contention that the reader's 'communicative and constitutive activities' are stimulated as Beckett shows us 'that something is being withheld' and challenges us 'to discover what it is'.[32] But how can the reader constitute a withheld truth of identity, which, whenever constituted becomes a fiction? It is as if the Judaic prohibition against naming God, discussed by Steiner in *Real Presences*, has decidedly come down to earth in Beckett: 'Once spoken, this name passes into the contingent limitlessness of linguistic play, be it rhetorical, metaphoric or deconstructive.'[33] The reader's communicative activities are profoundly baffled: it is literally impossible to paraphrase the withheld essence of Molloy or Moran, or the Unnamable. And lest the reader should find solace in the sense of profundity (a version of Ricks's 'wisely unfathomable'), Beckett resorts to plopping! 'It's like shit', notes the Unnamable a little later, 'there we have it at last, there it is at last, the right word' (p. 368).

As such it is one of the very few 'right words' in the *Trilogy*. The sense of cancellation affecting proper names is just one aspect of the whole problem of language. If this problem seems to invite the reader to participate creatively in substituting alternative 'right' words then it does so deceptively. 'Live and invent', urges Malone, '. . . Invent. It is not the word. Neither is live. No matter' (p. 195). The reader's predicament at such moments is irresolvable. In one sense the negation is comprehensibly cynical. The 'life' that Malone is forced to live can hardly be called a life! But, further, Malone's account of his life *is* an invention, inevitably cancelled by other 'lives', other 'fictions' which claim *him* as *their* invention. The recurring process then cancels the idea of invention itself. If all life stories, in the *Trilogy*, are essentially the same story repeatedly deferred, then the concept of invention is untenable: 'And truly it little matters what I say . . . Saying is inventing. Wrong, very rightly wrong. You invent nothing . . .' (p. 32). Here the reader faces a typical and inexhaustible paradox. If the expression 'saying is inventing' is true then it is false, itself an invention (and therefore true, and then again false . . .). Hence 'wrong, very *rightly* wrong'; but wrong also in the sense that 'saying' *invents* nothing. To invent is to lie, to fictionalize, but it is not, here, to originate (Malone or Molloy tell the same old story) or to constitute (they fail to invent themselves, or the world around them considering Malone's consoling but doomed attempt to give an inventory of his possessions). If, in the instruction 'live and invent', Malone can neither live (because he invents) nor invent (because he repeats the 'nothing new') then the negation does not allow alternatives. The reader is left hopelessly agreeing that neither 'live' nor 'invent' are the right words.

Neither do the paradoxes allow a resolving or comforting sense of literary truth. Moran explicitly denies the reader 'something worth reading' on the grounds that 'it is not at this late stage of my relation that I intend to give way to literature' (p. 152). Molloy suggests that it would be better 'to obliterate texts' than to fill them (p. 13); Malone describes his discourse as 'babble' (p. 236) and the Unnamable asks 'would it not be better if I were simply to keep on saying babababa' (p. 310). The recourse to 'nonsense' language superficially recalls the sound effects of Sterne and Rabelais. Tristram's violin tuning, like Rabelais's account of the frozen words which melt and give off their sounds, seems to explore the rudiments of the connection between sound and sense:

> Ptr..r..r..ing — twing — twang — prut — trut —— 'tis a cursed bad
> fiddle [. . .]
>   Diddle diddle, diddle diddle, diddle diddle — hum — dum —
> drum. (*Tristram Shandy*, pp. 306-7)

And Beckett's 'ba' is perhaps one of those earliest expressions of the speaking child. But whereas Sterne and Rabelais offer a celebration of linguistic freedom, Beckett gives an embittered assault against the impossibility of meaningful utterance. The reader's sense of literary relevance is completely baffled as he or she is forced to acknowledge the equally arbitrary nature of inclusions and exclusions. There *are* moments where significance seems truly literary, evoking, for instance, the lyrical and the symbolic – 'it would ill become me not to mention the awful cries of the corncrakes' (p. 17) – but where the formula *for* significance mocks itself. It 'ill becomes' Molloy whatever he mentions. Lyricism is victimized by cliché and obscenity: 'A stream at long intervals bestrid – but to hell with all this fucking scenery' (p. 279). The reader, here, faces the pointlessness of all novelistic scenery and descriptive detail, referred to elsewhere in Beckett as 'filthy circumstance'. When Molloy tells us that the valet wore white trousers he adds:

> It is not often that I take cognisance so clearly of the clothes that
> people wear and I am happy to give you the benefit of it. (p. 44)

So the reader is left to wonder what exactly the 'benefits' might be. Molloy feels the need to satisfy our yearning for accurate observation, to give, for instance, the breed of a dog which enters his story: 'a Pomeranian I think, but I don't think so' (p. 12). It is Iser's contention that 'as the negated statements remain present in his mind, so the indeterminacy of the text increases, thus increasing the pressure on the reader to find out what is being withheld from him'.[34] Molloy's Pomeranian reduces such an idea to banality: what remains in our mind is the pointless (and perhaps presumptuous) Pomeranian and its equally pointless alternatives. What would be the *point*, we might well ask, of a thoroughly determined and unequivocal Pomeranian? The 'pressure on the reader', here, borders on apathy. 'Shall I describe the room', asks Molloy, 'No'; and the refusal may *seem* perverse, but it causes no need for imaginative detection in the reader. Far from being a proactive imaginative participant, the reader is threatened with inertia, having nothing to do and nothing to contribute, left in a strange state anticipated by one of Beckett's titles: imagination dead imagine. 'No, I can't record this fatuous colloquy' (p. 33) leaves the colloquy fatuous and unrecorded: we certainly do not imagine what it might have been. As readers of novels we are used to being tested and teased by the withholding of information, but always, we sense, to some end. In the *Trilogy* all means are means to no end, so all narrative refusals and retractions deny us the meaningful process of prediction and confirmation.

> Now as to telling you why I stayed a good while with Lousse, no, I cannot. That is to say I could I suppose, if I took the trouble. But why should I? (p. 51)

Far from complaining that it is the responsibility of narrative to take such a trouble, and far from speculating on the absurd relationship with Lousse, the reader rather accepts the sense of the question: why indeed? 'Here', says the Unnamable, 'all things, no, I shall not say it, being unable to' (p. 296). Far from being perverse this is reasonable. The reader does not, *cannot*, rise to the challenge of inconclusiveness, being as helpless as the narrator. The part-statement, in its inexhaustibility, cannot be an invitation to imagine what all things do indeed do. When the thread returns it immediately exhausts its 'things' in the very process of its enunciation, leaving the reader equally redundant: 'I have said that all things here recur sooner or later, no, I was going to say it' (p. 301).

The reader is asked not to judge degrees of significance, but of insignificance: 'you must choose, between the things not worth mentioning and those even less so' (p. 41). Naturally it is a distinction impossible to preserve: 'these are things that do not seem at first sight to signify anything in particular. I record them all the more willingly' (p. 62). We have, in the *Trilogy*, a combination of imperatives and impotence. The reader has to conspire with the helplessness and pointlessness of what is said, finding it a problem *in proportion to* the urgency of saying the unsayable. The predicament the narrators find themselves in becomes our own, as *our* desires for order and coherence are disabled by *their* attempts to structure chaos.

To take Malone's narrative as our example, it pre-empts and silences our will to order in its hopeless attempts to follow its own rigorous order. Malone has a simple enough plan. He wants to tell four stories – one about a man, one about a woman, one about a thing, and one about an animal – and then give his inventory. The aim offers a universality which embraces the inanimate, the animal and the human. The inventory implies the written order we impose on the world of 'things' – Malone wants to make his account: 'draw the line and make the tot'. Immediately, though, a re-ordering takes place as the story about the man, and the other about the woman, become one and the same story (as we have seen, sexual distinctions are not easily made by Beckett's narrators). The reader is reassured that all is still in order by a revised repetition of the agenda. Now, however, Malone suddenly proposes to start with an account of his present state. This might seem to satisfy our sense of order more thoroughly, promising an overarching autobiographical structure moving from Malone's present life, to his inventory (a kind of will), to his death. But the new plan is seen as a potential problem: 'I think this is a mistake. It is a weakness. But I shall indulge in it' (p. 182). Malone's misgiving is prophetic. As long as one believes one can tell stories about others there should be no difficulty, as 'stories', unlike autobiographies, are not compelled by the need to tell the truth. The inventory, though risking quasi-personal reference, offers an (as it turns out, delusory) opportunity to exhaust a description, especially as Malone's possessions are so minimal. It belongs, therefore, with Beckett's many other mathematical sequences, as another potentially finite, closed, system. Malone's original aims, then, seem to give reasonable hope of success. So long as, in other words, one does not come to the real matter, structure, order and completion are possible. But to tell about self – one's present state – is to raise the unspeakable which then threatens to invade all that is said.

Here is a crucial paradox for the reader: the wish for narrative order and purpose conflicts with the search for relevance, meaning and truth which cannot be thus ordered. Malone's 'present state' will now infect all his other plans. It will not, of course, *be* a *present* state: Malone begins by speculating on his past, on the possible stories of how he came to be in this present (deplorable) state: 'But perhaps I was stunned with a blow, on the head, in a forest perhaps' (p. 184). Now Malone's state seems to link with the first part of the *Trilogy*, both narrators there – Molloy and Moran – having had a violent encounter in a forest. Malone later finds in his 'possession' a bloodied club, which he believes to be his own, implying that he, like most of Beckett's characters, is both victim and aggressor. The pen, as we will see, is an equally blunt instrument, as Malone will try to 'write off' the characters he 'invents' by having them murdered, so that the forest adventure has not only a narrative, but an allegorical, resonance. But the temptation such references bring for the reader to restructure the minimal pattern of events in the *Trilogy* is ultimately frustrated (there are, to quote Beckett's *Watt*, 'no symbols where none intended').[35] The narrative echoes confirm that 'all things here recur sooner or later', and that Malone's narrative is another version of Molloy's and Moran's. (In Beckett the *intra*textual relationship between the *Trilogy*'s own texts tends always towards this minimalist reduction: all the texts are versions of the *same* text: see the discussion of *Possession* in Chapter 8.) Soon, with a cry to 'leave me in peace', Malone tries to silence the 'not I' by beginning his first story – the story of Saposcat. Almost immediately this story fails to fill the void: Malone interjects the first of many withering critical asides: 'what tedium' (p. 187).

The tale of Saposcat's simpleton existence in a poor, sickly family becomes another version of Malone's 'present state': 'I wonder if I am not talking yet again about myself. Shall I be incapable, to the end, of lying on any other subject?' (p. 189). Saposcat is now the victim of Malone's unnamable: a 'pattern' of stops and starts indicates that Malone's plans are falling to ruins. He cannot tell four stories, nor three – all stories are the same: he cannot lie on any *other* subject. So Saposcat's story merges with that of the grotesque farming family of the Lamberts which is finally dropped: 'The Lamberts, the Lamberts, does it matter about the Lamberts? No, not particularly. But while I am with them the other is lost' (p. 216). But the 'other' returns, Saposcat 'becomes' Macmann and seeking the 'rare dispensation of waking madness' Macmann becomes Malone. As Macmann is axed to death by Lemuel (Malone's final agent of narrative doom) on an outing from the lunatic asylum, the falling axe merges with Malone's falling pencil:

> Lemuel is in charge, he raises his hatchet on which the blood
>   will never dry, but not to hit anyone, he will not hit anyone, he will
>   not hit anyone any more, he will not touch anyone any more, either
>   with it or with it or with it or with or
>   or with it or with his hammer or with his stick or with his fist or in
>   thought in dream I mean never he will never
>   or with his pencil or with his stick or
>   or light light I mean

> never there he will never
> never anything
> there
> any more . . . (p. 289)

There has been increasing panic before this seeming resolution. 'Quick quick my possessions', writes Malone after stopping the story of Macmann in mid-sentence (a sentence which is aptly discussing 'castles' in the air). But by now Malone is terminally incapable of finishing anything: 'I shall not finish this inventory either' (p. 250). The final straw is the loss of his stick which, since he is bedridden, he cannot retrieve and which, according to his own definitions, he cannot now include in the inventory (which demands proof positive of existence and ownership). 'My notes', notes Malone, 'have a curious tendency . . . to annihilate all they purport to record' (p. 261).

For the reader, as for Malone, all things return to the unspeakable. Malone, not able to speak himself into existence, is logically not able to die. The prayer of peace at his ending is cruelly followed by the recurring voice of the 'not I', as the Unnamable takes over the legacy:

> Where now? Who now? When now? Unquestioning. I, say I. Unbelieving. Questions, hypotheses, call them that. Keep going, going on, call that going, call that on. (p. 293)

The reader, too, keeps going, keeps going on, knowing like the Unnamable that the narrative will not be 'going' anywhere, and that 'on' is not progress. To read the *Trilogy* is to reach a recurring impasse. If the story of Saposcat (for instance) could have been told, then we could, perhaps, have escaped into the world of art with its compensatory and consoling order and sense. But such a story only *matters* when it cannot be told, as then it reveals its failure to speak the unspeakable truth of the 'reality' it mimics. The reader learns that to read on is to encounter the already read: that the Unnamable's Worm or Mahood will be another Saposcat, the Unnamable another Malone telling the same story that cannot be told.

Reading the *Trilogy* is to find the act of reading stripped of its usual purposes. Our imaginative wish for an involvement in others' lives and others' worlds is revealed to have the same motive as Malone's search for a narrative escape from a 'reality' which cannot be defined. Iser is right in discussing Beckett to refer to Kermode's thesis that we need fictions to cope with intolerable and unknowable ends.[36] Reading the *Trilogy*, we are both reminded of the uncomfortable motives for our narrative needs and divested of the escapist delusions that express them. We have learned not to expect Saposcat's story to lead anywhere. We understand why Malone can barely continue telling it. We know that its 'relevance' is its repetition of 'the convention that demands you either lie or hold your peace' (pp. 87–8). This, though, is a false alternative. If Malone or any other narrator *could* 'hold their peace' then all would be well. The structure of our reading experience is the confirmation that these fictions, these stories, do not allow us to hold our peace, that our peace exists in the same ineffable silence hopelessly reached for by Malone, Molloy, Moran and the Unnamable. When we read Beckett we have exactly the Unnamable's experience: we must go on; we can't go on; we go on.

8 Postmodernist Readings: *Possession*

> . . . there is an element of superstitious dread in any self-referring, self-reflexive, inturned postmodernist mirror-game or plot-coil that recognises that it has got out of hand, that connections proliferate apparently at random, that is to say, with equal verisimilitude, apparently in response to some ferocious ordering principle, not controlled by conscious intention, which would of course, being a good postmodernist intention, *require* the aleatory or the multivalent or the 'free', but structuring, but controlling, but driving, to some – to what? – end. Coherence and closure are deep human desires that are presently unfashionable. But they are always both frightening and enchantingly desirable. (pp. 421–2; Byatt's italics)

Possession, A. S. Byatt's 1990 Booker Prize winner, is a brilliant, sophisticated, complex postmodernist novel in which 'connections' do indeed 'proliferate', but not 'apparently at random', nor 'with equal verisimilitude'. The word 'multivalent' hardly does this particular novel justice: *Possession* is not merely *inter*textual but, as will be seen later, *intra*textual and *trans*textual. Supremely self-possessed, it reads itself, and other texts, and comments on the very process of all kinds of reading – in and of life, in and of literature. It eschews 'the aleatory' but its 'ferocious ordering principle' – and anti-theme (taking 'possession' as the theme proper, for the moment) – is, ironically enough, the indeterminate basis of readerly freedom. To quote Geoffrey Hartman, to whose seminal essay on indeterminacy in *Criticism in the Wilderness* we shall have occasion to return later in this chapter, '[r]eading itself becomes the project: we read to understand what is involved in reading as a form of life, rather than to resolve what is read into glossy ideas'.[1] This is not to reduce or traduce the novel's own busy agenda; on the contrary, it is to echo and confirm it. *Possession* is not, *pace* Randall Stevenson, 'more or less a love story';[2] rather, it is a novel pre-eminently about reading and the intertextual and indeterminate nature of the process. This is a claim often made about self-conscious fictional texts, of course (and indeed about other texts), but it is true of *Possession* in a double sense. First, the reader is invited to read the writings of no fewer than 17 fictional characters in the form of passages embedded in the novel's own textual fabric. Secondly, some of these extracts are themselves readings, or 'stories of readings', the interpretative products of compulsive, fiercely competitive readers, critics and theorists. What *Possession* offers, in other words, is an extended, elaborate and fascinatingly suggestive (even exhilarating) meditation on the pleasures and problems of 'reading as a form of life'.

Possession is a cluttered novel as befits a neo-Victorian artefact: that it teems with much else besides warring readings is a tribute to Byatt's fecund creativity. But the topic which might be termed 'the freedom to read' is to the fore throughout. This emphasis is scarcely surprising given Byatt's credentials as both academic critic and novelist. Like her contemporary David Lodge, she has tended to produce novels which draw on, reflect and comment upon her literary interests. (Lodge's *Nice Work* [1988] should be mentioned here as anticipating some of the concerns of *Possession*.) One way of understanding this tendency is to see it as part of a more general postmodernist movement towards an increasingly 'self-reflexive', knowing 'critical creativity', which finds its analogue in the switch to a 'creative criticism' in the writings of Hartman and others, as they strive to abolish the dividing line between *Dichter* (writer) and *Denker* (thinker). A more mundane explanation would simply involve pointing to Byatt's own appetite for reading. Like George Eliot, like Robert Browning (like Randolph Henry Ash, indeed), she is a voracious reader, and her tastes are eclectic. In an essay on Browning for the 'My Hero' column of the *Independent*, she writes:

> All my heroes, to begin with a half-truth, wrote long sentences. Proust, Shakespeare, Henry James, Donne, Balzac, George Eliot, Coleridge, Thomas Mann. I love them because I like people who make connections, who are interested in the way the mind puts the world together. Almost my first *frisson* of pleasure from following the clue of a long sentence from end to end came from Robert Browning.[3]

This stress on the pleasure of reading recurs in a volume of essays published after *Possession*, which Byatt entitled *Passions of the Mind*. Here she comments: '[g]reedy reading made me want to write, as if this was the only adequate response to the pleasure and power of books';[4] still more categorically, she later proclaims: '[w]riting is reading and reading is writing'.[5] In the same essay, she describes herself as an 'agnostic' where literary theory is concerned, and writes in defence of 'self-conscious realism', while castigating the 'solipsism' of writers such as Sterne, late Joyce, Woolf, and Beckett.[6] She elaborates (and her remarks, as nearly always, are worth quoting at length):

> I was recently at a conference where it was argued with some force and elegance that Sterne left space for the reader to be free and creative as George Eliot, an instructive narrator, did not. And yet if we think about it, which is really the more *coercive*, the more exclusive of mental activity in the reader, Eliot's measured exposition and solidly sensible embodiment, or Sterne's legerdemain playfulness? It is Sterne who manipulates, who teases the reader and demands total admiration and assent. Eliot lays out her evidence and conclusions, speaks sometimes as 'I', sometimes to 'you' and sometimes as 'we'. But despite her passionate morality, her reasonable proceedings leave room for dissent and qualification – indeed, she demonstrates and argues the case for independent thought, in reader as in characters and writer . . . But in Sterne's world, and in Beckett's . . . the reader's freedom is framed quite differently by the novelist's strategies. You – or I – may 'play freely' or 'create' – but with the freedom of the ludo player, or the magic slate-pencils of my childhood, rather than that of the moral daydreamer who temporarily inhabits the world of *Middlemarch*, feeling out its spaces and limitations, knowing that daydreaming is indeed daydreaming and is also discovery.[7]

This insistence of Byatt's on 'the reader's freedom' is something to which we shall return later in discussing *Possession*. Byatt's preference for Eliot (and Austen and Dickens) over Sterne and Joyce and Beckett is briefly developed in another essay in the same volume, 'George Eliot: A Celebration', in which she argues that 'Eliot was, I suppose, the great English novelist of ideas'.[8] As we shall see, *Possession*, like *Middlemarch* and *Daniel Deronda*, bristles with ideas, and many of the ideas have to do with the freedom of the reader to read and to misread, to interpret and to misinterpret.

Byatt's above remarks serve to underline how Beckett's *Trilogy* and

Possession differ as postmodernist projects. Beckett's difficult fiction, as we have seen, harks back to the alienated mood of high modernism itself, and is pervaded by a sense that reality is fragmentary, incoherent, absurd, challenging and disorienting the reader in the process; Gilbert Adair's phrase, 'the last gasp of the past' seems apposite here.[9] Byatt's novel, on the other hand, though similarly self-conscious and ludic (though nowhere near as darkly ironic), represents more of a break with modernism proper, along the lines of John Fowles's *The French Lieutenant's Woman* (1969) and Umberto Eco's 'palimpsest' *The Name of the Rose* (1983). As with these earlier novels, there is a renewed interest in complex plotting, a return to the traditions and conventions of Victorian/pre-modernist 'romantic realism', and an emphasis upon the intertextual nature of all fictions.

Possession can be seen as a postmodernist novel in two further senses. First, in common with many other postmodernist novels, it is an admixture or curious blend of different kinds of discourse, involving pastiche, parody and *bricolage*. Again, various parallels suggest themselves: Lodge's *The British Museum is Falling Down* (1965) and *Small World* (1984), D. M. Thomas's *The White Hotel* (1981), Graham Swift's *Waterland* (1983), Julian Barnes's *Flaubert's Parrot* (1984), Peter Ackroyd's *Hawksmoor* (1985), and Jeanette Winterson's *Oranges are not the only fruit* (1985) spring to mind. But perhaps the most striking similarities are with those contemporary British novels which attempt to rewrite the Victorian novel, such as Lodge's *Nice Work* (published two years before *Possession*), Charles Palliser's *The Quincunx* (1989), and, of course, Fowles's *The French Lieutenant's Woman* (which antedates *Possession* by 21 years). Like Fowles's influential novel, but to an even greater extent, *Possession* borrows from and incorporates different genres and sub-genres: lyrics, narrative poems, dramatic monologues, fairy-tales, journals, letters, academic lectures, critical articles . . . '[j]ust reeling off their names is ever so comfy', to quote W. H. Auden.[10] Many of the extracts are allusions to, or quotations from, actual literary and critical sources: references abound to Donne, Shakespeare, Milton, Wordsworth, Coleridge, Keats, Hawthorne, Tennyson, Browning, Freud, Graves, Lacan, and many others, in the crowded pages of this novel. But most of the passages, such as the poems, letters and diary entries of the novel's Victorian protagonists, 'originate' from Byatt herself, who proves to be an accomplished, skilful stylist in her imitations of Christina Rossetti and (especially) Robert Browning, among others.

The dense, fussy detail of this aspect of *Possession* might be adduced in support of Omar Calabrese's argument that 'neo-Baroque' is a preferable term to 'postmodern'.[11] (Alternatively, the novel as a 'treasure-house of detail' – to quote Henry James's famous description of *Middlemarch* – could be seen as Byatt's ultimate homage to Victorian aesthetics.) Two effects follow from the patch-work construction of *Possession*, both paradoxical. In the first place, the boundaries between discourse-types are blurred (though not obliterated), while their distinctive features are highlighted. In the second place, the novel comes across as containing different voices, as being 'dialogic' or 'polyphonic' in form (to use Bakhtinian terms); yet these disparate (and often ambiguous) voices resonate within a single overarching narrative framework with a double plot, wherein its twentieth-century plot parallels and comments upon its nine-teenth-century plot and vice versa. (The analogue this time is with Harold Pinter's ingenious screenplay version of *The French Lieutenant's Woman*.) To read *Possession*, as we shall see, is to read conscious of plurality, self-deconstruction and, ultimately, indeterminacy.

Secondly, *Possession* can be understood as a postmodernist novel from the point of view of its self-conscious reappraisal of an earlier period of history, or as a form of 'historiographic metafiction'. The relevant concept of postmodernism here is Umberto Eco's. He sees postmodernism as defined by its intertextuality, knowingness, and ironic revisiting of the past. In his essay, 'Postmodernism, Irony, the Enjoyable', he writes:

> I think of the postmodern attitude as that of a man who loves a very cultivated woman and knows he cannot say to her, 'I love you madly', because he knows that she knows (and that she knows that he knows) that these words have already been written by Barbara Cartland. Still, there is a solution. He can say, 'As Barbara Cartland would put it, I love you madly.' At this point, having avoided false innocence, having said clearly that it is no longer possible to speak innocently, he will nevertheless have said what he wanted to say to the woman: that he loves her, but he loves her in an age of lost innocence. If the woman goes along with this, she will have received a declaration of love all the same. Neither of the two speakers will feel innocent, both will have accepted the challenge of the past, of the already said, which cannot be eliminated; both will consciously and with pleasure play

the game of irony . . . But both will have succeeded, once again, in speaking of love.[12]

Eco's witty characterization of postmodernism, with its echoes of Barthes and the quotations within quotations, has a vibrant, moving equivalent in Chapter 28 of *Possession*, where Roland and Maud, the two postmodernist lovers, admit their love for one another, not only in quotation marks, but in between quotations from Milton, Tennyson and (finally) Lennon and McCartney (pp. 505–7). The pleasure that Eco's two lovers experience, and the pleasure that Byatt's two lovers knowingly feel, are as nothing to the pleasure of the reader of Eco, or the reader of Byatt.

Eco, in the same essay, asks whether there could 'be a [postmodernist] novel that was not escapist and, nevertheless, still enjoyable?'[13] *Possession*, like Eco's own *The Name of the Rose*, proves that postmodernist fiction can be pleasurable to read. Part of the pleasure of reading *Possession* derives from the reader's consciousness of its nature and status as 'historiographic metafiction'. Here, the work of Linda Hutcheon is apposite. In her essay, 'Telling Stories: Fiction and History', she poses a similar question to Eco's. She wonders 'how we can come to know the past today'.[14] For Hutcheon, postmodernist 'historical novels' do not offer escapist, nostalgic versions of the past, but neither do they merely ironize the past (as Eco suggests); instead, she argues, they reveal the past as ideologically and discursively constructed, by problematizing simplistic notions of narrative representation through their self-conscious, metafictional processes. In Hutcheon's quasi-new historicist view, then, a close study of postmodernist historiographical metafictions like *Possession* (which clearly has much to say about histories in general, and about Victorian history in particular) would show that nothing is 'natural' or given, and that everything is mediated, constructed, interpreted. This has partly to do with the 'radically indeterminate and unstable nature' of (inter)textuality itself:[15] all we have are readings of other readings, interpretations of other interpretations. But this is also related to Fredric Jameson's subversive recognition that narrative is not only the central function of the human mind, but also a 'socially symbolic act': there is, strictly speaking, no such thing as a non-historical, non-political telling of a story.[16] As we shall see, the 'politics of story' and the problems of historiography are among the main subjects explored by Byatt in her postmodernist novel.

Among the main subjects. For *Possession* (subtitled *A Romance*) is generously stocked with subjects, ideas, and motifs, as well as replete with readers and readings. The *OED* gives 14 senses of 'possession', and Byatt's novel deals with many of them, but along the way it takes in most aspects of Victorian society and culture (including geology, palaeontology, science, philosophy, religion, theology, history, poetry, mesmerism . . .) and not a few aspects of life in 1980s Britain – both within the groves of academe and without. It offers the reader two love stories (one Victorian, one postmodern), the two not-quite-symmetrical plots artfully patterned and cunningly interwoven to bring out their parallels and differences. The novel captures well the excitement and thrills of bona fide scholarly research and literary criticism, while satirizing ruthlessly the wilder excesses of certain kinds of theorists and ideologues, and the moral bankruptcy of the modern biography industry. It is a detective story of sorts, but without a murder (unless suicide can be thus classified), littered with secrets, melodramatic revelations, genuine clues and false leads. Its clever plotting is but one aspect of its careful planning: motifs which run throughout the novel, such as the forbidden or secret garden (and variants on it) contribute effectively and subtly to the novel's overall design. The novel's dramatis personae – its 'men and women', one might say – make up an impressively varied list, with the principal Victorian characters (Randolph Henry Ash, Christabel LaMotte, Ellen Ash and Blanche Glover) given intriguing twentieth-century parallels (respectively: Roland Michell, Maud Bailey, Val and Leonora Stern). But whereas the Victorian plot contains a relatively simple nexus of relationships involving the four main characters, the 1980s plot is (unsurprisingly) more complex in this respect, for there are further relationships involving Euan MacIntyre (with Val), and Fergus Wolff (with Maud). In addition, the 1980s plot is more richly served with (more than minor) characters such as Mortimer Cropper, Beatrice Nest and James Blackadder. The above list of names signals clearly enough the novel's literary interests, but still more indicative of its postmodern literariness are the many examples of writings by seven of the Victorian personae (Ash, Christabel, Ellen, Blanche, Sabine de Kercoz, Mrs Lees and Crabb Robinson) and the fewer, and generally slighter, excerpts by ten of the twentieth-century figures (Roland, Maud, Leonora, Fergus, Cropper, Blackadder, Ariane Le Minier, Beatrice, Lady Joan Bailey and Veronica Honiton). The extracts from Ash and Christabel (mostly poems and letters) make up the bulk of the interpolated material, and the success of *Possession* depends to a large extent on how the reader reads and responds to this material, and (equally important) how the reader processes and interprets the readings of the Ash/Christabel texts by Maud, Roland, Leonora, Fergus, Cropper and others. Thus, as pointed out earlier, the novel is not merely *inter*textual in the conventional sense (and its allusions to earlier literature will be touched on below), but *intra*textual (the novel is concerned with the network of relationships between its own constituent texts), and *trans*textual (the novel does not merely relate to other texts, it surveys and comments upon textuality and intertextuality in general).

This aspect of reading *Possession* deserves further elaboration here. So much in this novel – both for its own fictional readers and for the actual reader of the novel – depends on the ability to identify quotations, references, allusions (both 'marked' and 'unmarked'),[17] and on the facility for making connections within the text and between the text and other texts. '[T]he attempt to connect': the phrase is Hawthorne's, and is to be found in the novel's first epigraph.[18] All reading involves this 'attempt to connect', but connections abound to an extraordinary extent in *Possession*. Here is Roland speaking to Maud:

> 'I mean of course everything connects and connects – all the time – and I suppose one studies – I study – literature because all these connections seem both endlessly exciting and then in some sense dangerously powerful – as though we held a clue to the true nature of things?' (p. 253)

To paraphrase Barthes, to read any text is to read 'the already written elsewhere'. To read *Possession* is to read not merely the words (of) 'Roland' and 'Maud', but at the same time to read the words of Browning (author of ' "Childe Roland to the Dark Tower Came" ', published in *Men and Women* in 1855) and Tennyson (author of *Maud*, also published in 1855). This structuralist emphasis occurs earlier in the novel when the narrator comments on how

> it may seem odd to begin a description of Roland Michell with an excursus into the complicated relations of Blackadder, Cropper and Ash, but it was in these terms that Roland most frequently thought of himself. (p. 10)

This is Roland as 'latecomer' (p. 10), a word suggestive of the neo-Freudian psychoanalytic theories of the Harold Bloom of *The Anxiety of Influence: A Theory of Poetry* (1973) and *A Map of Misreading* (1975) – the latter book having a chapter on Browning's '"Childe Roland to the Dark Tower Came"'. We read of Roland busy forging connections as he reads Ash (also busy making connections), and make connections of our own – and not merely between Roland and Ash. The 'connections proliferate' (p. 421). In another passage, detailing Roland's and Maud's excursion (following their careful map reading) to 'Boggle Hole' in North Yorkshire, the narrator, sounding conspicuously like Fowles's narrator depicting the undercliff in *The French Lieutenant's Woman*, describes the scene thus:

> The cliffs themselves are grey and flaking. Roland and Maud noticed that the flat stones at their bases were threaded and etched with fossil plumes and tubes . . . A young man with a hammer and a sack was . . . busy chipping away at the rock-face, from which coiled and rimmed circular forms protruded everywhere. (pp. 268–9)

The cliffs with their rock strata and their fossils can be read as a metaphor for the layered, intertextual (*supra*textual? palimpsestic?) novel itself, each rift richly loaded with ore. The beach, too, with its 'proliferation' of highly coloured stones, which Maud and Roland pick up and enthuse over, before 'letting [them] fall back into the mass-pattern, or random distribution' (p. 269), is powerfully evocative, though (to adapt the metaphor slightly) reading *Possession* entails deeper mining than the 'open-cast' variety, as 'some that have deeper digged' may be better able to testify.

That this is so can be confirmed by considering some of the hundreds of allusions in the novel. Some allusions present the reader with specific interpretative difficulties; some appear relatively straightforward. An instance which falls into the latter category might be the quotation from Wordsworth's 'Preface' to *Lyrical Ballads* in Chapter 15: we are told of Ash that he looked as 'one who "had thought long and deeply"' (p. 274). The quotation is signalled as such, though the source is not mentioned; it is accurate, apart from the (presumably deliberate) omission of 'also' after 'had'; and it makes ready sense in context – Ash, after all, is a (post-)Romantic poet of sorts. But we know, from numerous other indications, that Ash is principally modelled on Robert Browning, and on the same page we are told that Ash 'looked out at the world steadily enough, fearless but with something held in reserve', and that he 'had a decided way of taking in the world'. This time no quotation is signalled. Is it a reference to Browning's (self-?)portrait of a poet in 'How It Strikes a Contemporary' (another poem from the *Men and Women* collection): '[s]centing the world, looking it full in face'?[19] There are enough unmarked quotations and near-quotations from Browning in *Possession* to make the supposition not unlikely. (A nice example in connection with Maud occurs early on: coming out of the shower, she 'loosed from her shower-cap *all her yellow hair*' [p. 57; our emphasis] – like, and yet unlike, Browning's Porphyria.) Further evidence in support of the above reading might be put together from later in the chapter, where we are told that Ash, when younger, 'had been much struck by the story of Wordsworth and his solitary Highland girl' but that

> [h]e himself, he had discovered, was different. He was a poet greedy for information, for facts, for details. Nothing was too trivial to interest him; nothing was inconsiderable . . . (p. 277)

This is very like the poet who

> took such cognizance of men and things,
> If any beat a horse, you felt he saw;
> If any cursed a woman, he took note . . .[20]

Examples such as this are very common in *Possession*. One further case must suffice here. Chapter 3 ends with Fergus's comment on Maud to Roland (who has yet to meet her): '"She thicks men's blood with cold," said Fergus with a lot of undecodable feeling' (p. 34). The line (with 'She' for 'Who' and 'men's' for 'man's') comes from Coleridge's main contribution to *Lyrical Ballads*, 'The Rime of the Ancient Mariner' (line 194); the comment refers to the female figure, Life-in-Death. An easy enough quotation for a reader well-versed in nineteenth-century poetry to pick up: but how is it to be interpreted in its context? Does it tell the reader more about Maud or more about Fergus? It is something of a truism to observe that there are no easy answers to questions like this, but it is true enough, none the less. Fergus's statement is only decodable up to a point. It can be read and interpreted only so far. To the question, 'how much significance should a reader attach to the quotation from Coleridge in this context?', there can be no satisfactory answer. At the point of 'intertext' misreadings are bound to occur: sooner or later an *aporia* (or impasse) will be reached, holding the reader back from arriving at a determinate, unambiguous meaning. Of course, it could be urged that what is true of specifically intertextual moments, is true of reading more generally. Given that all communication is mediated, and therefore subject to interpretation, it might be argued that it makes more sense to speak not in terms of possible readings, but in terms of the inevitability of misreadings, only distinguishing between the various kinds and degrees of misreading. As Vincent B. Leitch writes,

> reading is transmutation, not transportation, of truth . . . There can never be 'correct' or 'objective' readings, only less or more energetic, interesting, careful, or pleasurable misreadings . . .[21]

Not that this realization prevents readers from wanting to know, as *Possession* amply demonstrates. For one of the subjects the novel critically explores in great detail is the reader's will to knowledge and, particularly, the reader's desire for narrative closure. As Ash admits in a letter to Christabel, 'I cannot bear not to know the end of a tale' (p. 176). Related to his narrative inquisitiveness, it seems, is his compulsion to know the exact outcome of his sexual relationship with Christabel. The source this time is another, much later, letter to her:

> There is something I *must know* and you know what that is. I say 'I must know' and sound peremptory. But I am in your hands and must beg you to tell me. What became of my child? Did he live? How can I ask, not knowing? How can I not ask, not knowing? (p. 456; Ash's italics)

(Compare Elizabeth Bennet's not being able to know about Darcy and Wickham in *Pride and Prejudice*, which we discussed in Chapter 3.) The letters and the accompanying narrative at this stage of the novel, because so personal, are almost unbearably moving. Ash sums up his thoughts in more general terms in the poem which stands as epigraph to Chapter 27:

> We are driven
> By endings as by hunger. We *must know*
> How it comes out, the shape o' the whole . . .
>   We feel our way
> Along the links and we cannot let go
> Of this bright chain of curiosity
> Which is become our fetter.   (p. 476; Byatt's italics)

In the novel's terms the urge or need to know is fundamental and not a trait of Ash alone. Ash's American biographer, Mortimer Cropper, characteristically asserts his imperious intention to discover what Ash had been desperate to know, as he makes plain to his English academic rival, James Blackadder, sounding rather like Samuel Richardson's Mr B. in *Pamela* (1740):

> 'I intend to have those letters if I can,' he said. 'And I intend to find out the rest.'
> 'The rest?'
> 'What became of their child. What they concealed from us. *I intend to know*.' (p. 428; Byatt's italics)

Later, Cropper is again tantalized by 'the thought of *perhaps never knowing*' (p. 489; Byatt's italics). The italicization in all four of the extracts just quoted is revealing: the determination to *know* runs deeply, and is accompanied by powerful emotional undercurrents. Only Ellen Ash (pp. 455, 460), and her latter-day champion and editor, Beatrice Nest (p. 498), seem able and willing to resist reading the not-known, and in both cases it is because the knowledge in question is perceived by them to be morally dubious and/or emotionally threatening. Roland, for his part, justifies his 'dispossession' or 'theft' of the original manuscript letters by confessing, 'I felt possessed. I had to know' (p. 486). Maud makes a similar admission to Roland, as she too becomes caught up in the literary detective case:

> 'I want to – to – follow the – path. I feel taken over by this. I want to *know* what happened, and I want it to be me that finds out. I thought you were mad, when you came to Lincoln with your piece of stolen letter. Now I feel the same. It isn't professional greed. It's something more primitive.' (p. 238; Byatt's italics)

Roland's diagnosis is '[n]arrative curiosity', but Maud asserts that the explanation is more complicated than that. (We shall return to the 'something more primitive' shortly.) What is significant about Maud's speech is her feeling of the way – 'I want to – to – follow the – path'; she seeks a path through words (as she and Roland literally follow a path in Yorkshire) to define the meaning of what has been happening. But without success. She only manages to say what it is not ('professional greed') and, very vaguely, what it might be ('something more primitive'). What we have here, in fine, is a moment of *aporia* – a word which originally meant 'a pathless path'.

There is an irony in all this, of course. Roland wants to know, Maud wants to know – only once (p. 421) does she claim she positively does not want to know – yet, as late 1980s literary critics, they 'are so knowing', as Maud concedes (p. 253). On another occasion she elaborates to Roland:

> 'We are very knowing. We know all sorts of other things, too – about how there isn't a unitary ego – how we're made up of conflicting, interacting systems of things – and I suppose we *believe* that? We know we are driven by desire, but we can't see it as they did, can we?' (p. 267; Byatt's italics)

(The 'they' here refers to Ash and Christabel.) As good postmodernist readers Roland and Maud are 'very knowing', and they know that they are very knowing. They are also aware of the 'tiresome and bewitching endlessness of the quest for knowledge' (p. 4).[22] But that does not prevent them from wanting to know in some more 'primitive' sense.

What is this more 'primitive' sense? And what has all of this to do with postmodernist reading(s)? Here is Roland, with Maud, about to discover the letters of Ash and Christabel:

> He felt unable to urge the unbuckling of the trunk. He felt as though he was prying, and as though he was being uselessly urged on by some violent emotion of curiosity – not greed, curiosity, more fundamental even than sex, the desire for knowledge. (p. 82)

And here is Ash, meditating on the same theme in a letter to Christabel:

> [God] made us *curious*, did he not? – he made us questioning – and the Scribe of Genesis did well to locate the source of all our misery in

that greed for knowledge which has also been our greatest spur – in some sense – to good. To good *and* evil. We have more of both those, I must believe, than our primitive parents. (pp. 164–5; Byatt's italics)

The wish to know, for both Ash and Roland, is fundamental, it would seem, to what it is to be human. It is this which generates and impels reading and readings. And in Roland's view, while it is analogous with the sexual urge, it really runs even deeper – a difficult concept for contemporary readers to accept, perhaps, since (in Maud's words) 'we question everything except the centrality of sexuality' (p. 222) – a point unwittingly borne out by the extract from Leonora Stern's book, *Motif and Matrix in the Poems of LaMotte* (pp. 243–6). Cropper's violating of Ash's grave, out of a desperation to know, makes a further point:

> He poised his sharp spade above the earth and struck and struck with a terrible glee, slicing, penetrating the sloppy and the resistant . . . He struck, he struck, he struck. 'Steady on,' said Hildebrand, and 'Keep going,' hissed Cropper, pulling with his bare hands at a long snake of the yew's root system, getting out his heavy knife to cut it.
> 'It is here. I know it is here.' (p. 493)

A scene which takes us back to the epigraph to Chapter 1, and back still further to the forbidden tree of knowledge of good and evil in Genesis. Later, in the Rowan Tree Inn, it is again Cropper who opens the recovered package, 'insert[ing] the knife point under the join', then 'slipp[ing] his knife under the seal' (p. 498). The 'something more primitive' has to do with power: we read for pleasure, we read to know, but ultimately we read for the power the possession of knowledge gives us over others. Reading, according to this thesis, is a political act, just as narrative, in Jameson's view, is politically significant.

Of course, to put it thus is to oversimplify almost to the point of absurdity. *Possession* does indeed bring out startlingly the political dimensions of reading and interpretation, as quite a few other postmodernist novels do. But Byatt's sense of the nature of reading is more complex than the above account suggests. This becomes apparent on considering the detailed descriptions given of various readers actually reading. Fergus Wolff's reading of Christabel LaMotte's *The Fairy Melusina* is instructive (p. 33). His commentary on the tale ('the symbolism is obvious') confirms Maud's dictum that 'we question everything except the centrality of sexuality'. The tale's 'key' moment of revelation is when Raimondin, Melusina's husband, spies on her when expressly forbidden so to do:

> 'And in the end, of course, he looked through the keyhole – or made one in her steel door with his sword-point according to one version – and there she was in a great marble bath disporting herself. And from the waist down she was a fish or a serpent, Rabelais says an "andouille", a kind of huge sausage . . .' (p. 33)

Fergus, predictably, implies that the symbolism is basically sexual. But this conventional reading underplays the obvious: it is Raimondin's nosiness, his powerful wish to know which prompts him to look through the keyhole; the 'genesis' of his troubles, as he admits, is the 'horrible snake'. (Fergus refers to Rabelais. *We* might be reminded of Sterne's 'own' borrowing – his *Ec*[*h*]*o!* – of Rabelais in the shape of the Abbess of Andoüillets.) And, appropriately, Raimondin's act of piercing the door 'with his sword-point' neatly prefigures Cropper's investigation (with 'his knife point') of the secret of Ash and Christabel in the scene already examined. This makes Fergus's summing-up truer than he is in a position to realize: 'It's an odd affair – tragedy and romance and symbolism rampant all over it, a kind of dream-world full of strange beasts and hidden meanings . . .' (p. 33). Which is one way of describing *Possession* itself. Also of interest in this connection are the reported thoughts and conversations of the 'theoretically knowing' (p. 423) Roland and Maud on theories of narration and reading, as when they first read the Ash/Christabel correspondence, for example (pp. 129–31), and after their reading of Sabine de Kercoz's journal (pp. 421–5). But most telling is their discussion after reading Ellen's journal and Blanche's letters (pp. 236–8). Reading is seen here by them to be, first, unavoidably intertextual and, secondly, driven by the 'deep human desire' (p. 422) for narrative disclosure. 'Literary critics make natural detectives', Maud points out to Roland (p. 237), before proceeding to adumbrate 'the theory that the classic detective story arose with the classic adultery novel – everyone wanted to know who was the Father, what was the origin, what is the secret' (p. 238). Back to 'the will to power' inhering in 'the will to knowledge' (or 'meaning')? A 'phallogocentric' quest, by readers caught in the web of textuality, for a 'transcendental signified'?

The questions are raised, but not conclusively answered. And this is characteristic of *Possession*, and is partly what makes it so fascinating a postmodernist novel. This brings us back to the question of indeterminacy, and the relevance of Hartman's essay, 'Criticism, Indeterminacy, Irony', in *Criticism in the Wilderness*. In this important essay, Hartman argues that

> indeterminacy, though not an end to be pursued but something disclosed by liberal and thoughtful reading, is . . . like a traffic sign warning of an impasse. It suggests (1) that where there is a conflict of interpretations or codes, that conflict can be rehearsed or reordered but not always resolved, and (2) that even where there is no such conflict we have no certainty of controlling implications that may not be apparent or articulable at any one point in time.[23]

Later in the essay, he is at pains to stress that indeterminacy (which he defines as 'thoughtfulness itself', comparing it with Keats's 'negative capability')[24] 'does not doubt meaning'; rather, it takes adequately into account 'the resistance of art to the meanings it provokes'.[25] To read, and to write, is to experience 'the undoing of a previous understanding', Hartman claims. He continues:

> Indeterminacy, as a concept, resists formally the complicity with closure implied by the wish to be understood or the communication-compulsion associated with it . . . Indeterminacy functions as a bar separating understanding and truth. Understanding is not disabled but is forced back on the conditions of its truth: for example, the legitimacy of its dependence on texts.[26]

It is unfortunate, but not (Hartman thinks) surprising, that 'some are scared witless by a mode of thinking that seems to offer no decidability, no resolution'.[27] In the light of these remarks, the temptation at this stage might be to point the moral for those readers in *Possession* who express their need for closure, narrative certainty, and dogmatic interpretations so emphatically – from the neo-Fascist determination of Mortimer Cropper to the quieter fervour of Ash, Roland and Maud. But it would clearly be missing the point were the readers of this novel to overlook their own similar desires. What the reader is presented with in the closure of *Possession* we shall shortly examine. But it is worth pausing here to consider, in Hartman's memorable phrase, 'the resistance of art to the meanings it provokes'.

For *Possession* is comfortably indeterminate on numerous issues and occasions throughout. It has at least its fair share of silences and gaps – some of which the characters themselves are aware of (for example, p. 215), some of which they seem blithely unconscious of (amusingly, pp. 477–8). Then there are the prose dramatic monologues – minor masterpieces of ironic, unwitting self-revelation: Val's (pp. 19–20) is disturbing, while Leonora's performance (p. 403) is more comical; but the reader has work to do in interpreting both. The narrator's own urbane, nuanced discourse presents many interpretative difficulties – some of which defy resolution altogether. When we are told that Roland 'hated himself for these demeaning fantasies, and was reasonably afraid that [Val] might suspect he nourished them' (p. 14), what is the force of 'reasonably'? 'Reasonably' from whose point of view? On another occasion the reader is told that 'Maud was not experienced enough' to recognize the typical ploys of ex-lovers like Fergus (p. 140); the reader might be forgiven for wondering what constitutes being 'experienced enough'. Is the narrator or Blackadder the immediate source of the question, 'Why must the English now always apologise?' (p. 401). And when we read, 'The truth was, [Cropper] had come to love the bright transparencies of the things he had acquired, almost as much as the things themselves' (p. 386), whose 'truth' is being referred to here?

Other interpretative cruxes vary in difficulty: it is not hard to read the end of Chapter 6 as presenting Cropper in the guise of someone who habitually masturbates over pornographic photographs (p. 111). Nor is it difficult to read between the lines in Chapter 25, and so deduce that Randolph and Ellen Ash's marriage was not consummated, though the explanation given is not without ambiguity (see pp. 458–9). Re-reading Ellen's crossing-out in her journal, 'Despite all', before the sentence, 'We have been so happy in our life' (p. 229), in the light of what we later learn, it is not unreasonable to surmise from this 'present absence' that she was about to refer to the (complete) absence of a physical sexual relationship between her and Randolph; yet this is still guesswork at that point. But what about the account given of Randolph's own thoughts and feelings after sexual intercourse with Christabel, when he finds 'blood on his thighs'? The passage reads:

> He had thought, the ultimate things, she did *not* know, and here was ancient proof. He stood, sponge in hand, and puzzled over her. Such

delicate skills, such informed desire, and yet a virgin. There were possibilities, of which the most obvious was to him slightly repugnant, and then, when he thought about it with determination, interesting, too. He could never ask. To show speculation, or even curiosity, would be to lose her. Then and there. He knew that, without thinking. It was like Melusina's prohibition, and no narrative bound him, unlike the unfortunate Raimondin, to exhibit indiscreet curiosity. He liked to know everything he could – even this – but he knew better than to be curious, he told himself, about things he could not hope to know. (pp. 284–5; Byatt's italics)

The passage is rich indeed in its suggestiveness (every word counts), but it is the reference to the 'possibilities' (plural) which is intriguing, assuming that the words 'the most obvious' refer to a possible physical relationship with another woman, presumably Blanche Glover. Is Ash to be understood as mulling over how Christabel appears to be so sexually experienced, by weighing up the relative explanatory powers of (i) a previous lesbian relationship; (ii) a non-penetrative heterosexual relationship; (iii) some auto-erotic experience; (iv) an 'instinctive' imagination in this respect? To list some of the possibilities in this way is patently ridiculous: but doing so underlines one interpretative quandary, at least. It is worth noting that Ash finds the lesbian possibility only '*slightly* repugnant' momentarily; and as soon as he begins to think about it 'with determination', he finds it 'interesting'! Ash is, in Hartmanian terms, a model reader – determinedly staying with the indeterminacy (now that Christabel is, in one sense, 'known' to him), rather than pursuing the (futile?) quest to its (bitter?) end.

Finally, there is the most interesting *mis*reading of all, of course, which Beatrice and Leonora prompt, but with which other twentieth-century characters collude (including Maud, Roland, Blackadder, Cropper); and it leaves them with the utterly mistaken impression that Ash never learned that he had a daughter by Christabel – an impression of which none of them is ever disabused (p. 504). The wish to know has led each of them to misread the vital, but ambiguous, evidence: as literary detectives they are all 'failures' (as their diverse names suggest) – not remotely in the Inspector Morse class (let alone the Sherlock Holmes class). And of the Victorian cast, only Ash, as we learn from the poignant, joyful 'Postscript', 'knows that he knows' he has a daughter, and has met her, for May never passes on the message to her 'aunt' Christabel, and likewise Ellen must be supposed not to know that her husband knows. The novel's readers are the privileged spectators of all of these events, and for us the narrative may be said to reach a satisfactory conclusion both cognitively (the main loose ends are tied up neatly and, within the conventions of romance, reasonably convincingly) and emotionally. The ending is by no means a conventionally 'closed' one, however, as far as the knowledge and the destinies of the protagonists (especially the 1980s figures) are concerned: many questions are left unanswered, many possibilities are left open. In this respect, the ending of *Possession* is decidedly indeterminate.

Reviewing *Possession* in the *Sunday Times*, one critic remarked upon how the novel is 'eloquent about the intense pleasures of reading. And, with sumptuous artistry, it provides a feast of them.'[28] Reading *Possession* is indeed an intensely pleasurable experience: it is erudite (but wears its scholarship lightly); it is intelligent (but never merely clever); it is deeply moving (though never slipping into sentimentality); and it is often (but not too often) amusing and witty as well. It is, one might say, a *haunting* novel (to draw on one of the meanings of 'possession' given in the *OED*). If its presiding poetic genius is Robert Browning, the Victorian novelist Byatt comes closest to emulating is undoubtedly George Eliot. *Possession* presents a world as Eliot might have seen it, not so much through 'the spectacles of books', as through observant postmodernist eyes. Had Byatt wanted a third epigraph for the novel, to go with those from Hawthorne and Browning, she might have done worse than to have selected a moment from Lodge's *Small World* (subtitled *An* Academic *Romance*). It is taken from Morris Zapp's lecture on textuality and striptease:

> 'To read is to surrender oneself to an endless displacement of curiosity and desire from one sentence to another, from one action to another, from one level of the text to another. The text unveils itself before us, but never allows itself to be possessed; and instead of striving to possess it we should take pleasure in its teasing.'[29]

There is a precise postmodernist pleasure to be experienced from a reading of Byatt's endlessly intertextual, writerly novel. It teases, it leads on, it baffles, it frustrates – it acknowledges and confirms, in other words, the ultimately indeterminate nature of the human quest for meaning in theory, in the context of a sane, pragmatic analysis of why, and how, readers read (for pleasure, for knowledge, for power) in practice. 'Each work of art, and each work of reading, is potentially a demonstration of freedom', writes Geoffrey Hartman.[30] *Possession*, in presenting the reader with so many different kinds and examples of reading and misreading, draws attention to reading's infinite possibilities. It shows up restrictive, monologic, authoritarian, closed, coercive readings for what they are, and promotes an ideal that is the product of thoughtfulness – liberal, dialogic, democratic, open, pluralistic; in short, it exposes *possessiveness*, and encourages *freedom* – the freedom to criticize, the freedom to interpret. It shows good reading to be writing, and good writing to be reading: and 'no doubt that is what reading is: rewriting the text of the work within the text of our lives', as Roland Barthes pointed out; and, as Robert Scholes adds, not only must we strive to live up to that ideal, we must also 'keep on rewriting our lives in the light of those texts'.[31] *Possession* is a text fully worth thinking feelingly of in those terms. Malcolm Bradbury's comment on the novel is germane here:

> Amongst its other qualities, [*Possession*] is a criticism of the drab impersonality of a good deal of modern literary thought and theory, and a strong inward argument for the recovery of the creative principle – the fire of art and the imagination that should, indeed, restore romance to the disconnected, over-textualized world of the late-modern novel.[32]

Bradbury's comment returns us to Rorty's expression of his impatience with dreary theorized readings of Conrad's *Heart of Darkness*, quoted at the beginning of Chapter 1. Much of what passes for 'modern literary thought' (no Ricksian oxymoron intended) does indeed exhibit a 'drab impersonality', and Byatt's majestic novel provides an effective antidote for that condition. The novel's argument, as Bradbury rightly points out, *is* 'inward', and all the stronger for being so. But the last words on the subject of reading, for now, must come from the novel itself (the italics, again, are Byatt's):

> There are readings – of the same text – that are dutiful, readings that map and dissect, readings that hear a rustling of unheard sounds, that count grey little pronouns for pleasure or instruction and for a time do not hear golden or apples. There are personal readings, that snatch for personal meanings, I am full of love, or disgust, or fear, I

scan for love, or disgust, or fear. There are – believe it – impersonal readings – where the mind's eye sees the lines move onwards and the mind's ear hears them sing and sing.

Now and then there are readings which make the hairs on the neck, the non-existent pelt, stand on end and tremble, when every word burns and shines hard and clear and infinite and exact, like stones of fire, like points of stars in the dark – readings when the knowledge that we *shall know* the writing differently or better or satisfactorily, runs ahead of any capacity to say what we know, or how. In these readings, a sense that the text has appeared to be wholly new, never before seen, is followed, almost immediately, by the sense that it was *always there*, that we the readers, knew it was always there, and have *always known* it was as it was, though we have now for the first time recognised, become fully cognisant of, our knowledge. (pp. 471–2)

Conclusion

Criticism interested in the nature of reading and the role of the reader has nearly always had to return to questions about the source of meaning. The extent to which meaning is in the words on the page or the result of the reader's response has consequently been an issue of recurrent concern in this book. Taken together, the preceding chapters have suggested a range of possible variations on the combination of reader and text, and one of the aims in bringing together so many remarks from commentators of markedly different literary-critical backgrounds is to show the degrees of possible divergence. We can, in a sense, create the full spectrum of response: at one extreme we have someone like Steiner for whom response is a secondary activity, and critical response sometimes simply a parasitical one; next, perhaps, we have Christopher Ricks, who exemplifies in his practice the creativity of literary criticism, but who demands that we pay better attention to the text, since it is our primary responsibility to interpret the text sensitively and sympathetically; further up (or down) the line we have Wolfgang Iser, whose theory depends on the principle of an interaction between the text and the reader in the production of meaning; close to him would be Umberto Eco, who acknowledges the creativity of the reader, but believes that we must have some respect for, and some sense of, what the author intended and what the words mean; then we have Richard Rorty who makes a virtue of the impossibility of distinguishing between 'making' and 'finding' and pragmatically finds he can dispense with the idea of a meaning external to response; and, finally, close to *him*, but at the furthest remove from the position of Steiner, we have Stanley Fish, who argues that everything is the subject of a mediating response which makes it what it is, within a system which allows for such responses.

It is worth pausing for a moment here, because in practice the two ends of our progression meet at the text. Here, confirming the apparent extreme (where response creates the text, and where texts do not 'contain' meaning) is Fish at his most enjoyably polemical:

> The objectivity of the text is an illusion and, moreover, a dangerous illusion, because it is so physically convincing. The illusion is one of self-sufficiency and completeness. A line of print or a page is so obviously *there* – it can be handled, photographed, or put away – that it seems to be the sole repository of whatever value and meaning we associate with it. (I wish the pronoun could be avoided, but in a way *it* makes my point.) This is of course the unspoken assumption behind the word 'content.' The line or page or book *contains* – everything.[1]

But, despite what seems here to be an extreme anti-textualist position, this typical passage continues to constitute the text *as* an object – with print, lines and pages. Fish's parenthesis, with its regret that we have to talk as if 'it' – the text – existed independently of us, exactly recalls the problems Beckett's characters have with their pronouns. Robert Holub, then, is right to suppose that '[Fish] would presumably admit the existence of words or marks on a page or at least something that is there prior to interpretation'.[2]

We have already criticized, in Chapter 1, Holub's reading of Fish, but we can certainly see, here, the problematical source of his claim that Fish's practice depends 'on following closely the words printed on the page before him'.[3] Once we accept the existence of something to respond *to*, it is almost impossible to avoid talking *as if* the text created the response. This is a problem we have encountered before in this book, but it serves to remind us that pragmatists, like traditionalists, point to the text to validate their readings.

The difference between our critics, then, is not so much one of practice as of principle. Where Christopher Ricks would commend the text for creating such rich reading experiences, Fish would commend the mediating power of response for creating such rich texts; but both will support their arguments by textual analysis – a comparison all the more convincing, because they are both such masters of close, extremely detailed, reading.

So our list necessarily simplifies and even falsely discriminates between the positions of each of its critics, from Steiner to Fish, but it does hint at the variations possible within the argument about subjects and objects. Our approach, in this book, has been to consider the varieties of emphasis within this debate, sometimes asserting the apparent demands of the text, sometimes the freedom of the reader, but always with an interest in the resulting *experience* of reading: inevitably, then, our approach (more often than not) has tended to approximate to the Fishian end of the spectrum. Central to our discussions has been the idea that readers create texts as they read, that the meanings of words slip and slide before the versatility and freedom of our response and the inexpressibility of the world. Far from arguing that meaning is a fixed and external truth we have inclined to side with Maurice Zapp (as we have noted, himself a parody of Fish) in his view that literature is never simply about what it appears to be about.

In these last pages, though, we wish to reflect upon our own practice in the light of the finally unresolved tension between the novels which readers create and the novels which might exist beyond their reading. Therefore we need to examine the tendencies which seem most to counter the idea that meaning is the result of response. The moments where these trends are perhaps most obvious are of two main (interrelated) kinds. First, they are evident wherever there is an assertion of *textual* significance (this is what the words of the text 'really say' or 'really mean'). Secondly, they can be found in the conviction that certain interpretations are right, and others wrong (as if the text were the independent legislator of judgement about interpretations).

It is interesting that in nearly every chapter we have made use of the etymologies of words to help prove some nuance of interpretation, because recourse to etymology might seem the perfect example of a tendency to believe in a verifiable, objective, meaning external to response or interpretation. So, when Tristram finds a convenient midpoint in the conversational relationship between authors and readers we claim he is supporting a kind of 'mediated' response in line with the etymology of the word; 'prejudice' in Jane Austen's novel is not only bias, it is also, recalling the derivation of the word, pre-judgement; to 'read' *Great Expectations* is to 'consider' it with 'discernment', recalling *rǣdan*, the root in Old English; in Joyce all texts can be said to be portraits, from the Latin *pro trahere* – 'drawings from' life. Maud, in *Possession*, wants to 'follow the path' but the 'aporia', the 'pathless path' of the text, stops her.

This kind of technique, which reactivates sometimes forgotten meanings said to be 'in' words by virtue of their history, is typical critical practice. Steiner does it; Ricks does it brilliantly, as we shall see below; Derrida, famously, does it to such an extent that it has become something of a trademark of his. But is it therefore evidence that, whatever lip-service we pay to the reader's role in creating meaning, we resort to dictionaries and to a fixed and chronicled history of 'external meaning' to prove the aptness of our readings? The answer is, of course, partly yes and partly no. The text, as we have suggested elsewhere, becomes the s[c]ite (as soon as one thinks of Derrida one begins to see puns like this) of competing readings, and etymology is one of the devices of readerly rhetoric we bring to the competition – one of the ways of reading beyond the text. Here is proof, we say, even in the history of a word itself, of the truthfulness of our reading. The etymology of 'etymology', after all, is traceable back to the Latin *etymologia* borrowed from the Greek words *etumos* meaning 'true' and *logos*, here with the sense 'discourse'. We are not disputing that words have actual etymologies, but etymology itself testifies to the transforming power of usage, to the unfixed, changing nature of those marks on a page.

It is worth, here, watching a master at work with etymology. Christopher Ricks, in the following passage, is admiring Beckett's complaint '[t]o have vagitated and not be bloody well able to rattle':

> One word there, 'vagitated', has the air of having materialized from thin air. Even today it has not yet materialized – in Beckett's sense – within the *OED*, which still has only 'to roam or travel' (medieval Latin *vagitare*, Latin *vagari*, to wander), obsolete, with the one citation:
>
> > 1614 RALEIGH *Hist. World* Before the use of the compass was known it was impossible to vagitate athwart the Ocean.
>
> Not that roaming and travelling are beside the point at being born. But what Beckett needed was an Englishing of the French *vagir*: 'pousser un cri faible, semblable à celui des nouveau-nés'. This had been alive in his French in *Malone meurt*: 'Avoir vagi, puis ne pas être foutu de râler.'
>
> The English language delivers some words within this family. There is 'vagitus' (from Latin *vagire*, to utter cries of distress, to wail): 'A cry or wail; *spec.* that of a new-born child'. Within earshot is *vagient*: 'Of infants, infancy, etc.: Crying, squalling, wailing'; this with the Beckett-like earliest citation of 'nor vagient Youngling, nor decrepit Ageling' (1628).[4]

The scholarly paraphernalia of this passage – the italics, the inverted commas of citation, the use of dictionary abbreviations, the dates – all suggest the certainty of textual meaning. But the subject – the word 'vagitated' – is a neologism: 'even today' it has not materialized in the *OED*. But Ricks, though he clearly attributes the mastery to Beckett, masterfully materializes it! He brings the formidable range of his knowledge to bear on the word, to bring it into existence. It is etymologized, mythologized, and cited – it wanders, sails athwart the oceans, cries, wails, and *pousse un cri faible*. It is intertextualized, in French and in seventeenth-century English. Of course Ricks believes he is responding to the connotations of the word, and to Beckett's search for an English equivalent to the French. But the word is now more Ricks's than Beckett's, and we admire Ricks as well as Beckett when we read it. We can variously describe this process: in deconstructive terms, for instance, Ricks finds that the word needs the *supplement* of other texts, commentaries, and footnotes, and his ingenuity suggests that the word remains inexhaustible, that there is no final signifier which unequivocally (or univocally) will give its full meaning. But the technique belongs to no one branch of criticism – it is a tool of critical reading. In Ricks's case, as in all others, the reading of the word rhetorically fulfils the purpose of his agenda – his volume has the title *Beckett's Dying Words* and the inside dust flap advertises the paradoxical thesis:

> But how does a writer give life to dismay at life itself, to the not-simply-unwelcome encroachments of death? After all, it is for the life, the vitality, of their language that we value writers. As a young man, Beckett himself praised Joyce's words. 'They are alive.'
>
> Beckett became himself as a writer when he realized in his very words a principle of death.

What better proof for this argument than that reading of the word 'vagitated'! The word is given birth by Beckett, and its intertextual meanings suggest the cries of new-born infants, the wanderings of life, the wails and despair of suffering and the death rattle itself. This is not to decide, of course, on the issue of intentionality. It is probable that Beckett would have agreed with all the implications of Ricks's archaeological excavations of his word. But, whatever the authorial intentions, whatever the text is supposed to mean, Ricks has certainly made the word his own by his reading, and has certainly used his scholarship as part of a rhetorical strategy to prove the accuracy of his reading of the whole of Beckett.

This, too, is simply good reading. Admittedly it is reading 'as writing', and in two senses: Ricks writes down his reading; and his reading is a writing of the text – it makes the text what it will now be (we cannot read the word, now, without Ricks's associations).

The same applies to our own similar usages. Wherever we concentrate on the meanings of words, citing the dictionaries as if they supported our readings, we are not, ultimately, bearing witness to the fixedness of a meaning before reading. We are rather using the tools of the trade to re-write the text, to make it our own, to make it one with our interpretation. Let us take one of our own examples. Our argument in Chapter 6 suggests the limitations of readings of *A Portrait of the Artist as a Young Man* which insist on a certain absolute understanding of Joyce's protagonist Stephen. We argue that the very title of Joyce's novel shows that any one determined view *must* be limited, that there are unlimited possible emphases and readings of what this 'portrait' might, exactly, be a portrait *of*. At this point we move to a matter of etymology – portraits are not simple representations; they are rather 'drawings from' life and they 'draw from' the readers endlessly 'protracted' responses. Now obviously we believe that this etymology is *in* the word – that the word actually has these etymological associations. We also believe that this is a useful etymology – and would argue that it is revealing that the history of the word's derivation should contain within it a sense of the uncertainty of representations of external reality. The etymology of the word would seem to support our argument. But here is the crux: the use of this source serves a rhetorical function. It is used to persuade you that our reading, which sees Stephen as multifarious, is truer than those readings which see him as clearly definable. Our etymology does not *prove* this. It is used to persuade.

How, though, can we ever presume to dismiss or reject readings of a text or passage as 'wrong' or even 'daft'? It might be answered that we can do so when a reading depends on interpretations which have no corroborating sources. But this would be a hopeless assumption. Not only does current usage within a language offer a vast range of possible 'evidence' for interpretation (we note, for instance, that the word 'possession' has many active senses in Byatt's novel, each one with its own interlinguistic connections); but it is also legitimate practice to move from language to language, from text to text, and through a whole reference library to give support for our views. In any case the kinds of readings we have rejected have not been dismissed on the grounds that the individual words used simply do not mean what the interpretation would have them mean. To take one example, we found absurd a reading of Pip's 'I saw her pass among the extinguished fires, and *ascend some light* iron stairs', which suggested that Pip is ascending 'some light'. How can we defend this kind of critique: 'light', after all, certainly has the 'legitimate' meaning John Schad cites, and there *are* many other passages in *Great Expectations* where 'light' is important (giving a kind of intratextual support). Further, rhetorically, as our book is often concerned with reading as a *process*, might it not have served us better to agree with Schad's reading? Actually, on one level, the answer is easy – we do not think that this is how readers normally read these words; we do not think that they do normally dwell on 'light' as separate from 'iron stairs', but that their deep sense of grammar will force them to read 'light' as an adjective which qualifies 'iron stairs'. It will be noted that we cannot *prove* this by virtue of the assumed meanings of the words 'some light iron stairs' – the only test of the virtue of our argument will be the reading practice of those who read the phrase. Being cynical, there is another, rhetorical explanation for our rejection – it helps us to qualify our contention that reading is importantly a linear process, by suggesting that there are limits. It is an exception to prove a rule. In that different readings of a text compete with each other it is always useful to cite superficially similar readings – their dismissal carries the rhetorical force of implying greater discrimination on our part. When we say that 'the gap between "light" and "iron" is wholly of Schad's making' we are unmaking it. Of course we still feel we are right (and here, rhetorically, is the assumption that others will agree with our reading), but we should not confuse this feeling of rightness with a belief in indisputable textual proof.

When we support our readings, then, whatever our critical persuasion we cite 'evidence' *as if* it simply existed outside of us. Not only is this not bad practice; it is the *only* practice available to us.

In this book we have tried to show how the best reading practice is not necessarily practice which obeys with rigour the dictates of any critical orthodoxy of the moment. We believe that reading and interpretation always make use of some kind of theoretical discourse, and this book has made use of many of the often very different accounts of what we do when we read. What we find, finally, is that good readings from different perspectives have more in common than indifferent readings from the same perspective. In the end Richard Rorty and Christopher Ricks are fellow travellers, and we hope that we too journey along the same road, straggle as we may. The novels we have discussed are not a subject for indifference. Whatever responses they stimulate we should not end up in the position of John Berryman's speaker when he complains 'literature bores me, especially great literature'.[5] One of the reasons we admire the humour of this line is that we have all had the experience, maybe in our earliest studies of literature, of being told that we must admire this or that great work. The rebellion of Berryman's line lies in the assumption that this view projects a literature removed from us, the object of our admiration, not the creation of our response. We would like to think that this book has supported a different view of greatness, one which champions that experience of discovery which (really) is at the heart of the practice of reading.

Notes

Preface

1. Geoffrey Bennington, *Lyotard: Writing the Event* (Manchester, 1988), pp. 3-4.

1 Reading and Interpretation

1. Richard Rorty, 'The Pragmatist's Progress', in Stefan Collini (ed.), *Interpretation and Overinterpretation* (Cambridge, 1992), pp. 89–108 (p. 107).
2. Matei Calinescu, *Rereading* (New Haven and London, 1993), p. 110.
3. Patrocinio P. Schweickart, 'Reading Ourselves: Toward a Feminist Theory of Reading', in Andrew Bennett (ed.), *Readers and Reading* (London and New York, 1995), pp. 66–93 (p. 71).
4. Ibid., p. 79.
5. Ibid., p. 80.
6. Ibid., p. 85.
7. Ibid., p. 88.
8. Quoted by Schweickart, ibid., p. 78.
9. Ibid., p. 80.
10. Raman Selden and Stan Smith, 'General Editors' Preface' to Bennett (ed.), *Readers and Reading*, p. vii.
11. Wolfgang Iser, 'Interaction between Text and Reader', in *Readers and Reading*, pp. 20–31 (pp. 20–1).
12. Wolfgang Iser, 'The Reading Process: A Phenomenological Approach', in David Lodge (ed.), *Modern Criticism and Theory: A Reader* (London and New York, 1988), pp. 212–18 (p. 212).
13. Stanley Fish, *Doing What Comes Naturally: Change, Rhetoric, and the Practice of Theory in Literary and Legal Studies* (Oxford, 1989), p. 70.
14. Wolfgang Iser, *Prospecting: From Reader Response to Literary Anthropology* (Baltimore, Md and London, 1989), p. 6.
15. See, for instance, Mick Short, *Stylistics* (London, 1996).
16. Fish, *Doing What Comes Naturally*, p. 61.

17. Ibid., p. 60.
18. Ibid., p. 60.
19. Lennard J. Davis, *Resisting Novels: Ideology and Fiction* (New York and London, 1987), p. 11.
20. Quoted by Davis, *Resisting Novels*, p. 91.
21. Ibid., p. 92.
22. Ibid., p. 109.
23. Ibid., p. 109.
24. Fish, *Doing What Comes Naturally*, pp. 78–9.
25. Geoffrey H. Hartman, *Criticism in the Wilderness: The Study of Literature Today* (New Haven and London, 1980), p. 269. There is an excellent discussion of Hartman's ideas on indeterminacy in Elizabeth Freund, *The Return of the Reader: Reader-Response Criticism* (London and New York, 1987), pp. 152–6.
26. Umberto Eco, *The Tanner Lectures*, in Stefan Collini (ed.), *Interpretation and Overinterpretation* (Cambridge, 1992), pp. 23–43 (p. 39).
27. Ibid., p. 43.
28. Ibid., p. 88.
29. Ibid., p. 64.
30. Rorty, 'The Pragmatist's Progress', p. 97.
31. Quoted by Jonathan Culler in *On Deconstruction: Theory and Criticism after Structuralism* (London, 1983), pp. 77–8.
32. Ibid., p. 78.
33. Rorty, 'The Pragmatist's Progress', p. 95.
34. Stephen Knapp and Walter Benn Michaels, cited by Freund in *The Return of the Reader*, p. 17.
35. Freund, *The Return of the Reader*, p. 152.
36. Richard J. Goy, 'The "Reader's Edition" of *Ulysses*', the *Times Literary Supplement*, 18 July 1997, p. 17.
37. Quoted in Freund, *The Return of the Reader*, p. 12.
38. George Steiner, *Real Presences: Is There Anything In What We Say?* (London, 1989), p. 150.
39. Ibid., p. 23.
40. Ibid., p. 38.
41. Rorty, 'The Pragmatist's Progress', p. 95.
42. Ben Knights, *From Reader to Reader: Theory and Practice in the Study Group* (Hemel Hempstead, 1992), p. 6.
43. Ibid., p. 36.
44. Ibid., p. 44.
45. Freund, *The Return of the Reader*, p. 125.
46. Ibid., p. 126.
47. Bennett, *Readers and Reading*, p. 12.

48. Robert C. Holub, *Crossing Borders: Reception Theory, Poststructuralism, Deconstruction* (Madison and London, 1992), p. 20.
49. Freund, *The Return of the Reader*, pp. 62–3.
50. J. Hillis Miller, *The Ethics of Reading: Kant, de Man, Eliot, Trollope, James and Benjamin* (New York, 1987), p. 2.
51. Calinescu, *Rereading*, p. xii.
52. Holub, *Crossing Borders*, p. 193.
53. Knights, *From Reader to Reader*, p. 48.

2 The Role of the Reader: *Tristram Shandy*

1. Wolfgang Iser, *Sterne: Tristram Shandy*, trans. David Henry Wilson, *Landmarks of World Literature* series (Cambridge, 1988).
2. Quoted by Iser, *Sterne: Tristram Shandy*, p. 121.
3. Melvyn New, 'Sterne, Nietzsche, and Tartuffery', a paper given at the conference, *Laurence Sterne in Modernism and Postmodernism*, held at the University of York, April 1993. Both expressions are repeated by New in his published version of the paper, entitled 'Tartuffery' and included as Chapter 9 in *Tristram Shandy: A Book for Free Spirits* (New York, 1994), p. 132.
4. Viktor Shklovsky, 'A Parodying Novel: Sterne's *Tristram Shandy*', trans. W. George Isaak, in *Laurence Sterne: A Collection of Critical Essays*, ed. John Traugott (Englewood Cliffs, NJ, 1968), pp. 66–89 (p. 89).
5. Michael V. De Porte, *Nightmares and Hobbyhorses: Swift, Sterne, and Augustan Ideas of Madness* (San Marino, 1974), p. 132.
6. New, *Tristram Shandy: A Book for Free Spirits*, p.146.
7. John Traugott, *Tristram Shandy's World: Sterne's Philosophical Rhetoric* (Berkeley, 1954), p. 9.
8. New, 'Sterne, Nietzsche, and Tartuffery'. Again the expression is repeated in the published version, *Tristram Shandy: A Book for Free Spirits*, p. 128.
9. New, *Tristram Shandy: A Book for Free Spirits*, pp. 128–9.
10. Ibid., p. 132.
11. Ibid., p. 132.
12. Ibid., p. 133.
13. Iser, *Sterne: Tristram Shandy*, p. 10.
14. François Rabelais, *The Works of Francis Rabelais, M. D.*, trans. Thomas Urquhart and Peter le Motteux, rev. John Ozell, 5 vols (London, 1737).
15. Mikhail Bakhtin, *The Dialogic Imagination: Four Essays*, trans. Caryl Emerson and Michael Holquist, ed. Michael Holquist (Austin, Tex., 1981), p. 309.

16. Wolfgang Iser, *Prospecting: From Reader Response to Literary Anthropology* (Baltimore, Md and London, 1989), p. 6.
17. Fish, *Doing What Comes Naturally*, p. 82.
18. Bakhtin, *The Dialogic Imagination*, p. 276.
19. Rabelais, Vol. I, p. 255.
20. Mikhail Bakhtin, *Rabelais and His World*, trans. Helene Iswolsky (Bloomington, Ind., 1984), p. 10.
21. Iser, *Sterne: Tristram Shandy*, p. 91.
22. Gene Moore, 'Tristram Shandy's Narratees', a printed paper (since unpublished) given at the University of York conference, April 1993.
23. Moore, 'Tristram Shandy's Narratees'.
24. Ibid.
25. Iser, *Sterne: Tristram Shandy*, p. 84.
26. Taken from the first edition, observing the lineation, and number of asterisks: Laurence Sterne, *The Life and Opinions of Tristram Shandy, Gentleman*, Vol. III (London, 1761), p. 73. (This is the only quotation in this chapter taken from that edition.)
27. John M. Stedmond, *The Comic Art of Laurence Sterne: Convention and Innovation in Tristram Shandy and A Sentimental Journey* (Toronto, 1967), p. 126.
28. A. A. Mendilow, *Time and the Novel* (London, 1952), pp. 186–7.
29. Tzvetan Todorov, *The Poetics of Prose*, trans. Richard Howard (Oxford, 1977), p. 71.
30. Ibid., p. 71.
31. Northrop Frye, *Anatomy of Criticism: Four Essays* (Princeton, NJ, 1957), p. 244.
32. Stanley Fish, *Is There a Text in This Class?: The Authority of Interpretive Communities* (Cambridge, Mass. and London, 1980), p. 31.
33. Ibid., p. 91.

3 The Process of Reading: *Pride and Prejudice*

1. Quoted by Wolfgang Iser, 'The Reading Process: A Phenomenological Approach', repr. in *Modern Criticism and Theory: A Reader*, ed. David Lodge (London and New York, 1988), p. 213.
2. Lodge, p. 213; see also Wolfgang Iser, *The Implied Reader: Patterns of Communication in Prose Fiction from Bunyan to Beckett* (Baltimore, Md and London, 1978), p. 276.
3. Wolfgang Iser, *Prospecting: From Reader Response to Literary Anthropology* (Baltimore, Md, 1989), pp. 33–4.
4. Stanley Fish, *Doing What Comes Naturally: Change, Rhetoric, and the*

Practice of Theory in Literary and Legal Studies (Oxford, 1989), p. 77.

5. Matei Calinescu, *Rereading* (New Haven and London, 1993), p. 154.
6. Lennard J. Davis, *Resisting Novels: Ideology and Fiction* (London, 1987), p. 235
7. Ibid., p. 147.
8. Ibid., p. 238.
9. Stanley Fish, *Is There a Text in This Class?: The Authority of Interpretive Communities* (Cambridge, Mass., 1980), pp. 43–4.
10. Ibid., p. 144.
11. Iser, *The Implied Reader*, p. 288.
12. Fish, *Is There a Text in This Class?*, pp. 344–5.
13. Frank Kermode, *The Sense of an Ending: Studies in the Theory of Fiction* (Oxford and New York, 1967), pp. 54–5.
14. Ibid., p. 18.
15. Henry Fielding, *Joseph Andrews*, ed. Martin C. Battestin (Oxford, 1967), p. 42.
16. Quoted by Calinescu, *Rereading*, p. 191.
17. Penguin edition (1996), p. 336.
18. Robert C. Holub, *Reception Theory: A Critical Introduction* (London, 1984), pp. 40–1.
19. Robert C. Holub, 'Hermeneutics', in *The Cambridge History of Literary Criticism*, Vol. 8: *From Formalism to Poststructuralism*, ed. Raman Selden (Cambridge, 1995), pp. 255–88 (p. 269).
20. Ibid., p. 270.

4 The Experience of Reading: *Great Expectations*

1. From the introduction to Ian Gregor (ed.), *Reading the Victorian Novel: Detail into Form* (London, 1980), p. 9.
2. Stanley Fish, *Is There a Text in This Class?: The Authority of Interpretive Communities* (Cambridge, Mass. and London, 1980), p. 21. Compare Vincent B. Leitch's assertion that 'Critical writing is, in fact, narration of reading experience': *Deconstructive Criticism: An Advanced Introduction* (London, 1983), p. 184.
3. Jonathan Culler, *On Deconstruction: Theory and Criticism after Structuralism* (London, 1983), p. 67.
4. Philip Davis, *The Experience of Reading* (London and New York, 1992), pp. xiv, xi, xv, 303.
5. Ian Gregor, 'Criticism as an Individual Activity: The Approach through Reading', in Malcolm Bradbury and David Palmer (eds), *Contemporary Criticism* (London, 1970), pp. 195–214 (p. 197).

6. Fish, *Is There a Text in This Class?*, p. 22.

7. Christopher Ricks, '*Great Expectations*', in John Gross and Gabriel Pearson (eds), *Dickens and the Twentieth Century* (London, 1966), pp. 199–211 (p. 199).

8. W. K. Wimsatt, Jr and Monroe C. Beardsley, 'The Affective Fallacy', in W. K. Wimsatt Jr, *The Verbal Icon: Studies in the Meaning of Poetry* (London, 1970), p. 21.

9. See, for example, Fish, *Is There a Text in This Class?*, pp. 22–67.

10. See, for example, Norman Holland, *5 Readers Reading* (New Haven and London, 1975).

11. David Bleich, *Subjective Criticism* (Baltimore, Md and London, 1978).

12. John Reichert, *Making Sense of Literature* (Chicago, 1977), p. 87.

13. See F. R. Leavis and Q. D. Leavis, *Dickens the Novelist* (Harmondsworth, 1972), pp. 360–428.

14. Culler, *On Deconstruction*, p. 67.

15. For a useful introductory account of *Great Expectations* see Dennis Walder's 'Reading *Great Expectations*' in Dennis Walder (ed.), *The Realist Novel* (London and New York, 1995), pp. 135–65. There is a good concise discussion of Dickens's novel by Michael Wheeler in his *English Fiction of the Victorian Period 1830–1890* (London and New York, 1994), pp. 112–14. Anny Sadrin's monograph on *Great Expectations* in the Unwin Critical Library series (London, 1988) is probably the most exhaustive study of the novel to date. Steven Connor's *Charles Dickens* (Oxford and New York, 1985), pp. 109–44, offers a Lacanian analysis of the novel, including sections on 'the structures of looking' and on 'self and the other'. For those who find Lacanian approaches unhelpful, there is certainly scope for a rewarding interpretation of *Great Expectations*, drawing on the hermeneutics of Paul Ricoeur, especially *Oneself as Another*, trans. Kathleen Blamey (Chicago and London, 1992).

16. See Max Byrd, '"Reading" in *Great Expectations*', *PMLA*, Vol. 91 (1976), pp. 259–65.

17. Peter Brooks, *Reading for the Plot: Design and Intention in Narrative* (Oxford, 1984), p. 140.

18. Reproduced in Appendix F to Margaret Cardwell's edition of the novel for *The Clarendon Dickens* (Oxford, 1993), p. 510.

19. For a sensible, clear discussion of Derrida's *s'entendre parler* and the Lacanian split self in relation to *Great Expectations*, see Connor, *Charles Dickens*, pp. 109–44.

20. The preoccupation with actors, acting and the actorly in the novel has been perceptively discussed by William F. Axton in *Circle of Fire: Dickens' Vision and Style and the Popular Victorian Theater* (Lexington,

Ky, 1966), and by Robert Garis in *The Dickens Theatre: A Reassessment of the Novels* (Oxford, 1965).

21. Fish, *Is There a Text in This Class?*, pp. 344–5.
22. Wolfgang Iser, *The Act of Reading: A Theory of Aesthetic Response* (Baltimore, Md and London, 1978), p. 111.
23. Wolfgang Iser, *The Implied Reader: Patterns of Communication in Prose Fiction from Bunyan to Beckett* (Baltimore, Md and London, 1978), p. 278.
24. Ricks, '*Great Expectations*', p. 207.
25. John Schad, *The Reader in the Dickensian Mirrors: Some New Language* (Basingstoke and London, 1992), p. 61.
26. Fish, *Is There a Text in This Class?*, pp. 25–6.
27. See Hans-Georg Gadamer, *Truth and Method*, trans. William Glen-Doepel (London, 1979).
28. See Hans-Robert Jauss, *Toward an Aesthetic of Reception*, trans. Timothy Bahti (Brighton, 1982).
29. See, for example, Ian Maclean, 'Reading and Interpretation', in Ann Jefferson and David Robey (eds), *Modern Literary Theory: A Comparative Introduction* (London, 1986), pp. 139–40.
30. Paul Pickrel, '*Great Expectations*', in Martin Price (ed.), *Dickens: A Collection of Critical Essays* (Englewood Cliffs, NJ, 1967), pp. 158–68 (pp. 158–9).
31. The (anonymous) reviewer is E. S. Dallas, writing in *The Times* (17 October 1861); repr. in Philip Collins (ed.), *Dickens: The Critical Heritage* (London, 1971), pp. 430–4 (p. 433).
32. For the fullest account of the role of allusion in the experience of reading Victorian novels, see Michael Wheeler, *The Art of Allusion in Victorian Fiction* (Basingstoke and London, 1979).
33. Culler, *On Deconstruction*, p. 72. (Culler is being ironic here, at the expense of Stanley Fish; but, taken out of context, his comment makes a neat point.)

5 Deconstruction and Reading: *Daniel Deronda*

1. See, for example, the essays in Laurence Lerner (ed.), *Reconstructing Literature* (Oxford, 1983), and the polemical broadside by Peter Washington, *Fraud: Literary Theory and the End of English* (London, 1989).
2. See Harold Aram Veeser (ed.), *The New Historicism* (London and New York, 1989). The introduction to Richard Wilson and Richard Dutton (eds), *New Historicism and Renaissance Drama* (London and New York,

1992), pp.1–18, discusses informatively and lucidly the key influences of Michel Foucault, Raymond Williams and Stephen Greenblatt. David Gorman's essay, 'The Worldly Text: Writing as Social Action, Reading as Historical Reconstruction', in Joseph Natoli (ed.), *Literary Theory's Future(s)* (Urbana, Ill. and Chicago, 1989), pp. 181–220, surveys the impact of various theorists and critics, including Edward Said and Jerome McGann.

3. One of the more thoughtful ripostes to the anti–deconstruction lobbies is Alan Kennedy, *Reading Resistance Value: Deconstructive Practice and the Politics of Literary Critical Encounters* (Basingstoke and London, 1990).

4. See Raymond Tallis's essay, 'The Survival of Theory: (1) "He Never Said That"', in *Poetry Nation Review*, Vol. 20, No. 6 (July–August, 1994), pp. 61-4. (He is clearly exasperated.) Valentine Cunningham's *In the Reading Gaol: Postmodernity, Texts, and History* (Oxford and Cambridge, Mass., 1994) offers what is arguably the most balanced and judicious conspectus. Stanley Fish, in *Doing What Comes Naturally: Change, Rhetoric, and the Practice of Theory in Literary and Legal Studies* (Oxford, 1989) is one who clearly thinks that 'theory's day is dying' (p. 341), a notion he continues to pursue busily in *There's No Such Thing As Free Speech And It's A Good Thing, Too* (Oxford, 1994).

5. Barbara Johnson, *The Critical Difference: Essays in the Contemporary Rhetoric of Reading* (Baltimore, Md and London, 1980), p. 5.

6. Christopher Norris, *Deconstruction: Theory and Practice* (London, 1982), p. 31. (The metaphor in 'closely tied' – assuming that the phrase is *non*-tautological – is suggestive, given the frequent presentation of the practice of deconstruction in terms of 'untying the text'.)

7. Jonathan Culler, *On Deconstruction: Theory and Criticism after Structuralism* (London, 1983), pp. 213, 155.

8. J. Hillis Miller, *The Ethics of Reading: Kant, de Man, Eliot, Trollope, James, and Benjamin* (New York, 1987), pp. 9, 10. But earlier he notes: 'Reading itself is extraordinarily hard work. It does not occur all that often. Clearheaded reflection on what really happens in an act of reading is even more difficult and rare' (pp. 3–4). Elsewhere, he insists that 'the best places for discussing deconstruction are to be found in shared acts of reading, not in pure theory': 'On Edge: The Crossways of Contemporary Criticism', in J. Hillis Miller, *Theory Now and Then* (Hemel Hempstead, 1991), pp. 171–200 (p. 193).

9. From Lodge's (aptly titled) novel *Changing Places: A Tale of Two Campuses* (Harmondsworth, 1978), p. 48 – a novel in which Zapp (circumcised Jew) rescues one Mary Makepeace in an episode likened to 'some scene from a Victorian novel' (p. 139).

10. Jacques Derrida, *Positions*, trans. Alan Bass (Urbana, Ill. and Chicago, 1981), p. 63.
11. K. M. Newton (ed.), *George Eliot* (London and New York, 1991), p. 9.
12. David Carroll, *George Eliot and the Conflict of Interpretations: A Reading of the Novels* (Cambridge, 1992), p. 313.
13. Cited in David Carroll (ed.), *George Eliot: The Critical Heritage* (London, 1971), p. 33.
14. F. R. Leavis, *The Great Tradition: George Eliot, Henry James, Joseph Conrad* (Harmondsworth, 1993), p. 97. Leavis reprints Henry James's piece of 1876, '*Daniel Deronda*: A Conversation' in the Appendix to *The Great Tradition* (pp. 284–304). See also: U. C. Knoepflmacher, *Religious Humanism and the Victorian Novel: George Eliot, Walter Pater, and Samuel Butler* (Princeton, NJ, 1965), Ch. IV ('*Daniel Deronda*: Tradition as Synthesis and Salvation'); and Sally Shuttleworth, *George Eliot and Nineteenth-Century Science: The Make-Believe of a Beginning* (Cambridge, 1984), Ch. 8 ('*Daniel Deronda*: Fragmentation and Organic Union'). For a different perspective consult David Carroll, 'The Unity of *Daniel Deronda*', *Essays in Criticism*, Vol. 9 (1959), pp. 369–80.
15. In his introduction to the new Penguin edition, p. xvii.
16. Barbara Johnson, 'Nothing Fails like Success', *Deconstructive Criticism: Directions: SCE Reports*, Vol. 8 (Fall, 1980), pp. 9–10.
17. See Cynthia Chase, 'The Decomposition of the Elephants: Double-Reading *Daniel Deronda*', *PMLA*, Vol. 93 (1978), pp. 215–27, and K. M. Newton's reply, '*Daniel Deronda* and Circumcision', in his *In Defence of Literary Interpretation: Theory and Practice* (Basingstoke and London, 1986), pp. 197–211. Both articles are reprinted in Newton (ed.), *George Eliot*, pp. 198–231. J. Russell Perkin, in *A Reception-History of George Eliot's Fiction* (Ann Arbor, Mich. and London, 1990), pp. 154–5, offers a (briefer) critique of Chase's essay. The debate about circumcision in the novel is still continuing as we write: see John Sutherland, *Can Jane Eyre Be Happy?: More Puzzles in Classic Fiction* (Oxford, 1997), pp. 169–76, and K. M. Newton's commentary on Sutherland, 'Sutherland's Puzzles: The Case of *Daniel Deronda*', in *Essays in Criticism*, Vol. XLVIII (January, 1998), No. 1, pp. 1–12.
18. There is an insightful discussion of the novel's opening scene in A. S. Byatt and Ignês Sodre, *Imagining Characters: Six Conversations about Women Writers*, ed. Rebecca Swift (London, 1995), pp. 78–117 (pp. 80–6).
19. In her introduction to the earlier Penguin edition, p. 7.
20. William Wilkie Collins, *The Woman in White*, ed. Harvey Peter Sucksmith (Oxford, 1981), p. 113.
21. See Barbara Hardy, *The Novels of George Eliot: A Study in Form* (London and Dover, New Hampshire, 1963), p. 135.

22. Jane Austen, *Emma*, ed. Ronald Blythe (Harmondsworth, 1966), p. 351.
23. The Romantic feelings/knowledge hierarchy is prevalent throughout the novel: see especially pp. 364–5, 451. The most intelligent – and deconstructive – meditation on a variation of this theme (in the form 'emotional intellect'/'unemotional intellect') may be found on p. 514.
24. Norris, *Deconstruction: Theory and Practice*, p. 48.
25. See Alberto Manguel, *A History of Reading* (London, 1996).
26. As we write, an excellent collection of reflections on reading has just been published, offering diverse insights into the practice of reading today: see Philip Davis (ed.), *Real Voices On Reading* (Basingstoke and London, 1997).

6 Reading and Revelation: *A Portrait of the Artist as a Young Man*

1. Derek Attridge, 'Reading Joyce', in Derek Attridge (ed.), *The Cambridge Companion to James Joyce* (Cambridge, 1990), pp. 1–3.
2. John Paul Riquelme, 'The Preposterous Shape of Portraiture: *A Portrait of the Artist as a Young Man*', in Harold Bloom (ed.), *Modern Critical Interpretations: James Joyce's A Portrait of the Artist as a Young Man* (New York and Philadelphia, 1988), pp. 87–107 (p. 88). Riquelme's adroit essay examines the 'oscillating perspectives' and narrative/stylistic dislocations in *A Portrait*, paying particular attention to *le style indirect libre* in the context of the reader's experience of the novel.
3. Mark Schorer, 'Technique as discovery', in David Lodge (ed.), *20th Century Literary Criticism: A Reader* (London, 1972), p. 394.
4. Virginia Woolf, 'Modern Fiction', extract repr. in Miriam Allott, *Novelists on the Novel* (London and Henley, 1965), p. 77.
5. John Fletcher and Malcolm Bradbury, 'The Introverted Novel', in Malcolm Bradbury and James McFarlane (eds), *Modernism 1890–1930* (Harmondsworth, 1976), pp. 394–415 (p. 408). See also David Lodge's excellent essay in the same collection, 'The Language of Modernist Fiction: Metaphor and Metonymy', for a lucid elaboration of the characteristics of modernist fiction (pp. 481–96), and Christopher Butler's erudite conspectus, 'Joyce, Modernism, and Post-modernism', in Attridge (ed.), *The Cambridge Companion to James Joyce*, pp. 259–82.
6. See, for example, the selection of responses summarized in Morris Beja (ed.), *Dubliners and A Portrait of the Artist as a Young Man: A Casebook* (Basingstoke and London, 1973), p. 76.
7. All of these quotations are taken from Robert H. Deming (ed.), *James Joyce: The Critical Heritage*, Vol. I (London and Henley, 1970), pp. 81–129.

8. As far as literary history is concerned the chronological transition from late-nineteenth-century classic realism to early-twentieth-century high modernism is immensely complicated. Realism taken to one extreme led to naturalism (a mode which flourished more notably in French fiction than in English). But the transition from realism to modernism is via aestheticism and (to a lesser extent) impressionism. This might suggest a Hegelian dialectic: thesis – antithesis – synthesis. However, it is important to realize that modernism is in part a continuation or extension of aspects of realism, and not a wholesale reaction against the realist mode *tout court*. The emphases of modernism fall differently: generally speaking, greater stress is placed upon interiority than upon externals. But the point to note is that the mode of development is essentially organic. Realism itself grew out of those earlier forms of mimesis and representationalism which put a premium upon a high degree of verisimilitude (for example pseudo-history and autobiography in the fiction of Daniel Defoe). In a similar way, as we shall see in Chapter 8, postmodernism (as a literary phenomenon) grew out of modernism. The picture becomes even more complex, of course, once one starts to distinguish between varieties of realism, modernism, postmodernism, and so on. Not that, in the case of realism, the distinctions between (say) correspondent realism, expressive realism, neo-realism, romantic realism, socialist realism and symbolic realism (to name but six varieties) are watertight. Labels, it would seem, have only a limited usefulness.

9. See Bloom (ed.), *Modern Critical Interpretations: Joyce's A Portrait*, pp. vii, 1–4, 5–30. Wayne C. Booth, in his *The Rhetoric of Fiction* (Chicago and London, 1961), pp. 323–36, deals interestingly with this very problem.

10. George Eliot, *Middlemarch: A Study of Provincial Life*, ed. David Carroll (Oxford, 1988), p. 346.

11. According to Joyce's biographer, Richard Ellmann, Joyce much admired Henry James's presentation of Isabel Archer, the heroine of *The Portrait of a Lady*: see Richard Ellmann, *James Joyce* (Oxford, 1983), p. 193.

12. Joyce toyed with various alternative titles for *A Portrait*, including *Chapters in the Life of a Young Man*. According to Ellmann, one reason why Joyce felt uneasy with *Stephen Hero* as the title of his earlier version of *A Portrait* was that such a title 'might imply a more sardonic view of his hero than he intended' (Ellmann, *James Joyce*, p. 193).

13. Walter Pater, *The Renaissance: Studies in Art and Poetry* (Glasgow, 1961), p. 129.

14. For an elaborate and fascinating discussion of art as mirror, see M. H. Abrams, *The Mirror and the Lamp: Romantic Theory and the Critical Tradition* (Oxford, 1953), especially Ch. 2.

15. Eliot, *Middlemarch*, p. 575.
16. Ellmann, *James Joyce*, plate VIII.
17. For Joyce's definition of the epiphany, see James Joyce, *Stephen Hero*, ed. Theodore Spencer (London, 1977), p. 190.
18. Dorothy van Ghent, *The English Novel: Form and Function* (New York, 1961), p. 268.
19. In this Stephen is, perhaps, unlike Joyce who, on 7 September 1909, wrote from Dublin to Nora Barnacle as follows: 'Now, my darling Nora, I want you to read over and over all I have written to you. Some of it is ugly, obscene and bestial, some of it is pure and holy and spiritual: all of it is myself': *Selected Letters of James Joyce*, ed. Richard Ellmann (London, 1975), p. 169. (Compare the letter to Nora reprinted in Ellmann's biography, p. 287.)
20. Oscar Wilde, 'The Decay of Lying: An Observation', in *Complete Works of Oscar Wilde* (London and Glasgow, 1966), p. 970. (The speaker is Vivian.)
21. Anthony Burgess, 'Martyr and Maze-maker', in Bloom (ed.), *Modern Critical Interpretations: Joyce's A Portrait*, p. 45.
22. Arthur Power, *Conversations with James Joyce*, ed. Clive Hart (London, 1974), p. 98.
23. Riquelme, 'The Preposterous Shape of Portraiture', p. 88.
24. Ibid., pp. 94–5.
25. Ibid., pp. 102, 105.
26. *The Spiritual Exercises of Saint Ignatius*, trans. Thomas Corbishley, S.J. (Wheathampstead, 1973), pp. 7, 9.
27. Ibid., pp. 35–7.
28. William Shakespeare, *A Midsummer Night's Dream* (1600), V.i.14–15.
29. Anthony Burgess, like Joyce (like Stephen-as-Icarus, indeed) a *lapsed* Catholic, comments: 'I still find it difficult to read the hell chapter without some of the sense of suffocation I felt when I first met it, at the age of fifteen, myself a Catholic looking for emancipation. I was hurled back into conformity by this very sermon and this very vision' ('Martyr and Maze-maker', p. 52).
30. Chris Baldick's definition from *The Concise Oxford Dictionary of Literary Terms* (Oxford and New York, 1991), p. 150.
31. Attridge, 'Reading Joyce', pp. 23–5 (Attridge's italics).
32. Ibid., p. 27.
33. Paul Ricoeur, *Hermeneutics and the Human Sciences*, trans. John B. Thompson (Cambridge, 1981), pp. 190–3.
34. Georges Poulet, 'Criticism and the Experience of Interiority', in Richard Macksey and Eugenio Donato (eds), *The Structuralist Controversy* (Chicago and London, 1972), pp. 59–61.

7 Reading the Self: Beckett's *Trilogy* – *Molloy*; *Malone Dies*; *The Unnamable*

1. Matei Calinescu, *Rereading* (New Haven and London, 1993), p. 220.
2. Ibid., p. 220.
3. J. Hillis Miller, *The Ethics of Reading: Kant, de Man, Eliot, Trollope, James, and Benjamin* (New York, 1987), p. 56.
4. Ibid., p. 59.
5. Ibid., p. 59.
6. Gérard Genette, *Narrative Discourse*, trans. Jane E. Lewin (Oxford, 1980), p. 262.
7. Samuel Beckett, *Happy Days* (London, 1963), p. 33.
8. Jean-François Lyotard, *The Differend: Phrases in Dispute*, trans. Georges Van den Abbeele (Manchester, 1988), p. 47.
9. Christopher Ricks, *Beckett's Dying Words: The Clarendon Lectures 1990* (Oxford, 1993), p. 7.
10. Lyotard, *The Differend*, pp. 41–2.
11. Lennard J. Davis, *Resisting Novels: Ideology and Fiction* (New York and London, 1987), p. 102.
12. Ben Knights, *From Reader to Reader: Theory and Practice in the Study Group* (Hemel Hempstead, 1992), pp. 109–10.
13. John Locke, *An Essay Concerning Human Understanding*, ed. Peter H. Nidditch (Oxford, 1975), pp. 585–6.
14. Ibid., p. 583.
15. Lyotard, *The Differend*, p. 51.
16. Ibid., p. 45.
17. Ibid., p. 54.
18. Wolfgang Iser, *Prospecting: From Reader Response to Literary Anthropology* (Baltimore, Md and London, 1989), p. 143.
19. Quoted by Ricks in *Beckett's Dying Words*, pp. 150–1.
20. Ibid., p. 151.
21. Ibid., p. 148.
22. Christopher Norris, *The Truth about Postmodernism* (Oxford, 1993), p. 18.
23. Ibid., pp. 98–9.
24. Samuel Beckett, *Watt* (London, 1988), p. 47
25. Norris, *The Truth about Postmodernism*, p. 48.
26. See particularly *The Truth about Postmodernism*, pp. 24, 218–20, 240–2.
27. Lyotard, *The Differend*, p. 13.
28. Bill Readings, *Introducing Lyotard: Art and Politics* (London, 1991), p. 127.
29. Norris, *The Truth about Postmodernism*, p. 271. (Norris is praising Paul de Man's deconstruction of Martin Heidegger.)

30. Ibid., p. 88.
31. Iser, *Prospecting*, pp. 142, 141.
32. Ibid., p. 141.
33. George Steiner, *Real Presences: Is There Anything In What We Say?* (London, 1989), p. 57.
34. Iser, *Prospecting*, p. 141.
35. Beckett, *Watt*, p. 255.
36. Wolfgang Iser, *The Implied Reader: Patterns of Communication in Prose from Bunyan to Beckett* (Baltimore, Md and London, 1978), pp. 259–60.

8 Postmodernist Readings: *Possession*

1. Geoffrey Hartman, *Criticism in the Wilderness: The Study of Literature Today* (New Haven and London, 1980), p. 272.
2. Randall Stevenson, *A Reader's Guide to the Twentieth-Century Novel in Britain* (Hemel Hempstead, 1993), p. 122.
3. A. S. Byatt, 'My Hero: Robert Browning', in the *Independent*, 26 November 1988 (magazine supplement).
4. A. S. Byatt, *Passions of the Mind: Selected Writings* (London, 1991), p. 1.
5. Ibid., p. 2.
6. Ibid., pp. 2, 4.
7. Ibid., p. 4 (Byatt's italics).
8. Ibid., p. 75.
9. The phrase is taken from *The Post-Modernist Always Rings Twice: Reflections on Culture in the 90s* (London, 1992), cited in Roger Scruton's review article, 'In Inverted Commas', the *Times Literary Supplement*, 18 December 1992, pp. 3–4 (p. 4).
10. W. H. Auden, 'Lakes', in 'Bucolics', from *The Shield of Achilles* (1955).
11. See Scruton, 'In Inverted Commas', p. 4.
12. Umberto Eco, 'Postmodernism, Irony, the Enjoyable', repr. in Peter Brooker (ed.), *Modernism/Postmodernism* (London and New York, 1992), pp. 225–8 (p. 227; Eco's ellipsis).
13. Ibid., p. 226.
14. Linda Hutcheon, 'Telling Stories: Fiction and History', in Brooker (ed.), *Modernism/Postmodernism*, pp. 229–42 (p. 230).
15. Ibid., p. 231.
16. Ibid., p. 233.
17. For an elaboration of this distinction, see Michael Wheeler, *The Art of Allusion in Victorian Fiction* (Basingstoke and London, 1979), p. 3.
18. Prefiguring E. M. Forster's 'Only connect . . .' epigraph to *Howards End* (1910) – a novel with clear intertextual relationships with both Elizabeth

Gaskell's *North and South* (1854–5) and David Lodge's *Nice Work* (1988).

19. Robert Browning, *The Poems*, ed. John Pettigrew and Thomas J. Collins (Harmondsworth, 1981), Vol. I, p. 605.
20. Ibid., p. 605.
21. Vincent B. Leitch, *Deconstructive Criticism: An Advanced Introduction* (London, 1983), p. 59. A more cautious position is taken by Robert Crosman in 'Is There Such a Thing as Misreading?', in Jeremy Hawthorn (ed.), *Criticism and Critical Theory* (London, 1984), pp. 1–12.
22. These are Roland's thoughts. The word 'tiresome' contrasts nicely with Ash's phrase, 'our tireless quest to *know*' (p. 209; Ash's italics).
23. Hartman, *Criticism in the Wilderness*, p. 265.
24. Ibid., p. 270.
25. Ibid., p. 269.
26. Ibid., pp. 271–2.
27. Ibid., p. 283.
28. The extract is quoted before the title page in the paperback edition.
29. David Lodge, *Small World: An Academic Romance* (Harmondsworth, 1985), p. 27. The part-parody of Stanley Fish is deft and astute. Compare Beatrice's words on Ellen Ash: *Possession*, p. 485, and Blackadder's reply to Euan's query, pp. 482–3. Another highly appropriate choice for a further epigraph would have been from T. S. Eliot's 'East Coker' (III), in *Four Quartets* (1943):

> In order to possess what you do not possess
> You must go by the way of dispossession.

30. Hartman, *Criticism in the Wilderness*, p. 2.
31. See Robert Scholes, *Protocols of Reading* (New Haven and London, 1989), pp. 1, 155.
32. Malcolm Bradbury, *The Modern British Novel* (London, 1993), p. 440.

Conclusion

1. Stanley Fish, *Is There a Text in This Class?: The Authority of Interpretive Communities* (Cambridge, Mass. and London, 1980), p. 43.
2. Robert C. Holub, *Crossing Borders: Reception Theory, Poststructuralism, Deconstruction* (Madison and London, 1992), p. 27.
3. Ibid., p. 20.
4. Christopher Ricks, *Beckett's Dying Words: The Clarendon Lectures 1990* (Oxford, 1993), pp. 111–12 ['*pousser un cri faible, semblable à celui des nouveau-nés*' – 'to utter a feeble cry, like that of new-born babies'].
5. John Berryman, *The Dream Songs* (New York, 1969), p. 16.

Select Bibliography

Listed here are all those secondary sources (mainly critical books and articles) cited in this study, together with those items consulted in the course of writing the book but not explicitly referred to above which readers might find of interest. A list of the editions of the seven main primary texts used can be found at the beginning of the book.

Abrams, M. H., *The Mirror and the Lamp: Romantic Theory and the Critical Tradition* (Oxford, 1953).

Allott, Miriam, *Novelists on the Novel* (London and Henley, 1965).

Atkins, G. Douglas, *Geoffrey Hartman: Criticism as Answerable Style* (London and New York, 1990).

Attridge, Derek (ed.), *The Cambridge Companion to James Joyce* (Cambridge, 1990).

Axton, William F., *Circle of Fire: Dickens' Vision and Style and the Popular Victorian Theater* (Lexington, Ky, 1966).

Bakhtin, Mikhail, *The Dialogic Imagination: Four Essays*, trans. Caryl Emerson and Michael Holquist, ed. Michael Holquist (Austin, Tex., 1981).

Bakhtin, Mikhail, *Rabelais and His World*, trans. Helene Iswolsky (Bloomington, Ind., 1984).

Baldick, Chris, *The Concise Oxford Dictionary of Literary Terms* (Oxford and New York, 1991).

Beja, Morris (ed.), *Dubliners and A Portrait of the Artist as a Young Man: A Casebook* (Basingstoke and London, 1973).

Bennett, Andrew (ed.), *Readers and Reading* (London and New York, 1995).

Bennington, Geoffrey, *Lyotard: Writing the Event* (Manchester, 1988).

Bleich, David, *Subjective Criticism* (Baltimore, Md and London, 1978).

Bloom, Harold (ed.), *Modern Critical Interpretations: Joyce's A Portrait of the Artist as a Young Man* (New York and Philadelphia, 1988).

Booth, Wayne C., *The Rhetoric of Fiction* (Chicago and London, 1961).

Bradbury, Malcolm, *The Modern British Novel* (London, 1993).

Bradbury, Malcolm and McFarlane, James (eds), *Modernism 1890–1930* (Harmondsworth, 1976).

Bradbury, Malcolm and Palmer, David (eds), *Contemporary Criticism* (London, 1970).

Brooker, Peter (ed.), *Modernism/Postmodernism* (London and New York, 1992).

Brooks, Peter, *Reading for the Plot: Design and Intention in Narrative* (Oxford, 1984).

Burgess, Anthony, 'Martyr and Maze-maker', in Harold Bloom (ed.), *Modern Critical Interpretations: Joyce's A Portrait of the Artist as a Young Man* (New York and Philadelphia, 1988), pp. 43–54.

Butler, Christopher, 'Joyce, Modernism, and Post-modernism', in Derek Attridge (ed.), *The Cambridge Companion to James Joyce* (Cambridge, 1990), pp. 259–82.

Byatt A. S. and Sodre, Ignês, *Imagining Characters: Six Conversations about Women Writers*, ed. Rebecca Swift (London, 1995).

Byatt, A. S., 'My Hero: Robert Browning', in the *Independent*, 26 November 1988 (magazine supplement).

Byatt, A. S., *Passions of the Mind: Selected Writings* (London, 1991).

Byrd, Max, ' "Reading" in *Great Expectations*', *PMLA*, Vol. 91 (1976), pp. 259–65.

Calinescu, Matei, *Rereading* (New Haven and London, 1993).

Carroll, David, *George Eliot and the Conflict of Interpretations: A Reading of the Novels* (Cambridge, 1992).

Carroll, David (ed.), *George Eliot: The Critical Heritage* (London, 1971).

Carroll, David, 'The Unity of *Daniel Deronda*', *Essays in Criticism*, Vol. 9 (1959), pp. 369–80.

Chase, Cynthia, 'The Decomposition of the Elephants: Double-Reading *Daniel Deronda*', *PMLA*, Vol. 93 (1978), pp. 215–27.

Collini, Stefan (ed.), *Interpretation and Overinterpretation* (Cambridge, 1992).

Collins, Philip (ed.), *Dickens: The Critical Heritage* (London, 1971).

Connor, Steven, *Charles Dickens* (Oxford and New York, 1985).

Crosman, Robert, 'Is There Such a Thing as Misreading?', in Jeremy Hawthorn (ed.), *Criticism and Critical Theory* (London, 1984), pp. 1–12.

Culler, Jonathan, *On Deconstruction: Theory and Criticism after Structuralism* (London, 1983).

Cunningham, Valentine, *In the Reading Gaol: Postmodernity, Texts and History* (Oxford and Cambridge, Mass., 1994).

Davis, Lennard J., *Resisting Novels: Ideology and Fiction* (New York and London, 1987).

Davis, Philip, *The Experience of Reading* (London and New York, 1992).

Davis, Philip (ed.), *Real Voices On Reading* (Basingstoke and London, 1997).

Deming, Robert H. (ed.), *James Joyce: The Critical Heritage*, 2 vols (London and Henley, 1970).

De Porte, Michael V., *Nightmares and Hobbyhorses: Swift, Sterne, and Augustan Ideas of Madness* (San Marino, 1974).

Derrida, Jacques, *Positions*, trans. Alan Bass (Urbana, Ill. and Chicago, 1981).

Eco, Umberto, 'Postmodernism, Irony, the Enjoyable', in Peter Brooker (ed.), *Modernism/Postmodernism* (London and New York, 1992), pp. 225–8.

Eco, Umberto, *The Tanner Lectures*, in Stefan Collini (ed.), *Interpretation and Overinterpretation* (Cambridge, 1992), pp. 23–43.

Eigner, Edwin M., *The Metaphysical Novel in England and America: Dickens, Bulwer, Hawthorne, Melville* (Berkeley and Los Angeles, 1978).

Ellmann, Richard, *James Joyce* (Oxford, 1982).

Fish, Stanley, *Doing What Comes Naturally: Change, Rhetoric, and the Practice of Theory in Literary and Legal Studies* (Oxford, 1989).

Fish, Stanley, *Is There a Text in This Class?: The Authority of Interpretive Communities* (Cambridge, Mass., 1980).

Fish, Stanley, *There's No Such Thing As Free Speech And It's A Good Thing, Too* (Oxford, 1994).

Fletcher, John and Bradbury, Malcolm, 'The Introverted Novel', in Malcolm Bradbury and James McFarlane (eds), *Modernism 1890–1930* (Harmondsworth, 1976), pp. 394–415.

Freund, Elizabeth, *The Return of the Reader: Reader-Response Criticism* (London and New York, 1987).

Frye, Northrop, *Anatomy of Criticism: Four Essays* (Princeton, NJ, 1957).

Gadamer, Hans-Georg, *Truth and Method*, trans. William Glen-Doepel (London, 1979).

Garis, Robert, *The Dickens Theatre: A Reassessment of the Novels* (Oxford, 1965).

Genette, Gérard, *Narrative Discourse*, trans. Jane E. Lewin (Oxford, 1980).

Gorman, David, 'The Worldly Text: Writing as Social Action, Reading as Historical Reconstructions', in Joseph Natoli (ed.), *Literary Theory's Future(s)* (Urbana, Ill. and Chicago, 1989), pp. 181–220.

Goy, Richard J., 'The "Reader's Edition" of *Ulysses*', the *Times Literary Supplement*, 18 July 1997, p. 17.

Gregor, Ian (ed.), *Reading the Victorian Novel: Detail into Form* (London, 1980).

Gregor, Ian, 'Criticism as an Individual Activity: The Approach through Reading', in Malcolm Bradbury and David Palmer (eds), *Contemporary Criticism* (London, 1970), pp. 195–214.

Gross, John and Pearson, Gabriel (eds), *Dickens and the Twentieth Century* (London, 1966).

Hardy, Barbara, *The Novels of George Eliot: A Study in Form* (London and Dover, New Hampshire, 1963).

Hartman, Geoffrey, *Criticism in the Wilderness: The Study of Literature Today* (New Haven and London, 1980).

Hawthorn, Jeremy (ed.), *Criticism and Critical Theory* (London, 1984).

Holland, Norman, *5 Readers Reading* (New Haven and London, 1975).

Holub, Robert C., *Crossing Borders: Reception Theory, Poststructuralism, Deconstruction* (Madison and London, 1992).

Holub, Robert C., 'Hermeneutics', in *The Cambridge History of Literary Criticism*, Vol. 8: *From Formalism to Poststructuralism* , ed. Raman Selden (Cambridge, 1995), pp. 255–88.

Holub, Robert C., *Reception Theory: A Critical Introduction* (London, 1984).

Hutcheon, Linda, 'Telling Stories', in Peter Brooker (ed.), *Modernism/ Postmodernism* (London and New York, 1992), pp. 229–42.

Iser, Wolfgang, *The Act of Reading: A Theory of Aesthetic Response* (London, 1978).

Iser, Wolfgang, *The Implied Reader: Patterns of Communication in Prose Fiction from Bunyan to Beckett* (Baltimore, Md and London, 1978).

Iser, Wolfgang, 'Interaction between Text and Reader', in Andrew Bennett (ed.), *Readers and Reading*, (London and New York, 1995), pp. 20–31.

Iser, Wolfgang, *Prospecting: From Reader Response to Literary Anthropology* (Baltimore, Md and London, 1989).

Iser, Wolfgang, 'The Reading Process: A Phenomenological

Approach', in David Lodge (ed.), *Modern Criticism and Theory: A Reader* (London and New York, 1988), pp. 212–18.

Iser, Wolfgang, *Sterne: Tristram Shandy*, trans. David Henry Wilson, *Landmarks of World Literature* series (Cambridge, 1988).

James, Henry, '*Daniel Deronda*: A Conversation', in F. R. Leavis, *The Great Tradition: George Eliot, Henry James, Joseph Conrad* (Harmondsworth, 1993), pp. 284–304.

Jauss, Hans-Robert, *Toward an Aesthetic of Reception*, trans. Timothy Bahti (Brighton, 1982).

Jefferson, Ann and Robey, David (eds), *Modern Literary Theory: A Comparative Introduction* (London, 1986).

Johnson, Barbara, *The Critical Difference: Essays in the Contemporary Rhetoric of Reading* (Baltimore, Md and London, 1980).

Johnson, Barbara, 'Nothing Fails like Success', *Deconstructive Criticism: Directions: SCE Reports*, Vol. 8 (Fall, 1980), pp. 9–10.

Kennedy, Alan, *Reading Resistance Value: Deconstructive Practice and the Politics of Literary Critical Encounters* (Basingstoke and London, 1990).

Kermode, Frank, *The Sense of an Ending: Studies in the Theory of Fiction* (Oxford and New York, 1967).

Knights, Ben, *From Reader to Reader: Theory and Practice in the Study Group* (Hemel Hempstead, 1992).

Knoepflmacher, U. C., *Religious Humanism and the Victorian Novel: George Eliot, Walter Pater, and Samuel Butler* (Princeton, NJ, 1965).

Leavis, F. R., *The Great Tradition: George Eliot, Henry James, Joseph Conrad* (Harmondsworth, 1993).

Leavis, F. R. and Leavis, Q. D., *Dickens the Novelist* (Harmondsworth, 1972).

Leitch, Vincent B., *Deconstructive Criticism: An Advanced Introduction* (London, 1983).

Lerner, Laurence (ed.), *Reconstructing Literature* (Oxford, 1983).

Lodge, David, 'The Language of Modernist Fiction: Metaphor and Metonymy' in Malcolm Bradbury and James McFarlane (eds), *Modernism 1890–1930* (Harmondsworth, 1976), pp. 481–96.

Lodge, David (ed.), *Modern Criticism and Theory: A Reader* (London and New York, 1988).

Lyotard, Jean-François, *The Differend: Phrases in Dispute*, trans. Georges Van den Abbeele (Manchester, 1988).

Macksey, Richard and Donato, Eugenio (eds), *The Structuralist Controversy* (Chicago and London, 1972).

Maclean, Ian, 'Reading and Interpretation', in Ann Jefferson and David Robey (eds), *Modern Literary Theory: A Comparative Introduction* (London, 1986).

Manguel, Alberto, *A History of Reading* (London, 1996).

Mendilow, A. A., *Time and the Novel* (London, 1952).

Miller, J. Hillis, *The Ethics of Reading: Kant, de Man, Eliot, Trollope, James and Benjamin* (New York, 1987).

Miller, J. Hillis, *Theory Now and Then* (Hemel Hempstead, 1991).

Moore, Gene, '*Tristram Shandy*'s Narratees', unpublished paper given at the *Laurence Sterne in Modernism and Postmodernism* conference, University of York, April 1993.

Natoli, Joseph (ed.), *Literary Theory's Future(s)* (Urbana, Ill. and Chicago, 1989).

New, Melvyn, *Laurence Sterne as Satirist: A Reading of 'Tristram Shandy'* (Gainesville, Fla, 1969).

New, Melvyn, 'Sterne, Nietzsche, and Tartuffery', paper given at the *Laurence Sterne in Modernism and Postmodernism* conference, University of York, April 1993.

New, Melvyn, *Tristram Shandy: A Book for Free Spirits* (New York, 1994).

Newton, K. M. (ed.), *George Eliot* (London and New York, 1991).

Newton, K. M., *In Defence of Literary Interpretation: Theory and Practice* (London, 1986).

Newton, K. M., 'Sutherland's Puzzles: The Case of *Daniel Deronda*', *Essays in Criticism*, Vol. XLVIII (January, 1998), No. 1, pp. 1–12.

Norris, Christopher, *Deconstruction: Theory and Practice* (London, 1982).

Norris, Christopher, *The Truth about Postmodernism* (Oxford, 1993).

Pater, Walter, *The Renaissance: Studies in Art and Poetry* (Glasgow, 1961).

Perkin, J. Russell, *A Reception-History of George Eliot's Fiction* (Ann Arbor, Mich. and London, 1990).

Pickrel, Paul, '*Great Expectations*', in Martin Price (ed.), *Dickens: A Collection of Critical Essays* (Englewood Cliffs, NJ, 1967), pp. 158–68.

Poulet, Georges, 'Criticism and the Experience of Interiority', in Richard Macksey and Eugenio Donato (eds), *The Structuralist Controversy* (Chicago and London, 1972), pp. 59–61.

Power, Arthur, *Conversations with James Joyce*, ed. Clive Hart (London, 1974).

Price, Martin (ed.), *Dickens: A Collection of Critical Essays* (Englewood Cliffs, NJ, 1967).

Readings, Bill, *Introducing Lyotard: Art and Politics* (London, 1991).

Reichert, John, *Making Sense of Literature* (Chicago, 1977).

Ricks, Christopher, *Beckett's Dying Words: The Clarendon Lectures 1990* (Oxford, 1993).

Ricks, Christopher, '*Great Expectations*', in John Gross and Gabriel Pearson (eds), *Dickens and the Twentieth Century* (London, 1966), pp. 199–211.

Ricoeur, Paul, *Hermeneutics and the Human Sciences*, trans. John B. Thompson (Cambridge, 1981).

Ricoeur, Paul, *Oneself as Another*, trans. Kathleen Blamey (Chicago and London, 1992).

Riquelme, John Paul, 'The Preposterous Shape of Portraiture: *A Portrait of the Artist as a Young Man*', in Harold Bloom (ed.), *Modern Critical Interpretations: Joyce's A Portrait of the Artist as a Young Man* (New York and Philadelphia, 1988), pp. 87–107.

Rorty, Richard, 'The Pragmatist's Progress', in Stefan Collini (ed.), *Interpretation and Overinterpretation* (Cambridge, 1992), pp. 89–108.

Sadrin, Anny, '*Great Expectations*', in the Unwin Critical Library series (London, 1988).

Schad, John, *The Reader in the Dickensian Mirrors: Some New Language* (Basingstoke and London, 1992).

Scholes, Robert, *Protocols of Reading* (New Haven and London, 1989).

Schorer, Mark, 'Technique as Discovery', in David Lodge (ed.), *20th Century Literary Criticism: A Reader* (London, 1972), pp. 386–400.

Schweickart, Patrocinio P., 'Reading Ourselves: Toward a Feminist Theory of Reading', in Andrew Bennett (ed.), *Readers and Reading* (London and New York, 1995), pp. 66–93.

Scruton, Roger, 'In Inverted Commas', the *Times Literary Supplement*, 18 December 1992, pp. 3–4.

Selden, Raman (ed.), *From Formalism to Poststructuralism*, Vol. 8 of *The Cambridge History of Literary Criticism* (Cambridge, 1995).

Semmel, Bernard, *George Eliot and the Politics of National Inheritance* (Oxford and New York, 1994).

Shklovsky, Viktor, 'A Parodying Novel: Sterne's *Tristram Shandy*', trans. W. George Isaak, in *Laurence Sterne: A Collection of Critical Essays*, ed. John Traugott (Englewood Cliffs, NJ, 1968), pp. 66–89.

Short, Mick, *Stylistics* (London, 1996).

Shuttleworth, Sally, *George Eliot and Nineteenth-Century Science: The Make-Believe of a Beginning* (Cambridge, 1984).

Stedmond, John M., *The Comic Art of Laurence Sterne: Convention and Innovation in Tristram Shandy and A Sentimental Journey* (Toronto, 1967).

Steiner, George, *Real Presences: Is There Anything In What We Say?* (London, 1989).

Stevenson, Randall, *A Reader's Guide to the Twentieth-Century Novel in Britain* (Hemel Hampstead, 1993).

Sutherland, John, *Can Jane Eyre Be Happy?: More Puzzles in Classic Fiction* (Oxford, 1997).

Tallis, Raymond, 'The Survival of Theory: (1) "He Never Said That"', in *Poetry Nation Review*, Vol. 20, No. 6 (July-August, 1994), pp. 61–4.

Todorov, Tzvetan, *The Poetics of Prose*, trans. Richard Howard (Oxford, 1977).

Traugott, John, *Tristram Shandy's World: Sterne's Philosophical Rhetoric* (Berkeley, 1954).

Traugott, John (ed.), *Laurence Sterne: A Collection of Critical Essays* (Englewood Cliffs, NJ, 1968).

Van Ghent, Dorothy, *The English Novel: Form and Function* (New York, 1961).

Veeser, Harold Aram (ed.), *The New Historicism* (London and New York, 1989).

Walder, Dennis, 'Reading *Great Expectations*', in Dennis Walder (ed.), *The Realist Novel* (London and New York, 1995), pp. 135–65.

Walder, Dennis (ed.), *The Realist Novel* (London and New York, 1995).

Washington, Peter, *Fraud: Literary Theory and the End of English* (London, 1989).

Wheeler, Michael, *The Art of Allusion in Victorian Fiction* (Basingstoke and London, 1979).

Wheeler, Michael, *English Fiction of the Victorian Period 1830–1890* (London and New York, 1994).

Wilson, Richard and Dutton, Richard (eds), *New Historicism and Renaissance Drama* (London and New York, 1992).

Wimsatt Jr, W. K. and Beardsley, Monroe C., 'The Affective Fallacy', in W. K. Wimsatt Jr, *The Verbal Icon: Studies in the Meaning of Poetry* (London, 1970).

Woolf, Virginia, 'Modern Fiction', extract repr. in Miriam Allott, *Novelists on the Novel* (London and Henley, 1965) pp. 76–7.

Index

Index

17

Byatt, A. S., xi, 30, 43, 141, 200n
column for the *Independent*, 164
Passions of the Mind, 165
Possession, xi, xii, 25–6, 39, 63–4,
71, 123, 163–83, 189

Calabrese, Omar, 167
Calinescu, Matei, 3, 26, 57–8, 66,
141–2
Calvino, Italo, 26
canon, *see* literary canon
Carey, John, 117–18
carnivalesque, *see* Bakhtin, Mikhail
Cartland, Barbara, 167
Cave, Terence, 100
Cervantes, Miguel de, 26
Chase, Cynthia, 200n
Cohen, William A., 88–9
Coleridge, Samuel Taylor, 164, 166
'The Rime of the Ancient
Mariner', 172–3
Collini, Stefan, 13
Collins, Wilkie
The Woman in White, 112–13
Connor, Steven, 197n
Conrad, Joseph
Heart of Darkness, 1–2, 20, 182
constatives, 9–10
criticism
Blackmur's idea of 'technical'
criticism, 25
Steiner on criticism as a
secondary activity, 19–20
Crosman, Inga, *see* Suleiman,
Susan R.
Crosman, Robert, 206n
Culler, Jonathan, 15, 77, 79, 80, 95,
97
Cunningham, Valentine, 199n
Curran, C. P., 127

Dallas, E. S.,198n
Davis, Lennard, 10–11, 58–9, 146–7
Davis, Philip, 77–8, 118, 201n
deconstruction, 4, 80, 95, 96–118,
124–6, 155, 167, 188
defamiliarization, 34–5
deferral, 27, 38, 42, 48–50, 65, 82–3,
93–4, 156

Defoe, Daniel, 202n
Moll Flanders, 101
De Man, Paul, 96, 142
De Porte, Michael V., 31
Derrida, Jacques, 23, 98, 139, 151,
187, 197n
Dial, The, 122
Dickens, Charles, 165
All the Year Round, 78, 93
David Copperfield, 77
Great Expectations, xi, 26, 42,
59–60, 76–95, 121, 127, 128,
190
Oliver Twist, 10–11
Dickinson, Emily, 3–5
diegesis, 40
différance, 98
digression, *see* reading process
Donne, John, 164, 166
Dumas, Alexandre (père)
The Count of Monte Cristo, 132
Dutton, Richard, *see* Wilson,
Richard

Eco, Umberto, 7, 13–16, 20–1, 167,
184
The Name of the Rose, 166, 168
'Postmodernism, Irony, the
Enjoyable', 167–8
Eliot, George (Mary Ann(e), or
Marian Evans), 90, 91, 126,
133, 164, 165, 181
Daniel Deronda, 95, 96–118, 121,
124, 125, 127, 131, 134, 165
Middlemarch, 21, 81, 108, 125,
165, 167
The Mill on The Floss, 105
Eliot, T. S., 69
Four Quartets, 206n
Ellmann, Richard, 127, 202n, 203n
epiphany, *see* Joycean epiphany
embedding, 46–9
Empson, William, 125
etymology, 186–9
of 'aporia', 175, 186
of 'etymology', 187
of 'expectation', 84
of 'mediated', 28, 186
of 'portrait', 127, 186, 189